The Age of Culture

THE AGE OF CULTURE

D. Paul Schafer

Foreword by Federico Mayor
Introduction by David Stover

A New Road Book
Rock's Mills Press

A New Road Book
PUBLISHED BY
Rock's Mills Press

The author and publisher gratefully acknowledge permission to reproduce previously published material in this book:

"Functioning of a Cultural Age" and "Priorities for a Cultural Age" were originally published in *Revolution or Renaissance: Making the Transition from an Economic Age to a Cultural Age*. Copyright © 2008 by University of Ottawa Press. Reproduced with permission from the University of Ottawa Press.

"The Millennium Challenge: Making the Transition from an 'Economic Age' to a 'Cultural Age'" was originally published in *World Futures: The Journal of General Evolution* 51: 3–4 (1998). Copyright © 1998 by O. P. A. (Overseas Publishers Association) Amsterdam B. V. Reproduced with permission of Taylor & Francis.

"Towards a New World Order: The Age of Culture" was first published in *Cultures* 2: 3 (1975). Copyright © 1975 by UNESCO. Reproduced with permission of UNESCO.

"The Culturescape: Self-Awareness of Communities" was first published in *Cultures* 5: 1 (1978). Copyright © 1978 by UNESCO. Reproduced with permission of UNESCO.

Library and Archives Canada Cataloguing in Publication

Schafer, D. Paul (David Paul), 1937-, author
 The age of culture / D. Paul Schafer ; foreword by Federico Mayor ; introduction by David Stover.

"A new road book".
Includes bibliographical references.
ISBN 978-0-9881293-2-0 (pbk.)

1. Culture. 2. Social change. I. Title.

HM626.S33 2014   306   C2014-902815-6

Cover: "Sunrise in Venice," by Jose Antonio Galan. Venice was the site of the first major international conference on culture and cultural policy, held in 1970.

First Edition
ISBN-13: 978-0-9881293-2-0

Contents

Introduction

"One day we shall realize . . . that the essential options in any truly democratic, truly national development policy are cultural." So declared René Maheu, director-general of UNESCO, in his address to the first world conference on cultural policy in Venice in 1970.

The conference was a harbinger of things to come. While the prevailing attitude at the time was that culture was the responsibility of individuals, not-for-profit organizations, wealthy patrons, and the private sector, delegates at this historic event foresaw the need for governments and the public sector generally to play a large and forceful role in the cultural affairs of nations and in the world of the future, even if they were as yet unsure about what this role should be.

Making culture the centrepiece of a global conference was a bold step. At that time, the views of governments, politicians, and people in general about how the world worked were dominated by the theories and practices of economics, as indeed is all too often still the case. Economic ideas and metrics were seen as the chief means of valuing everything in the world, from the worth of individuals to the importance of nations. To be fair, this economic view of human values and motivations has, over the course of the last two hundred years, produced unprecedented improvements in human productivity, longevity, wealth, and sheer numbers. More people are better off materially than ever before. Moreover, we have walked on the moon, plumbed the depths of oceans, and unravelled the mysteries of the atom. And yet, even setting aside the question of whether this vast increase in wealth and power is, in fact, sustainable, there is something cold and hollow about it.

The new emphasis on culture has been affirmed and deepened at numerous municipal, regional, national, and global conferences on culture and cultures in general—and cultural development and policy in particular—over the decades since the Venice conference. This growth in interest reached a climax in May, 2013 when delegates at the International Congress on Culture in China adopted the Hangzhou Declaration, which placed culture at the "heart of sustainable development policies." This call was reinforced several months later at a session initiated by the president of the United Nations General Assembly, when several hundred participants, many of them government ministers responsible for cultural policies in their home countries, resolved that culture should be accorded "top priority in the post-2015 global development agenda."

Remarkably, in the space of less than fifty years, culture has moved from being seen as a peripheral activity in the world to something utterly indispensable to the achievement of vital social and development goals. It is now apparent that culture—and by this is meant culture in the broadest sense, as the sum of human experience and achievement—is intimately connected to all the world's most pressing and debilitating problems.

Those problems are legion in the modern world: climate change, environmental degradation, glaring inequalities in income and wealth, growing shortages of natural resources, conflicts between different countries, religions, and ethnic groups, and the need for meaningful and positive transformation and change at every level—individual, institutional, governmental, and corporate. None of these problems can be addressed effectively, much less solved, without recourse to the holistic perspective culture provides. Narrow views no longer suffice, and the status quo is unacceptable.

Paul Schafer has spent much of his life wrestling with these problems and demonstrating why culture has a crucial role to play in coming to grips with them. In *The Age of Culture*, he draws on many different disciplines and strands of thought to frame the ongoing discussion about culture and the central role it can play in bringing a more human—and humane—world into existence. We ignore the book's timely, urgent, yet hopeful message at our peril.

David Stover
2014

Foreword

"Man cannot be, if not free," proclaimed Salvador Espriu in one of his most memorable poems. Each unique human being has the capacity for creation, that distinctive ability that only the human race possesses. It is this ability, which must be nourished through education in philosophy and the arts, that has enabled humanity to progress over the course of history, especially with regard to medical and preventive measures that have resulted in increased longevity for a very significant portion of the world's population.

Article 1 of the UNESCO Constitution splendidly defines education as contributing to the creation of "free and responsible" human beings.

"Only those with knowledge are free and freer still are those with more knowledge," wrote Miguel de Unamuno in 1902. An in-depth knowledge of reality enables us to act effectively upon our own reflections and to fulfill our corresponding responsibilities.

Learning to know, to do, to be, to live together, to undertake new endeavours. . . . Daring to know, and knowing when to dare because—and I must insist on this—taking risks without the proper knowledge is dangerous, but knowledge without risk is meaningless.

And now, for the first time in history, thanks to digital technology, the peoples of the world may cease to be invisible, anonymous, subjected and confined territorially and intellectually, and may finally freely express themselves.

Manifestations of cultural identity, of what one thinks, imagines, and invents, which until very recently were the exception, may now progressively but rapidly become the rule.

And not only manifesting one's own cultural traits but becoming aware of the cultural identity of others is necessary, so that we can better appreciate what unites us and what distinguishes us. Global consciousness and worldwide citizenship are essential components of the great transformations that await us on the horizon. But the cultural development of a society will never be complete until gender equality is achieved. With a very few fleeting exceptions, women have not been a part of the "cultural profile" of humankind. But this biased situation is also changing.

We are now at the right point in history to usher in a new era: the era of culture. This book, *The Age of Culture*, addresses three aspects of this change: the prerequisites for a cultural age; the fundamental character- istics of a cultural age; and glimpses into what a cultural age might be like. As the author states in this book:

> One of the biggest challenges for a cultural age will be piecing to- gether, making known, and using a cultural worldview to replace the economic worldview. . . .
>
> While construction of this worldview from ideas and practices across such a wide range of disciplines is fraught with difficulties, and is subject to numerous qualifications and generalizations, it simply must be done if we are to ascertain the way in which the world would be viewed from a cultural perspective.
>
> From anthropology, sociology, history, and philosophy there is the concern with the whole. . . . From the arts there is the concern with excellence, creativity, beauty, diversity, and the search for the sublime, as well as the ways in which knowledge and understanding of cultures are enhanced through signs, symbols, and stories that stand for the whole. From the humanities there is the concern with people, cooperation, equality, and the connection between spirit- ualism and materialism. From ecology, biology, and other dis- ciplines that have a close historical and contemporary affinity with culture there is the concern with the natural environment, other species, and the relationships, including the similarities and dif- ferences, between these and human beings. . . .
>
> *When these concerns are looked at in totality, they provide the basis for the construction of a cultural worldview.* In contrast to the economic worldview, a cultural worldview would be predicated on the conviction that the best way to view the world and everything in it is through the prism of culture. The priority would be placed on the whole, not just on economics or any other part of the whole, and on the need to achieve balanced, harmonious, and equitable relationships between the parts and the whole. This would then be used to address the complex challenges and opportunities involved in making improvements in society, the human condition, and the world system. . . .
>
> The development and use of a cultural worldview in this collec- tive sense could prove valuable and timely at the present juncture in

history. In the first place, it would place humanity in a much stronger position to make sensible and sustainable decisions about future courses and directions in planetary civilization. In the second place, it would provide an opportunity to make a breakthrough in environmental matters because a high priority would be placed on the relationship between people and the natural environment. In the third place, it would render a better perspective on the numerous conflicts between groups of people, countries, and cultures. . . .

A cultural worldview would place the priority on unity, synthesis, inclusion, and holism, rather than division, separation, exclusion, and polarization.

Developing culture in depth *and* breadth is essential if we are to be able to create and use the new cultural model of development that the author aptly describes as one of the pillars of the new era.

It was Federico García Lorca who, in an interview in the Granada daily *La Voz* a month before his assassination in August 1936, underscored the fact that the situation in the world at that time was untenable, that it was impossible to accept that a large part of mankind lived in extreme poverty, dying of starvation. But, he added, "There will come a great revolution: a spiritual revolution that will give sense to human existence."

In my book *The World Ahead: Our Future in the Making*, written with Jérôme Bindé and published in 2000, I proposed four new contracts to achieve the radical change of course that the systemic crisis of neoliberal globalization required: a new social contract, a new environmental contract, a new cultural contract, and a new ethical contract. I heartily welcome Paul Schafer's ideas on these matters. They are particularly opportune at this time, when it is possible to express ourselves freely, when gender equality is advancing to enable one of the essential components of the "cultural age" to play its full role, and, above all, when we as global citizens can admire that unlimited cultural diversity—each unique human being with his or her own creative abilities—that is our greatest wealth. Together with the great universal principles, these opportunities provide us force and strength.

We already have several diagnoses of the human dilemma but are lacking an appropriate treatment. Paul Schafer, consistent with the unparalleled perspective provided by UNESCO, here offers a global view of the infinite cultural diversity and values that guide the destiny of the human race. He articulately and enthusiastically promotes the World Culture Project, which, with the approaching end of the systemic crisis confronting humanity at the dawn of this new century and millennium, will undoubtedly provide one of the principal avenues leading us to that other possible world we all desire.

Federico Mayor
2014

Federico Mayor served as director-general of UNESCO from 1987 to 1999, following a distinguished career in Spanish academic and political life. A biochemist by profession, he holds numerous honorary degrees, has written more than a dozen books, and after retiring from UNESCO returned to Spain to create the Foundation for a Culture of Peace, which he chairs.

Preface

When Victor Hugo said "greater than the tread of mighty armies is an idea whose time has come," it was not a cultural age he had in mind. Nevertheless, there is mounting evidence to indicate that a cultural age is truly "an idea whose time has come."

Hence this book. It is designed to show why a cultural age is necessary and how it might be achieved, as well as the way my thoughts on this matter have evolved over many years. In order to do this, a number of articles and chapters from books I have written on this subject are reproduced here. It is hoped that they make a compelling case for a cultural age and the many benefits that can be derived from it.

While I didn't realize it at the time, the education I received in the arts when I was young was the ideal preparation for someone who seemed destined to spend the bulk of his life wrestling with the complexities of culture and making the case for a cultural age. This is due to the intimate connection between culture and the arts, and the fact that the arts act as a "gateway to culture" in many ways. Recently, I have even begun to wonder if the arts might provide the centrepiece for a cultural age in much the same way that science provides the centrepiece for the current economic age.

When I taught economics in the 1960s, I found myself thinking about the need for a new kind of age very often. This was because I felt a much broader perspective was required on the world situation—a perspective that included all human activities as well as the natural environment in public and private planning, policy, and decision-making. Could culture provide this perspective? Years later, I learned that many cultural scholars have viewed culture in holistic terms, and there has been a strong bond between culture and nature dating back to classical times.

My first real foray into this area occurred in 1975 when an article of mine—"Towards a New World Order: The Age of Culture"—was published in UNESCO's journal *Cultures*. This was reinforced when Jack Fobes,

Deputy Director-General of UNESCO at the time, ordered a special printing of the article for distribution to delegates attending a Roundtable on Cultural and Intellectual Cooperation and the New International Economic Order, organized by UNESCO. It was reinforced even more when Guy Métraux, editor of *Cultures*, asked me to write a second article—"The Age of Culture: Prospects and Implications"—for publication in *Cultures* later in 1975.

These events, which happened in rapid succession, were a defining factor in my life. They convinced me that I should spend the rest of my life trying to broaden and deepen knowledge and understanding of culture and making the case for a cultural age.

This was not possible, however, without learning much more about culture than I knew at that time. Fortunately, an opportunity to do this opened up when I went to the University of Toronto in the early 1980s to teach courses in arts administration and cultural policy and act as coordinator for two new cooperative programs being developed there in arts administration and international development. Whenever I had some spare time, I would head off to the Bladen Library to read about culture and what cultural scholars had to say about it.

What I discovered there amazed me. I learned that cultural scholars have had an enormous amount to say about culture and its actual and potential role in the world. The problem was that their thoughts on this subject were spread across many disciplines—the arts, humanities, history, philosophy, sociology, anthropology, ecology, and biology—rather than located in a single place. This was because of the incredible amount of complexity that exists in the world and culture's capacity for helping us to understand and deal with this complexity.

What amazed me even more was that when I pulled all the contributions of cultural scholars together and looked at them collectively, I found that all the ingredients were there to make a compelling case for a cultural age. This was true not only with regard to the nature and meaning of culture, but also for the impact culture has on every aspect of the world situation and human condition, from the individual and institutional level to the municipal, regional, national, and international level.

I also became aware of something else. There was a very different way of seeing the world and valuing things in the world contained in the thoughts and ideas of cultural scholars. I began to refer to this as "the cultural way of looking at the world" or a "cultural worldview" (as Federico Mayor has noted in his Foreword) because it included all human activities and the natural environment in its purview. It also placed a great deal of emphasis on humanity's greatest, wisest, and most inspiring achievements and ideals, thereby making it possible to predicate the case for a cultural age on the contributions of countless cultural scholars and practitioners rather than wishful thinking on my part.

This ultimately led to the publication of a book called *Culture: Beacon of the Future*. Published in 1998, this book was designed to present my findings on culture up to that point in my life, make the case for a holistic understanding of culture in general and cultures in particular, and demonstrate the crucial importance of culture and cultures in the development of people, communities, countries, the state, the world system, and a cultural age. The title of the book was chosen deliberately to emphasize that there are risks as well as rewards to be experienced when dealing with culture. Hence the need to warn of possible danger and institute the necessary safeguards as well as illuminate a vital, viable, and safe path to the future.

Once *Culture: Beacon of the Future* was out and circulating, I turned my attention to a cultural age in earnest. This led to the publication of a number of articles relevant to this matter, as noted in the appendix and posted on the World Culture Project website, as well as a second book, *Revolution or Renaissance: Making the Transition from an Economic Age to a Cultural Age*. This book was published in 2008, and was intended to show that a cultural age should constitute the next step in global development and human affairs because it possesses the potential to deal with the world situation in broader, deeper, and more fundamental terms.

At the heart of this book was a problem that had bothered me for years and still bothers me today. It is this. How can we create an age that makes it possible for *all* people and *all* countries to enjoy reasonable standards of living and a decent quality of life without straining the globe's fragile ecosystems, scarce resources, and finite carrying capacity to the breaking point?

I believe that a cultural age can do this, but only if we can create a more effective balance between the material and non-material dimensions of life and realize much more caring, sharing, compassion, and cooperation in the world. The distinguished Dutch cultural historian, Johan Huizinga, gave us an inkling of what is required to do this when, following his examination of numerous cultures throughout the world, he declared that "the realities of economic life, of power, of technology, of everything conducive to man's material well-being, must be balanced by strongly developed spiritual, intellectual, moral, and aesthetic values." Such a balance, in my view, is the key to a cultural age, as well as to achieving a great deal more harmony, stability, sustainability, equality, and well-being in the world.

Clearly we have only scratched the surface of the rich potential that culture possesses to create the conditions for a better world. This is especially important now that developments in communications technology have made it possible for people in all parts of the world to tap into humanity's greatest historical and contemporary accomplishments in every field of cultural endeavour, as well as to express their own thoughts, creativity, and ideas, and share them with others throughout the world.

In effect, that is what I have attempted to do in this book. I have tried to draw on the insights and ideas of countless generations of cultural scholars and practitioners, and blend them with my own personal, professional, and often profound experiences with culture and cultures over the years.

It is my hope that this approach—and this book—will prove helpful in generating fruitful discussion on why a cultural age is so desperately needed at this time and what is most essential to achieve in such an age. This is imperative now that culture has become a powerful force in the world and we are standing on the threshold of a whole new era in global development and human affairs.

D. Paul Schafer
2014

Culture, however we define it, is central to everything we do and think. It is what we do and the reason why we do it, what we wish and why we imagine it, what we perceive and how we express it, how we live and in what manner we approach death. It is our environment and the patterns of our adaptation to it. It is the world we have created and are still creating; it is the way we see that world and the motives that urge us to change it. It is the way we know ourselves and each other; it is our web of personal relationships, it is the images and abstractions that allow us to live together in communities and nations. It is the element in which we live.

—Bernard Ostry, *The Cultural Connection*

Part One

PREREQUISITES FOR A CULTURAL AGE

CHAPTER ONE
Foundations for Life

*The arts are not for the privileged few but for the many. . . . Their place
is not at the periphery of society but at its center. . . . They are not just
a form of recreation but are of central importance to our well-being
and happiness.*

—Rockefeller Panel Report,
The Performing Arts: Problems and Prospects[1]

T he best thing my parents did for me when I was young was give
me an education in the arts. I have been reaping the benefits of
this all my life.

Awareness of this fact has not suddenly vaulted into my consciousness.
It has always been there, progressively broadening and deepening over the
years as I have come to understand my good fortune and appreciate how
much this has helped me in life.

My parents were not well-to-do. Nor were they well-educated. They
came from farming stock—my mother from Manitoba and my father from
Saskatchewan—and were forced to leave school rather early to earn a liv-

---

[1] Rockefeller Panel Report on the Future of Theatre, Dance, Music in America, *The
Performing Arts: Problems and Prospects* (New York: McGraw-Hill, 1965), p. 1.

ing and help support their parents. However, my mother did manage to go to normal school and teach for a number of years before she got married, although my father was forced to leave school in grade ten, despite the fact that he had done very well in school up to that point in time.

Both my parents understood the value of an education in the arts, just as many parents do. It is not coincidental that the large majority of parents want music lessons, singing lessons, dance lessons, or art lessons for their children, even if they have been deprived of such opportunities themselves. They understand the value of the arts for happiness, fulfillment, and well-being in life.

My parents certainly did. I don't know where this came from, but it was definitely there. Perhaps it was because they came from European stock, and were able to benefit from the high value Europeans generally place on the arts. Perhaps it was because they saw people around them whose children had benefitted from an education in the arts and wanted their children to benefit from this as well. Or perhaps it was because they taught themselves to play musical instruments or paint pictures and wanted this for their children.

Interestingly, my mother taught herself to play both the piano and the violin, and played in a dance band and community orchestra for a number of years when she was young despite the fact that she didn't have any lessons on either instrument. My father taught himself to play the piano too—although not as well as my mother—and would often sit down at the piano after dinner and play the first movement of Beethoven's *Moonlight Sonata*, Claude Debussy's *Clair de Lune*—or as Victor Borge called it, "Clear the Saloon"—and the first few pages of Chopin's *Étude in E Major* before it got too difficult. He also taught himself to paint pictures, and produced many beautiful pastel and water colour paintings without the benefit of any lessons. He cultivated a keen interest in classical music later in life, although he had no opportunities to listen to classical music when he was young.

It is not surprising, then, that my parents wanted their children to have an excellent education in the arts—the kind of education that was deeper, richer, and broader than the one provided by elementary and secondary schools at the time and probably even today. They commenced their quest to achieve this by arranging for me and my brother Murray to have art classes at the Art Gallery of Toronto, now the Art Gallery of Ontario. These classes took place every Saturday morning when Murray was eleven or twelve and I was seven or eight. I seem to recall a teacher there called A. Y.

Jackson and another called Arthur Lismer. What I didn't know at the time was that these two talented individuals were not just art teachers, but distinguished members of Canada's Group of Seven, undoubtedly the most famous group of artists Canada has ever produced.

I enjoyed the classes at the Art Gallery very much. I also enjoyed all the paintings displayed there, as well as the many different rooms in which they were displayed. Since authorities at the Gallery were anxious to emulate European masters, styles, galleries, and tastes, most of the paintings were by artists such as Gainsborough, Constable, Turner, Goya, Vermeer, Van Dyck, and others. I even recall a painting by Rembrandt, and one or two by French Impressionists. These paintings had a lasting effect on me, since they exposed me to some of the finest paintings and painters in the world, despite the fact that they were European in origin and there were few if any paintings by Canadian artists that I can remember.

Taking lessons at the Art Gallery of Toronto and seeing the many beautiful paintings on display there was not the only experience that had a lasting effect on me. I also remember being asked by a little old Jewish lady on Dundas Avenue to light her stove every Saturday morning on our way to the Gallery because she was not allowed to light her stove on the Sabbath. While this seems trivial or insignificant, it had a profound effect on me because it exposed me to a person who had very different religious beliefs and cultural convictions than I did. When I look back on it now, I can see that it was experiences like this that were instrumental in inculcating in me a strong desire to learn more about the many diverse cultures and religions of the world at a very early age.

It was about this time that my mother enrolled me in Grace Church on-the-Hill choir. This was one of the most important—if not the most important—experiences in my life. It filled me with an appreciation for music in general—and religious music in particular—that has grown steadily over the years and endured to the present day. Whenever I am bored or depressed, I usually end up realizing it is because I am not listening to enough music to keep my spirits high. Today, I enjoy music of all types, styles, genres, and parts of the world: popular and classical; sacred and secular; ancient, medieval, and modern; and African, Asian, Latin American, Middle Eastern, and North American. However, I am aware that it was my early encounter with "religious music" that made all this possible.

One of the best things about Grace Church on-the-Hill was all the music there was in the service, which is true for most Anglican churches. Not only was much of the liturgy sung rather than spoken, but also there were many wonderful hymns and anthems. I enjoyed singing these hymns and anthems immensely, although I didn't have a good singing voice. The organist and choir master at Grace Church—John Hodgins—said it was because the doctor cut too deep when he removed my tonsils. I don't know how much truth there is in this, but my voice did become a good singing voice—momentarily—just before it changed. Unfortunately, it wasn't long enough for John Hodgins to take advantage of it as far as any solos or separate parts were concerned. Nevertheless, I count the experience I had in the choir among the richest and most valuable I have had in life.

There were many other reasons for enjoying the choir. One was singing *The Messiah* every Christmas at Massey Hall in Toronto when I was young, although we were so far up in the second balcony that it was virtually impossible to see the conductor—Sir Ernest MacMillan—who was one of Canada's most outstanding musicians and distinguished conductors at the time. Another was singing at weddings at Bishop Strachan School across the street from Grace Church on-the-Hill. Like the services at the Church, this involved singing a great deal of beautiful music, and being paid handsomely for the privilege of doing so.

Yet another was going to choir camp every summer. The best thing about this—quite apart from getting out of Toronto and the heat of the city for two weeks in July or August—was being out in nature and enjoying everything nature had to offer. Since the camp was held in a different location each year, this provided an opportunity to get acquainted with a great deal of beautiful scenery in Muskoka and other areas north of Toronto, as well as to enjoy many pristine lakes and rivers, take long walks in the country and the forest, learn how to paddle a canoe and row a boat, and eat freshly grilled fish for breakfast most mornings.

There were pranks, too, as there are in all choirs. They occurred often, but not without devastating consequences in some cases. The best example of this was the time the rector caught me playing a boogie bass my brother had taught me on the chimes of the organ at Grace Church before choir practice one afternoon. I was so anxious to hear what a boogie bass would sound like on the chimes that I failed to realize that the sound would reverberate throughout the Church and the entire neighbourhood around the Church, which was located in Forest Hill, one of Toronto's most fashionable and upscale areas. Although I thought I was alone in the Church at the time, it turned out that the rector—Dr. Dowker—was working in his office that day. As soon as he heard the chimes, he came flying across the chancel to put an instant stop to it. He came so fast, in fact, that he didn't even stop at the centre of the chancel to bow to the cross. It was the first and only time I ever saw him do this during the six or seven years I spent in the choir. Boy, did I get it that day! I got severely reprimanded by the organist and choir master, John Hodgins, following the tongue-lashing I received from Dr. Dowker.

While the experience I had in Grace Church on-the-Hill choir was one of the most memorable and valuable experiences in my life, listening to classical music with my father was another. We would lie on the couch in the living room together listening to classical music on the old "78's" for what seems like hours on end. The records had to be changed frequently in those days, since each record played for only a couple of minutes before it had to be changed. Unfortunately, this was before the days of automation, which made it possible to stack many records on the record player and play them one after another without having to change them by hand.

My father loved the music of Brahms, Beethoven, Schubert, Rachmaninoff, and Chopin, and instilled this love in me. He was particularly fond of Schumann, who he said had a remarkable capacity for creating musical problems for himself and then extricating himself from these problems with great beauty, imagination, and ingenuity.

There were piano lessons too, paid for in carefully-calculated monthly installments by my parents. Unfortunately, I couldn't play the piano any better than I sang. My piano teacher said it was because I had short fingers and a "lazy left hand." This irked me immensely because I was—and still am—left-handed, and one of the most outstanding pianists in the world at the time was Arthur Rubinstein, who had the shortest fingers I have ever seen. Nevertheless, I did manage to pass the grade eight piano exam and grade two theory exam at the Royal Conservatory of Music in Toronto. However, the most memorable experience I had with the piano was being paid in peanuts to practice. This was recorded on a blackboard in the kitchen. One day I remember getting 9½ peanuts for practicing 4¾ minutes. I was far more interested in playing ball hockey on the street.

These were not the only experiences I had in the arts that my parents arranged for me when I was young. My mother also read to Murray and myself for hours when we were young, much as many parents do for their children. Murray and I would lie spellbound on the bunk beds my father had built for us listening to stories like *Ali Baba and the Forty Thieves*, *Aladdin's Wonderful Lamp*, *Tales of the Arabian Nights*, *The Seven Voy-*

ages of Sinbad the Sailor, Peter Pan, Tom Thumb, The Scarlet Pimpernel, and many others. I think the name of the red-covered books these stories were in was *Journeys Through Bookland.* They were compiled by Charles H. Sylvester, and were part of a universal anthology that was put together especially for children with some of the finest literary masterpieces in the world in them.

These masterpieces ran the gamut of possibilities. There were short stories, long stories, epic tales, everyday adventures, poems, and virtually everything else. They were drawn from every conceivable part of the world—western, eastern, northern, and southern—and, like the experience with the little old Jewish lady, filled me with a keen desire to learn more about the diverse cultures, traditions, customs, and countries of the world. They also instilled in me an appreciation for great literature that has persisted to this day. It is difficult to see how a comprehensive education in the arts can be achieved without it.

My parents also saw to it that I was able to enjoy a number of theatrical performances when I was young. One of the most memorable of these was a performance by an aboriginal group on the Six Nations Reserve near Brantford, Ontario one crisp, fall evening in September. I cannot remember the subject matter of the performance, but it had a profound effect on me. Perhaps it was about Hiawatha, the legendary chief of the Onondaga tribe who founded the Iroquois Confederacy and was immortalized in a famous poem by Henry Longfellow called *The Song of Hiawatha.* But much more likely it was about Joseph Brant, the brilliant Mohawk leader and political strategist who was friendly with the British and led the colonial Loyalists and Indian troops against the American troops during the great American Revolutionary War.

After the war, Brant relocated in Ontario and became a prominent advocate and tireless negotiator for the Six Nations Indians. He also built a farm and homestead on a large tract of land that had been given to him in the Burlington-Brantford area by John Graves Simcoe, Governor of Ontario. He became so well known, in fact, that the City of Brantford and Brant County are named after him. But what stands out most clearly in my mind was the incredible setting that was selected for the aforementioned performance. It took place on and around a lake well after dark. The site was lit with huge torches and candles, with the audience seated on the shore of the lake. It was a captivating experience, which kept me in a state of rapture and suspense for the entire production.

There is one final area that deserves mention because it is so fundamentally related to the education I received in the arts when I was young. It has to do with the home my parents created for us. Although this was not as specific or concrete as taking piano lessons, art lessons, singing in a choir, listening to classical music, being exposed to a great deal of wonderful literature, or seeing an enthralling theatrical production, it seemed to incorporate everything my parents knew about the arts rolled into one.

We have all been in enough family residences to know that there is a huge difference between a "house" and a "home." A house has all the accoutrements and trappings that are required for life and living—tables, chairs, beds, sofas, lamps, pots, kettles, a stove, a refrigerator, a furnace, carpets, wall hangings, paintings, and the like. However, this doesn't make it a home. It only becomes a home when these things are arranged with consummate care, attractively displayed, cleverly presented, and a great deal of artistry and creativity goes into ensuring that they serve aesthetic functions and not just practical or commonplace functions.

This is seldom a matter of money. More often than not, it is a matter of taste. Many people who have a great deal of money to spend on family abodes and household items are incapable of making a house a home. Conversely, many people who do not have a lot of money to spend are more than capable of doing this. We have all experienced family dwellings where people have an enormous amount of money to spend on furnishing and decorations and end up creating a place that is cold, impersonal, and unattractive rather than warm, enjoyable, and inviting. And the more money they spend, often the worse things get! Unfortunately, they lack the artistic sensibilities and aesthetic sensitivities that are required to make a house a home.

Not so my parents. They knew exactly how to make our house a home and had an incredible knack for this, which I believe was intimately tied up with their awareness of, and appreciation for, the arts. They seemed to know where everything fit, what went with what and what did not, and how to achieve the maximum effect. This was especially true for my mother. Although she had very little money to work with and had to be extremely careful with every penny, she knew exactly how to use pictures, wall-hangings, knick-knacks, craft objects, carpets, and so forth to warm a room, create intimacy and aesthetic appeal, make every room distinctive and unique, and blend all the various parts together to form a harmonious and integrated whole. As a result, we enjoyed living in Toronto immensely. Although our home was not in the best of neighbourhoods and was semi-detached, this didn't matter to us. It had an artistic appeal and aesthetic ambiance about it that was as cherished as it was rare. It made life and living for me, Murray, and my parents far more memorable and satisfying than it otherwise would have been.

While the education I received in the arts when I was young was provided primarily by my parents, it was supplemented at elementary and secondary school. There were the usual art and music classes—which were largely concerned with how to play a musical instrument and paint pictures—as well as a number of opportunities to engage in extramural activities, such as going to a community drama production, joining a photography club, or participating in the school play or annual music night. This was especially true at secondary school. Indeed, it was at secondary school that my musical horizons were broadened quite considerably. Although I had listened to a great deal of classical music and sung an enormous amount of religious music, I had not been exposed to much music of other kinds. This changed dramatically when I was in secondary school, and I have been grateful for this ever since.

It was at secondary school that I was exposed to musicals for the first time, which were extremely popular when I was growing up in the 1950s and '60s. Most of these musicals were created by American composers and lyricists, such as Richard Rodgers, Oscar Hammerstein II, Alan Jay Lerner, Frederick Loewe, and others. Three of my favourites were *Carousel*, *Brigadoon*, and *Oklahoma*, which were performed at the secondary school I attended although I was not involved in any of the productions. But they filled me with a love for musicals in general—and American musicals in particular—that has grown steadily since that time, including *South Pacific*, *The King and I*, *My Fair Lady*, *Porgy and Bess*, and somewhat later, *The Sound of Music* and *Camelot*. These musicals, and others, have many wonderful songs in them, such as "If I Loved You" and "You'll Never Walk Alone" from *Carousel* and "Some Enchanted Evening" from *South Pacific*. I wish these and other musicals were performed more often than they are now, since they are filled with many exquisite songs and melodies that linger on in the mind and memory for decades.

It was also at secondary school that I was exposed to a great deal of popular music for the first time, and developed a keen appreciation for it. As a result, I enjoy popular music today as well as classical music, and don't make much distinction between the two. If I like a piece of music and I think it is beautiful, I will listen to it regardless of what people think or whether it is popular or classical in nature.

Many popular songs were all the rage when I was in secondary school, including "Love is a Many-Splendored Thing," "Shangri-La," "Unchained Melody," "Band of Gold," "Mr. Sandman," "My Prayer," "Sh-Boom," "I Believe," "I'm a Stranger in Paradise," and "Three Coins in the Fountain." Numerous singers and groups were also popular, such as Debbie Reynolds, Rosemary Clooney, Patti Page, Perry Como, Frank Sinatra, Frankie Laine, the McGuire Sisters, The Four Lads, The Four Coins, The Platters, and others. I enjoy listening to these singers and groups when-ever I hear them—which regrettably is far too seldom—as well as the music of many other singers who were popular at the time.

I am sure this is true for all young people and all musical eras, be it the 1950s and '60s, the '70s and '80s, the '90s, and the new millennium. Every era produces its own pop stars who are favourites, such as Elvis Presley, the Beatles, the Rolling Stones, the Bee Gees, Abba, Ella Fitzgerald, Bob Dylan, Ray Charles, Barbra Streisand, Madonna, Céline Dion, Beyoncé Knowles, Lady Gaga, Justin Bieber, and countless others who have been popular over the last half century or are popular today. This may have something to do with the fact that many people have romantic attractions and love affairs when they are young—romantic attractions and love affairs that often last a lifetime—and these are usually tied up with music or the arts in some way. I am always amazed at how many people end up marrying their childhood or high school sweethearts and spending the rest of their lives together.

Although there were many other opportunities to enjoy the arts when I was in secondary school, most of the students did not have the intensive education in the arts that I did when I was young, due to the strong com-mitment that was made to this by my parents. And I was aware of something else. I was aware of how much friction there was between the arts and sports when I was in school.

This is best demonstrated by the experience I had with the French horn in secondary school. When I was in grade eleven, I decided to take music as an option. I was told that I would have to learn to play a musical instru-ment as a fundamental prerequisite of this option. So I decided to take the French horn because it had a mellow tone and sounded nice. I was also in-volved in a number of sports at the time, especially football and basketball. Whenever I had to take the French horn home to practice, I would leave school early on those days because I didn't want my teammates on the football or basketball team to see me carrying an awkward-looking French horn case home from school for fear of being ridiculed and teased too much. So I would slink along side streets and over backyard fences with this cumbersome-looking French horn case under my arm, always being eternally grateful it wasn't a tuba or a double bass. You can imagine how embarrassing it would have been for me to be seen carrying a French horn, tuba, or double bass home from school when I was the quarterback of the football team and we were well on our way to winning a T. D. I. A. A. —Toronto District Intercollegiate Athletic Association—football championship.

This friction between the arts and sports was palpable when I was in secondary school. And it wasn't confined to athletes. It affected every boy and girl at the school because sports were generally deemed to be "male activities" whereas the arts were generally deemed to be "female activities." But the consequences were the same. It kept boys out of the arts, and girls out of sports. I have often wondered if things have changed significantly in this respect now that girls are much more involved in sports than they were in those days. My impression is that things haven't changed all that much, although I have no factual evidence or empirical documentation to back this up.

When I went to university, my education in the arts was curtailed somewhat, although I continued to enjoy listening to music and visiting art galleries and museums whenever I had the opportunity to do so. Nevertheless, I didn't take any formal classes in the arts because I was enrolled in a very heavy commerce and finance and then economics program and there was simply no provision for courses in the arts. As a result, I had to settle for enjoying the arts in my spare moments and leisure time, although they were never far from my mind. However, I did have one experience in the arts at university that had a profound effect on me. Like many other experiences, it was in the field of music. It did a great deal to expand my musical horizons even more, largely by exposing me to an area of music that was not well known to me at the time but has been an integral part of my life ever since.

It happened one day when I was walking past Hart House at the University of Toronto. Suddenly I heard some exquisite music lofting out of one of the windows at Hart House. I stood there for the longest time listening to this music because it was so incredibly beautiful and I had never heard it before. When it was over, I went to the music room at Hart House to find out what it was and who had composed it. It turned out to be *The Four Seasons* by Antonio Vivaldi, one of the world's greatest composers of baroque music. While I had been exposed to a great deal of baroque music through composers like Johann Sebastian Bach and George Frideric Handel during my years in the choir, I had not been exposed to much baroque music by other composers and certainly nothing by Vivaldi that I can remember.

Hearing *The Four Seasons* opened up a whole new musical world for me. It instilled in me an avid desire to learn more about the music of Vivaldi—the so-called "Red Priest"—as well as other baroque composers such as Arcangelo Corelli, Alessandro Scarlatti, and Tomaso Albinoni from Italy, François Couperin and Jean-Philippe Rameau from France, Henry Purcell and John Stanley from England, Georg Philipp Telemann from Germany, Domenico Scarlatti from Italy and Spain—and the son of Alessandro Scarlatti—and Dietrich Buxtehude from Denmark. This turned out to be a real "find" for me, as baroque music has played a prominent role in my life ever since. I love the music of baroque composers. It is so uplifting, majestic, and accessible that it never fails to move me and fill me with a great deal of joy and inspiration whenever and wherever I hear it. This is confirmed by many other people. In fact, contemporary research is revealing that baroque music has a very favourable and exhilarating effect on people because it is very regal and evocative and affects that part of the brain that produces positive feelings, emotions, and sensations.

Looking back on the many different experiences I had in the arts in my youth—both inside and outside the formal educational system—makes me realize how fortunate I was to be exposed to the arts when I was young, as all people are even if they have not had the good fortune to experience the rich and varied education in the arts that I did. There is only one thing I would change if it was possible to do so. I would see to it that every person was given a solid education in the architectural, cinematographic, culinary, and horticultural arts, as well as in the material arts or crafts. For although I had a comprehensive education in the visual, musical, and literary arts, and was exposed to a fair amount of drama, I didn't have any education in these other areas. It was only later in life that I realized what I had missed. Unfortunately, I had to wait until I was well into my thirties and had travelled a great deal before realizing how important the architectural, cinematographic, culinary, horticultural, and material arts are for life and living.

All this raises a very interesting question. What is it about the arts in general—and arts education in particular—that make it so imperative for every person in the world to have a comprehensive education in the arts? Since there are many reasons, it pays to examine these reasons in depth because the arts and especially arts education provide an incredible foundation for life.

First of all, the arts and arts education bring an enormous amount of fulfillment and happiness in life, not only when people are young but in all stages of life. The joy and satisfaction that comes from music, paintings, plays, literature, dance, and the like is immense, especially if we open our hearts, minds, souls, spirits, senses, and intellects to them and allow them to penetrate into the interior of our beings. Exposure to the arts during our youth is an investment that yields myriad benefits throughout life. There is simply no substitute for it.

This doesn't always require a great deal of money. In fact, while attending professional concerts and plays and taking private singing, dance, and music lessons can be expensive, there are usually ample opportunities to enjoy the arts in all communities and countries that are not too expensive if we search them out and hunt for them. The satisfaction that derives from this over the course of a lifetime is incalculable, and is evident on the faces of young people, children, adults, and seniors whenever we encounter them enjoying a concert, a play, a painting, a piece of music, a dance, or some other captivating artistic work.

Fortunately, this is much easier to achieve today than it was in the past, due largely to developments in modern technology. There is hardly a person in any part of the world who is not able to access the arts through radio, television, film, computers, iPhones, iPods, BlackBerries, the Internet, YouTube, Facebook, Twitter, tablets, or some other technological device owned by family, friends, schools, local groups, or people in the community. The ability to gain access to works of art of the highest calibre by virtually every artist and arts organization in the world—past and present, ancient and modern, Asian, African, Latin American, Caribbean, North American and Middle Eastern—is an achievement of monumental proportions, as people everywhere in the world are discovering to their pleasure and delight.

This is enhanced many times over when people get involved in the arts in a participatory way. The ability to play a musical instrument, sing in a choir, paint a picture, perform in a theatrical production, or make a craft object can bring an immense amount of pleasure and satisfaction in life. To actually be able to sit down and play a piece of music on the piano, draw a picture of birds, animals, landscapes, or people, dance in the street, participate in making a film or television program, take photographs, or fashion gifts from small bits of paper, cloth, wood, or other materials is an asset of major proportions. There is simply no substitute for this or time limit on it. It can be done at any time in one's life, as elderly people are discovering in seniors' homes and retirement centres in virtually all parts of the world today.

The arts also provide excellent vehicles for developing our communication skills and abilities. They make it possible for us to speak more clearly, write more concisely, and express our thoughts and ideas more cogently and convincingly. While I have never taken a drama course, my neighbour next door tells me that the drama course her daughter took in high school was *the most important class she ever took in school.* It helped her come out of her shell, perform effectively in groups, communicate more easily with the public, and develop a strong sense of identity, confidence, belonging, and self-worth.

This is enriched by the fact that the arts are excellent vehicles for expressing our emotions and feelings. It is impossible to participate in any artistic endeavour without learning to express one's feelings and emotions in sensitive, moving, and caring ways, as well as connect with people on a deeper, richer, and more profound and compassionate level. While the arts can be provocative at times—and must be if they are to perform one of their most essential functions in society—the feelings and emotions that are evoked through the arts are usually far more positive than negative. They seldom injure people, destroy things, or produce irrational or violent forms of behaviour.

One of the most interesting things about the arts is the fact that different instruments, plays, paintings, colours, and so forth can evoke different feelings and emotions. There is a significant difference, for example, between the feelings and emotions that are evoked by an oboe or a saxophone—which are often soothing, haunting, and melancholy in nature—and the feelings and emotions that are evoked by a cello or a trumpet, which tend to be more assertive and strident in nature. All that is required to confirm this is to listen to an oboe concerto by Tomaso Albinoni, a musical composition played by saxophonists like Charlie "Bird" Parker, John Coltrane, or Stan Getz, a cello work performed by Yo-Yo Ma, or a trumpet voluntary played by Wynton Marsalis. And what is true for musical instruments is equally true for paintings, plays, colours, and so forth. Think, for example, of the different emotions and feelings that are evoked by looking at a painting by Hieronymus Bosch compared to one by William Turner, watching a play by William Shakespeare compared to one by August Strindberg, or just looking at the colours red, green, blue, yellow, and black. Advertising executives and marketing experts are fully aware of this latter capability, and use it all the time to develop advertising tactics and marketing strategies that are designed to elicit specific responses from customers, consumers, and clients.

Developing communication skills and abilities and expressing feelings and emotions are not the only advantages to be derived from participation in the arts and a first-class education in the arts. The potential exists to develop many other capabilities as well. While some art forms tend to be more individual in character—the visual and material arts for example—others tend to be more collaborative in character. Take drama, music, and opera for instance. It is impossible to put on a play, perform a symphony, or stage an opera without engaging in a great deal of cooperation and teamwork. This cooperation and teamwork ranges all the way from working together on the creation of sets and props and rehearsing scenes and movements to practising parts and putting on final performances. Through the preparation and production of works of art, people learn to work collectively in the realization of common causes, goals, and objectives, thereby developing collaborative skills and cooperative abilities that are in great demand throughout the world today. This also provides a great deal of social interaction and human cohesion, thereby counteracting the isolation that comes from contemporary technology and is such a major problem in the world today.

It is impossible to engage in the arts without learning to discipline oneself and use one's time, talents, and faculties effectively. This doesn't always mean discipline by an authoritarian teacher. More often than not, it means mastering tools, techniques, methods, instruments, materials, and the like for oneself. This helps to develop our physical and mental capabilities to a much greater extent, as well as realize more effective use of hands, legs, feet, arms, eyes, ears, minds, and bodies. Small wonder educators, social workers, psychologists, and health care providers are using the arts more and more frequently to help people deal with a whole host of mental, physical, emotional, and spiritual problems.

What is true for people in general is equally true for people suffering from many different types of illnesses, diseases, and ailments. Recent research is revealing that people suffering from depression, anxiety, autism, Alzheimer's, or multiple sclerosis, living out the final stages of their lives, or who are housed in penal and mental institutions profit immensely from exposure to the arts and particularly participation in the arts. This is true for every art form, but especially for music. Listening to music, playing a musical instrument, singing in a choir, and so forth are powerful elixirs and great tonics for people in such circumstances because they activate chemical changes and physical reactions in the body and the brain that counteract negative images and stereotypes. And the more scientific research that is conducted in this area, the more the evidence accumulates that the arts produce mental and physical changes in the body and the mind that enhance people's quality of life and their ability to withstand some of the most difficult trials, tribulations, and challenges in life.

There is also the possibility of developing our critical faculties and sense of awareness, discrimination, and taste more effectively. This enhances our ability to make better judgements and assessments concerning a whole range of issues affecting our lives, our families, our communities, our social situations, and our environmental difficulties. This often morphs into a greater sense of awareness and appreciation for the skills, abilities, and accomplishments of others. It is impossible to participate in any artistic activity—be it a production, a performance, or an exhibition—without respecting the quest for excellence and perfection that lies at the heart of all artistic endeavours. This is invaluable, regardless of one's occupation, position, job, or station in life.

There is also much to be learned from the arts about life, living, and the world around us. Not only do the arts open up vast vistas and fertile avenues for exploration and discovery, but they also provide an unbelievable window on the world and everything contained in the world. Everything is there in one form or another: the universe, nature, the human species, other species, countries, cultures, history, geography, time, space, the past, the present, the future, and virtually everything else.

Take, for example, what can be learned about the universe, nature, and other species. There is an incredible amount to be learned about this from Hildegard von Bingen's *Symphony of the Harmony of Heavenly Revelation*, Gustav Holst's *The Planets*, Antonio Vivaldi's *Four Seasons*, Ludwig van Beethoven's *Pastoral Symphony*, Franz Schubert's *Trout Quartet*, Camile Saint-Saëns' *Carnival of the Animals*, Allan Hovhannes' *Mysterious Mountain*, Vaughan Williams' *The Lark Ascending*, Claude Debussy's *La Mer* (*The Sea*), Vincent d'Indy's *Symphony on a French Mountain Air*, and countless other works. It can also be achieved by studying the nature paintings of Claude Monet, Vincent van Gogh, and a host of other painters, the poetry of William Wordsworth, Samuel Taylor Coleridge, Percy Bysshe Shelley, John Keats, and Walt Whitman, the writings of Ralph Waldo Emerson, Henry David Thoreau, and John Muir, the photographs of Ansel Adams, and the works of wildlife artists such as John James Audubon, Owen Gromme, Robert Bateman, and Glen Loates. While much more might be said about this, suffice it to say that artists of all types have a great deal to teach us about the extraterrestrial and natural worlds in all their diverse aspects and manifestations.

The same holds true for life, living, human beings, and virtually everything related to human beings. There is an enormous amount to be learned about such matters from authors like William Shakespeare, George Bernard Shaw, Oscar Wilde, Jean-Baptiste Molière, Miguel de Cervantes, Dante Alighieri, Charles Dickens, Omar Khayyám, Jalal al-Din Rumi, Mark Twain, and numerous others. They teach us a great deal about things that are both extraordinary and commonplace, real and imagined, simple and complex, and encountered time and again in our lives regardless of where we live in the world or what we work at. Take Shakespeare, for instance. His plays are full of insights into different personality types, diverse social, political, and societal situations, human triumphs and tragedies, and personal foibles and insecurities, which helps to explain why his plays are as revered today as they were the day they were first performed. His deep insights into life, living, the human condition, and personal strengths and weaknesses in plays such as *Hamlet, Macbeth, King Lear, Romeo and Juliet, Othello, The Tempest*, and *Twelfth Night* are phenomenal to say the least.

And this is not all. The arts also have a great deal to teach us about different countries, cultures, and civilizations. This is because artists and arts organizations create many of the signs, symbols, myths, legends, metaphors, rituals, and stories that are needed to shed light on these and other human collectivities as "dynamic and organic wholes" or "overall ways of life." There is an enormous amount to be learned about France and French culture, for instance, from the works of Jean-Baptiste Racine, Claude Debussy, Maurice Ravel, Cécile Chaminade, Victor Hugo, Alexander Dumas, Edgar Degas, and Henri de Toulouse-Lautrec, just as there is a great deal to be learned about United States and American culture from the works of William Faulkner, Scott Fitzgerald, Ernest Hemingway, Aaron Copland, George Gershwin, Irving Berlin, Ken Burns, and Frank Lloyd Wright. These countries and cultures would not come alive for us the way they do if it was not for the aforementioned works and others dealing with the same matter.

This is equally true for history. Like the writing of history itself, the arts have a great deal to pass on about the past, as well as the historical development and evolution of every country, culture, and civilization in the world and the world as a whole. Every country, culture, and civilization in the world has a precious legacy of artistic works—paintings, plays, novels, sacred and secular texts, architectural edifices, musical masterpieces, craft objects, and the like—that say "this is who we are." These legacies provide a running commentary on how every country, culture, and civilization in the world came into existence, evolved historically, and what it cherishes most today. Since these legacies bring the histories of these human collectivities to life, they must be preserved, protected, and promoted as one of the most effective vehicles for understanding the past and seeing its relevance for the present and the future of all.

To this should be added what can be learned from the many different qualities that exist in the arts that enhance our knowledge, understanding, and mastery of other disciplines. From the visual arts, architecture, and the crafts, there is a great deal to be learned about colour, shape, mass, texture, form, proportion, and perspective; from dance, drama, and literature, there is much to be learned about balance, movement, muscle control, physical coordination, tragedy, comedy, satire, and pathos; and from music, there is much to be learned about sound, rhythm, harmony, counterpoint, and composition. These qualities can be used to great advantage in studying and mastering other disciplines—especially disciplines like physics, chemistry, geometry, mathematics, and so forth—which is why philosophers and scholars have long recognized the intimate connection between the arts, the sciences, mathematics, and other disciplines. Indeed, contemporary research is revealing that children's ability to master complex subjects and concepts and difficult theories, ideas, and systems escalates rapidly when they are able to benefit from an education in the arts.

The arts also have a great deal to teach us about excellence, diversity, change, specialization, integration, and creativity—properties and characteristics that are of crucial importance in the modern world.

Take excellence as an example. Regardless of what occupation or profession people decide to pursue, learning to pursue and achieve excellence is imperative for every occupation and profession in the world. The arts value excellence more than any other discipline and activity in society. This is because excellence is imperative for the mastery of every art form and the performance of every artistic endeavour. No one likes to watch artistic performances that are mediocre or inferior in nature, since this leaves much to be desired. In order to prevent this, it is essential to aspire to and achieve excellence in every artistic discipline, which often turns out to be the key to mastering excellence in other disciplines and subjects as well. It is also the key to understanding what is meant by "the art of science," "the art of politics," "the art of engineering," "the art of business," and so forth, since these activities become art forms in their own right when they are conducted and practiced at the highest level of excellence. This can be achieved in any area, subject, or activity if we are wise enough to recognize it and learn from the arts what must be learned to realize excellence and perfection in everything we do.

This is equally true for diversity and change. The arts are incredibly diverse and are always changing, evolving, and mutating, thereby exposing us to new ways of thinking, doing, and altered forms of consciousness. While many techniques in the arts must be repeated over and over again to master them, one of the most important things about the arts is the fact that they are in a constant state of flux, not only in time but also in space. What is commonplace today may not be commonplace tomorrow, as the history of music, drama, the visual arts, opera, literature, and other art forms constantly reminds us. The arts are always on the move, so to speak, thereby helping people to deal effectively with diversity, change, and a world that is in perpetual motion.

The same is true for specialization. Depending on the problem at hand and specific needs and circumstances, the arts can be sufficiently focused to develop highly specialized skills and abilities. Through the material arts or crafts, for example, specialization can be developed in the use of hands and eyes, and therefore in the use of mechanical and technological tools and hand and eye coordination. Through music, specialization can be achieved in the utilization of the ear, and therefore improvements in aural acuity and awareness of acoustic ecology. And what is true for these art forms is also true for other art forms. Every art form can be sufficiently focused to provide refinement in any of our sensory, intellectual, or physical faculties and capabilities.

The arts also teach us a great deal about integration. By stretching across all human faculties, they can be used to great advantage to assist us in becoming "whole people" and "total human beings" in the best and most complete sense of these terms.

Since the arts engage the mind, body, heart, soul, intellect, spirit, and senses, they provide a way of bringing together all our human faculties to create a harmonious and organic whole. This makes us more balanced within ourselves, as well as more in tune with the world. This is why artists, arts institutions, and the arts have been in the vanguard of the movement to educate "the whole person" ever since Matthew Arnold, the great nineteenth century British scholar and poet, espoused the need for the harmonious development of all the powers that comprise human nature. He was strongly opposed to the development of any one of these powers to the exclusion of others, and equally fully in favour of promoting excellence, perfection, and sharing the best humanity has to offer through the arts and education or "sweetness and light." Not bad advice for people living in a fragmented, disconnected, and disoriented world.

If the arts are the key to developing the whole person, they are also the key to developing the creative person. As such, they represent one of the best vehicles of all for helping people in general—and young people in particular—to respond imaginatively to the complexities and uncertainties of the modern world, not to mention the rapidly-changing nature of local, regional, national, and international events.

Many people feel that education should be directed towards preparing people for specific jobs, professions, disciplines, and activities. With the rapid rate of technological change and occupational turnover in recent years—it is now estimated that people will have fifteen to twenty different jobs during the course of their lives—this traditional view has started to change. It is now apparent that narrowly-trained and highly-specialized people are incapable of adjusting to the stresses, strains, and realities of the modern world, with totally different employment situations and jobs that are radically being transformed, restructured, or eliminated. In consequence, far more attention is being paid today to educating people who are creative—people who can respond creatively to whatever circumstances or conditions they are confronted with because they have learned to use their mental, physical, emotional, and spiritual powers and capabilities in new, original, and highly inventive ways. It is creativity—not conformity—that enables people to perform effectively in jobs and occupations today, as well as fashion new forms of living and altered forms of behaviour and consciousness.

I had my own experience with this many years ago. While I did not lose my job or have it terminated, I decided I no longer wanted to work in the area I was trained to work in at university. I was originally trained as an economist and taught economics for several years before making this decision. After a great deal of soul-searching and discussion, I finally decided that I wanted to work in the arts. But how? All my formal training had been in economics and I had no formal training, qualifications, or certification in the arts. So how would it be possible for me to make the transition from an area I no longer wanted to work in to an area I desperately wanted to work in? In short, how was it possible to turn my *avocation* into a *vocation* and *occupation*? It is a question that many people are confronted with, but few take the time and trouble to wrestle with and resolve.

In my case, the answer came through a bit of creative ingenuity on my part. Why not design a study of "the economics of the arts" and propose it to a number of arts organizations and institutions? This would enable me to draw on my knowledge of economics while simultaneously taking advantage of the experience I had gleaned through the education I received in the arts when I was young. While friends in the economics profession told me there was no such thing as "the economics of the arts," I persisted and went ahead and designed the study anyway. It was a good thing I did, because it was picked up by the Ontario Arts Council, which eventually hired me to undertake the study.

As luck would have it, this study morphed into a much larger study of theatre in Ontario—*The Ontario Theatre Study*—which was concerned with all aspects and manifestations of theatre in the province, from the economic and social to the psychological, educational, and political. I was asked to design this study as a result of my training in economics and the social sciences, and was then asked to become actively involved in its development and execution. This eventually led to my appointment as assistant director of the Ontario Arts Council and director of the Council's Centre for Arts Research in Education. Within a few short years, I had made the successful transition from economics to the arts, which ultimately resulted in spending the rest of my life in the arts and cultural field. My life, my life's work, and the focus of all my energies and efforts were totally transformed, largely as a result of some creative thinking and ingenuity on my part.

I doubt very much whether this would have been possible had it not been for the education I received in the arts in my youth. This education helped me to develop my creative faculties to a much greater extent than would have been the case if I had not had this education. It also made it possible for me to pursue an entirely different career path—a path that has brought me an enormous amount of fulfillment and happiness in life because I am doing what I want to do and doing it to the best of my ability, thereby confirming Confucius's wise advice to "find a job you love and you will never work a day in your life." This career path has been filled with many creative challenges, opportunities, jobs, and projects over the years. While some of these have been created by myself—such as the World Culture Project—others have been created in conjunction with other people and other institutions, most notably the development of two highly innovative programs in arts administration at York University and the University of Toronto.

Without the education I received in the arts, I doubt very much if I would have been able to create these projects, jobs, and programs, or to confront the challenges and opportunities I have been presented with in life in imaginative and innovative ways. Much of this has come from my early exposure to the arts in general and artistic qualities such as creativity, excellence, beauty, and the quest for the sublime in particular. But the quality that has taught me the most about life and the world around me is *holism*. Not only did I learn very early that every work of art is a holistic entity composed of many interconnected and interrelated parts, but also I learned a great deal about holism that has been extremely valuable at each and every stage of the life process, primarily in terms of how to bring things together rather than split them apart.

As I reflect back on these experiences, I am in a much better position to understand why a comprehensive education in the arts is so essential for every person. Not only does it enable us to reap enormous benefits and numerous rewards over the course of a lifetime, but also it provides the foundations that are imperative for a happy, healthy, productive, and fulfilling life. These foundations are both practical and theoretical in nature.

By enabling us to develop all our faculties and not just some faculties, the arts make it possible for us to become whole people and find balance, harmony, meaning, synergy, and symmetry in life. By making it possible to express our feelings and emotions in positive and constructive rather than negative and destructive ways—as well as to react imaginatively and creatively to complex problems and possibilities—the arts facilitate our adjustments to a world that is in perpetual motion and continuous flux. And by assisting us to learn an incredible amount about life, living, and the world around us—in both human and non-human terms—the arts broaden, deepen, enrich, and intensify our knowledge, understanding, and appreciation of many things that are of quintessential importance in life. In other words, the arts give us all the equipment we need to live complete, constructive, compassionate and caring lives, not only in the internal and personal sense, but also in the external and professional sense. They also enable us to reduce the huge ecological footprint we are making on the natural environment because they are primarily labour-intensive rather than capital-intensive or material-intensive in nature, thereby reducing our consumption of scarce natural resources and providing excellent models for environmental sustainability and human happiness.

It is for reasons such as these that every child and young person in the world should receive a comprehensive education in the arts. This education should not be limited to a few art forms, but spread liberally across all art forms. It should also include opportunities to participate actively in the arts on both an informal and formal basis. Every child and young person in the world, be it in Africa, Asia, Latin America, North America, the Caribbean, or the Middle East, should have enough opportunities to participate in the arts that the arts become the foundation for life. As Des McAnuff, former artistic director of the Stratford Shakespeare Festival in Stratford, Ontario, said:

> To deny young people first-hand encounters with art of the highest order is to hobble their powers of imagination. And since those young people will be the citizens and leaders of tomorrow, the future vision and vigour of our society are ultimately at stake. . . . Encouraging universal and affordable access to art should be a public priority.[1]

It was convictions like this that caused delegates at the Second World Conference on Arts Education—which was convened by UNESCO in Seoul, South Korea, in 2010—to articulate what is now called "the Seoul Agenda." This Agenda set out a number of fundamental goals and strategies for arts education, as well as a detailed action plan to implement them. Included among these goals and strategies are the need to:

- Ensure that arts education is accessible as a fundamental and sustainable component of a high quality renewal of education;

- Apply arts education principles and practices to contribute to resolving the social and cultural challenges facing today's world;

[1] Des McAnuff, "Wake up young minds with the arts," *Toronto Star*, September 19, 2010, p. A15.

- Support and enhance the role of arts education in the promotion of social responsibility, social cohesion, cultural diversity, and intercultural dialogue;

- Affirm arts education as the foundation for balanced creative, cognitive, emotional, aesthetic, and social development of children, youth, and life-long learning.

Goals and strategies like these confirm what is required to create a strong and firm foundation for life. If every child and young person in the world were given a comprehensive education in the arts, they would have all the equipment they need to live rich, full, meaningful, and creative lives. The result would be much happier people and a far more harmonious world, with a great deal more peace, order, stability, and civility, and far less violence, destruction, devastation, and war. In the final analysis, this is what an arts education is all about. It is about making the world a better, safer, more secure place for all the world's diverse peoples and countries.

CHAPTER TWO

Towards a New World Order:
The Age of Culture

If I seem to take part in politics, it is only because politics encircle us today like the coil of a snake from which one cannot get out, no matter how much one tries. I wish therefore to wrestle with the snake.

To me, political power is not an end in itself, but one of the means of enabling people to better their condition in every department of life.
—Mahatma Gandhi

L ike politics and philosophy, culture plays a fundamental role in shaping the personality of the individual and the character of the world. How, then, are we to account for the growing interest in culture that is springing up around the world? Like some, are we to assume that it flows naturally, perhaps inevitably, out of earlier preoccupations with economic growth, educational enlightenment, and social change? Or, are we to conclude that the escalating interest in cultural practices and policies in prominent political and public circles throughout the world must be viewed as an early warning signal that all is not right in the world as we know it? In effect, is this interest merely reinforcing the existing world order or is it setting in motion forces which may soon conspire to create an entirely new international pattern, a different system of world values?

Needless to say, the fact that culture can be used in positive and negative ways, like many other activities in society, betrays a dual realization of the incredible capacity culture contains for influencing individual actions as well as conditioning mass behaviour. Given the manipulative potential of culture, it is remarkable that as individuals and as nations, we seem prepared to gamble with such risks in order to pursue cultural interests.

Of course, viewed from the opposite optic, this willingness to incur risks may really reflect the severity of world problems as well as the necessity for immediate and imaginative action.

A New World Perspective

In the mid-1960s, much of the social scientific literature pouring out of the western world was filled with explicit statements or implicit suggestions about the imminent emergence of a world Nirvana. It was scarcely possible to pick up a book or read an article without encountering the belief that the western world was passing over the threshold to an entirely new social order, a kind of post-industrial society. How was this Nirvana being achieved? Through advanced automation or cybernation—the effective application of self-regulating technologies to diverse economic processes—it was assumed that western man was being liberated rather quickly from traditional dependency on the work ethic. Once achieved, it was concluded that this liberation from menial bondage to economic necessity could be extended, albeit with greater difficulty, to the rest of the world so that all people could get on with the more essential aspects of life and living.

Less than a decade later, the western world—indeed, the entire world—seemed precariously poised on the brink of an economic-political crisis about to assume gigantic proportions. Suddenly, almost without warning, the post-industrial Nirvana of the middle and late '60s seemed to be rapidly disintegrating into a pre-industrial Hades of the '70s, as industrial expansion and political optimism gave way to pronounced economic dislocations and public pessimism. As these disruptions took place, words like depression, crisis, catastrophe, and doomsday slipped slowly but surely from private discourse into the public vernacular.

As time presses on, it becomes more and more obvious that a matrix of world problems has emerged on the global horizon which defies existing, practical solutions. Deep down, there is a sinking feeling that these problems stand well beyond the known, theoretical systems designed for dealing with them. It would seem that the conventional twentieth-century solution for coping with industrial dislocations and economic depressions and cycles—the Keynesian economics—has already outlived its effectiveness.

In its most elementary form, the Keynesian and post-Keynesian system has been built on three fundamental factors: the establishment of an impartial, public body to regulate economic activity and settle disputes between labour and capital; the encouragement of consumption and investment practices which consume world resources at an accelerated or multiplied rate; and the promotion of technologies which subordinate human values to mechanical means, thereby encouraging conformity in public tastes.

Rapidly changing world conditions make these solutions totally unacceptable or untenable. How can governments effectively balance and regulate economic activity when they have grown to the point where they are in rather drastic need of regulation themselves? How can public authorities act as impartial mediators in disputes between labour and capital when they have vested interests in the outcome of almost all disputes and consequently lack credibility in both camps? More fundamentally, how can an economic system based on excessive levels of consumption and investment and needless and irrational wastage of world resources by a privileged few be justified when the plight of the underprivileged many is still poverty, starvation, and perpetual resource shortage? And how can technological forms be sanctioned which preclude active involvement in the decision-making process and prevent any real fulfillment from human industry and effort?

In a philosophical sense, there is nothing particularly new or startling about these general observations. What is new is the way in which more and more people around the world, either through passive dissent or active resistance, are refusing to cooperate with the dominant value system and the traditional world order.[1]

At present, this new world consciousness, this emerging counterculture is viewed by those in positions of economic and political power as little more than a set of temporary and isolated disturbances in the existing world balance. Somehow they seem unaware of the paramount need for new forms of economic activity which spring more from the human imagination and depend less on mindless and monotonous mechanical repetition. They are slow to realize that they are actually sanctioning pointless resource wastage by encouraging technologies which reward obsolescence and penalize permanence. Furthermore, they confuse the basic human need for greater participation in the creation of new economic and political structures and cultural practices with a drift towards blind and thoughtless nationalism.

This resistance to the dominant world value system must be confronted

[1] T. Roszak, *The Making of a Counter Culture* (New York: Doubleday & Company, 1969).

for what it really represents: a deep and basic struggle between present and future world orders. Given our proximity to the present, our propensity for clinging to the secure, and our penchant for avoiding risks, it is perhaps understandable that initially we should try to preserve the old and familiar, rather than confronting the new and the uncertain. Even the Club of Rome seems more preoccupied with documenting the decay of the existing world order through its statistical collections of relative rates of resource utilization than it does with developing viable and effective plans for contributing to the emergence of a new world order. Before long, however, we will be forced to confront the fact that an entirely new world perspective must unfold which flows from a different set of perceptions, principles and priorities.

The Snow Thesis

There can be little doubt that the history of the world during the past several centuries has been dominated by a preoccupation with scientific, economic, and political priorities. No sooner had the religious-humanistic revolution failed to develop a value system based on inherent worth or qualitative judgment than the door was thrust open for the emergence of a value system predicated first on an attempt to discover the "value free" truths of science and later to accommodate the "value free" decisions of economics and politics.

In his fascinating book, *The Two Cultures and the Scientific Revolution*,[2] C. P. Snow contends that there is a basic conflict in the modern world between the scientific value system and the literary-intellectual (artistic-humanistic) value system.

Snow argues that the scientific value system is predicated on the external, the objective, and the altruistic. According to Snow, the scientist is concerned with discovering the laws which govern the external environment in order that we may better understand the way in which the universe functions. In the final analysis, Snow proposes that the scientist can only achieve this knowledge and understanding through total impartiality. Hence the need to suppress all emotions and perceptions as

---

[2] C.P. Snow, *The Two Cultures and the Scientific Revolution* (Cambridge: Cambridge University Press, 1959). In all fairness to Snow, it must be pointed out that, like Marx and Freud before him, he modified his original dialectical position in the face of personal reflections and refinements in the '60s. Like Snow, however, this author treats the dialectic as a relative tendency and epistemological device, rather than as an absolute truth or scientific law.

subjective or sensorial qualities unfit for true scientific inquiry. Detachment becomes the key to successful scientific investigation.

At the other extreme, there is the literary-intellectual value system which is predicated on the internal, the subjective, and the egocentric. For Snow, artists, humanists, and literary-intellectuals are aware of the tragic predicament of man. Ultimately, man is born alone and must die alone. This fundamental realization forces artists and writers inward, rather than outward. Unlike scientists, the challenge for artists is to explore the full range of human emotion as well as to expose the subjective side of human nature. Since this involves personal feelings and experiential processes, objectivity is clearly impossible.

Nowhere is the clash between these two dichotomous value systems better studied than in universities in the modern world. There can be little debate over which value system has reigned supreme in most universities. It has been science that has provided the real impetus for the exponential growth of most universities in the twentieth century. Scientific subjects of study are known around most universities as "hard" disciplines. To the extent that scientific methods and techniques have been transmitted to the study of psychology, anthropology, sociology, economics, and politics, these disciplines are now also accepted as "hard" disciplines. Most other subjects of study, including all of the arts and humanities, are seen and treated as "soft" disciplines. In fact, for Snow followers, "disciplines" is really a misnomer since by implication these subjects of study are viewed as intellectually flabby: it is tacitly assumed that they lack any rigorous method or require any systematic training.

This ridiculous notion is so superficial that it has lost all connection with the real needs of universities or contemporary society. Unfortunately, however, it still largely governs the disposition of educational funds. The more scientific an educational department is, the "harder" a discipline is willing to become, the greater the probability of acquiring funds. Conversely, the more artistic or humanistic a department is, the "softer" a discipline has become, the lesser the possibility of acquiring funds. Variations in this pattern are merely variations in personality, not in principle. Herein lies the critical problem. There is nothing wrong with science *per se*. The problem starts when the disposition of funds—in institutions of higher learning, in governments, and in corporations—is predicated on an exclusive adherence to scientific methods or acceptance of values and priorities derived solely from empirical procedures.

The fact that Snow's thesis aroused heated controversy when it was first published and has generated a prolonged debate which has persisted until today, bears vivid testimony to its ability to touch the central nerve of contemporary society. In part, this ability results from the use of a philosophical method that has always fascinated scholars: the dialectical process as it is known in the West or the principle of *yin* and *yang* in the East. Recently, this powerful theory of opposites—Marx and Freud precipitated revolutions around it—has been popularized in the notion of polarization. Perhaps a fitting tribute to its intellectual prowess!

Through this clever device of pushing tendencies to their logical conclusion, Snow concludes that the modern world must be developed through a progressive extension of the scientific value system rather than the artistic-humanistic value system. Since the former system produces altruism and optimism and the latter induces egoism and pessimism, according to Snow the solution is obvious. Diffuse science and suppress art. Set in motion those forces that will extend scientific methods and techniques to all parts of the world and all segments of society while simultaneously holding in check artistic and humanistic forces.

Whether or not pure science should provide the intellectual basis and moral foundation for future world development is a moot philosophical point that extends beyond the confines of this particular investigation. However, there can be little debate over the effect that science has had on past and present developments and herein lies the full force behind Snow's thesis. Through the use of a specific argument with profound general ramifications, Snow really uncovered the tip of a much more gigantic iceberg. We can now turn our attention more generally to world value systems.

World Value Systems
As the dominant discipline over the past two centuries, science found its corporeal form and practical application in economics and politics. Any glance at statistics on governmental expenditures or cursory examination of how decisions are made in public and private institutions will reveal how effectively this triad of dominant disciplines—science, economics, and politics—has combined to monopolize consumption and investment patterns and conditions the decision-making process.

This combination of theoretical and applied disciplines has produced a contemporary world order and dominant value system which has the following characteristics:

D. Paul Schafer

Present World Order and Dominant Value System

Dominant Disciplines	Science, Economics, Politics
Basic Biases or Tendencies	Centralization
	Specialization
	Imitation
	Standardization
	Conspicuous Consumption and
	Forced Obsolescence
Basic Method	Scientific (Quantitative)
Model Countries	Economically and
	Technologically Developed

The bias of centralization of the dominant value system causes all other forces to move to, or emanate from, certain accepted centres of activity. Internationally, this leads to the identification and acceptance of a small set of dominant countries and centres of economic, political, and cultural power which exercise an influence throughout the world out of all proportion to their actual size or significance. Success is then measured almost exclusively by winning recognition in one of the accepted international centres or in one of the dominant countries. Within each country, there is a similar tendency to assert the superiority of one or two prominent regions or metropolitan areas over the remaining hinterland. Migration and population movement studies of the last few decades confirm this universal tendency towards unilateral flow from small towns and rural areas to a few large urban environments.

Modern developments in communications, particularly in such media as radio and television, serve to reinforce this centralizing trend in population movement and human settlement. Followers of McLuhan would argue that this bias toward spatial centralization is inherent in the particular form of the communication instrument. Proponents of the Marxian ideology might counter that it is much more a question of who controls the means of communications and how these forms are used to exploit economic classes and geographical areas. In either case, the result is clear: the nature of the communication forms and the effective control of these forms combine to strengthen and fortify the ability of a handful of dominant countries and centres to define world values and determine the fate of nations.

Those in control of the dominant value system equally recognize the advantages of specialization or the division of labour and ideas. At first blush, the bias of specialization appears to be inconsistent with the bias of centralization. This inconsistency is quickly resolved through a realization that the important consideration is the degree of specialization, rather than absolute specialization. For the dominant value system, power depends on promoting a greater degree of specialization away from the centre than at the centre. Parkinson recognized the practical implications of this neat theoretical device when he developed his law of pyramidal growth of organizations: the employee below must always be slightly more specialized than the employee above. In economic terms, over the past several centuries, the dominant countries have capitalized on the law of comparative advantage (specialization) to encourage a greater degree of specialization at the margin. Hence the great dependency and economic vulnerability of colonial satellites.

In the modern world, the vehicle utilized for extending the dominant biases of centralization and specialization through space and over time is the institution. In effect, the institution is an instrument for temporarily arresting the law of entropy, or the universal tendency for less and less order and more and more chaos in the dominant value system. Not only does this produce a value system which overwhelmingly favours the institution over the individual, but it also yields a value system which excessively rewards conformity as opposed to creativity. When this is combined with the tendency toward centralization, it is easy to understand why institutional and technological forms are readily imitated and transferred from country to country, as well as how the problems of "model" countries are quickly transmitted around the world to produce instant crises of international proportions.

Finally, there is the bias of conspicuous consumption—as it was originally articulated by Thorstein Veblen—and forced obsolescence. Taken separately, each of these biases contributes to a value system which places an inordinate emphasis on the material side of human existence. Taken in combination, they yield a way of life in the dominant or "model" countries that is incredibly demanding on the environment and downright wasteful of the world's renewable and non-renewable resources. The enormous drain on global resources that this way of life produces has been well documented in *The Limits to Growth*[3] and need not delay us here.

---

[3] D.H. Meadows, D.L. Meadows, J. Randers and W.W. Behrens III, *The Limits to Growth* (New York: The New American Library, Inc., 1972).

Suffice it to say that these biases link to form a frightening picture of the world of the future if they are not contested at present.

Before we consider the newly emerging value system of the future, a word about how the dominant value system perpetuates itself in space and over time. The dominant value system depends on remaining highly organized and tightly structured through concentration on basic similarities. It keeps all other systems subservient or subordinate by dividing on the basis of differences. Moreover, those in control of the dominant value system manage to pass these biases off not as biases at all, but rather as relative laws or absolute truths. Since the dominant value system is predicated on scientific detachment and objectivity, rather than on human perception and subjectivity, it is increasingly assumed that these tendencies have universal validity and applicability which makes them eternal in time and immutable in space. Eventually, people accept them not as biases at all, but rather as beliefs and behavioural patterns to be revered and even worshipped.

If the attempt to pass off temporal and situational biases as absolute truths or basic beliefs is not enough, those in control of the dominant value system also attempt to promote an acceptance of these biases as "productive," while simultaneously treating all other value system biases as "unproductive" or "counterproductive." As a result, in contemporary society, it is easy to see why representatives of the dominant value system have been anxious to treat the arts and humanities as unproductive at best, but more likely than not, as counterproductive, even dangerous.

Given this particular constellation of accepted values, over the last two centuries the arts and humanities have been confronted with a dilemma not unlike the dilemma they presently face in most educational situations. There are two discernible alternatives. First, join the dominant value system, employ the quantitative method and become merely extensions of the scientific-economic-political value system. In this case, a patterned perception of the arts emerges which is highly centralized (art is international and universal), specialized (an urban centre is not really an urban centre without its full complement of theatre and dance companies, operas, symphony orchestras, galleries and museums), conformist (it brought rave reviews in London, Paris or New York), and opulent (great art can only truly be appreciated in grand facilities). Alternatively, it is always possible to remain small, esoteric, and out of the main stream of life. What has been true for the arts in particular has been equally true for the humanities and culture in general.

However disheartening this dilemma has been for the arts, the humanities, and culture, it is obvious that the dominant value system has weakened considerably during recent decades. The signs are everywhere.

There is public consternation over the lack of integrity in the political process as well as increased political instability throughout the world. Acute shortages of natural resources, inflation, and unemployment are beginning to place a tremendous strain on national and international economic structures. There is growing concern over the need for resource conservation as well as increased disenchantment with useless human waste. Moreover, there is the anti-scientific and anti-technological rebellion of the younger generation, which, more than anything else, results from the implicit imperialism of the dominant value system, the constraint imposed on the expression of true feelings and honest emotions, and the growing suspicion over the irresponsible or amoral nature of applied scientific methods.

As a response to these fundamental pressures, a new world value system is starting to take shape and is vigorously challenging the traditional supremacy of the dominant value system. It is based on the following general characteristics:

Future World Order and Emerging Value System

Dominant Disciplines	Arts, Humanities, Ecology, Culture
Basic Biases or Tendencies	Decentralization
	Integration
	Innovation
	Diversification
	Conservation
Basic Method	Artistic (Qualitative)
Model Countries	Culturally and Humanistically Developed

The movement towards these new biases represents a shift from the scientific to the artistic-humanistic value system, thereby refuting the central conclusion of the Snow thesis. Contrary to Snow, there is every reason to believe that the future of the world will be dominated more and more by a value system that will extend the arts and humanities, and the fundamental biases on which these activities are based, and will constrain the further extension of science, economics, politics, and quantitative method. Language used in prominent corporate and public circles is revealing. It is far from coincidental that actors, performers, and scenarios have replaced programmers and plans!

At the core of this newly-emerging value system lie the biases of de-centralization, integration, and innovation. For almost all artists and humanists, there is a great concern for the expressive, creative, intuitive, and integrative capabilities of modern man. Implicitly, and herein lies the critical importance of a discipline like ecology, there is a growing aware-ness that human creation does not take place in an intellectual vacuum, but rather grows out of local conditions and immediate surroundings, thereby expressing a fundamental relationship between the individual and his environment. When the desire for integration of the intellect, the senses, and the emotions is added to the need for a creative expression which is authentic and indigenous, it is easy to see how these concerns for innovation, integration, and decentralization combine to form the back-bone of this new world order of the future.

It is also readily apparent that this new value system must tend toward diversity in human expression rather than conformity to the general hypotheses or "laws" of scientific investigation. Perhaps this is what prompted T. S. Eliot in his *Notes Towards the Definition of Culture*[4] to conclude that the major challenge confronting the world is to find unity of human purpose through diversity of creative, cultural expression. This point proves most interesting in view of the recent trend in many countries away from the notion of a "uniculture" and toward an appreciation of "multicultures" or cultural pluralism.

The bias towards conservation rather than conspicuous consumption of the globe's natural resources represents a problem of some complexity. Let us proceed to it directly through the use of an informative example. It is one of thousands of similar examples.

During World War II, the major razor blade companies produced razor blades capable of several weeks of comfortable shaves by all accounts. To-day, after a great many years of continuous technological innovation, the new super, deluxe blades are capable of no more than two or three com-fortable shaves! Sound paradoxical? This is much more than the inverse relationship between quality and commercial success. Obviously, as indicated earlier, an economy based on increased obsolescence and material waste is only capable of producing a technology based on the same underlying values.

[4] T.S. Eliot, *Notes Towards the Definition of Culture* (London: Faber and Faber, 1948).

It is immediately apparent that there are two streams of technological innovation. One stream, about which we hear a great deal, is based on an exponential use of the world's natural resources, since it is based on rapid deterioration of products. The other, about which there is nothing but silence, is based on a fundamental concern for conservation of world resources. Why do we hear nothing about this latter technological stream at a time when acute global shortages are causing pronounced international tensions? Precisely because inventions conserving resources are bought off by vested interests before they arrive on the market, since they represent threats to profit margins and cause problems in economic dislocation and industrial reorganization.

There is a profound principle hidden here—a principle which is basic to all genuine artistic and humanistic method. For the artist or humanist, the challenge is to create the maximum effect with the minimum use of resources. This illustrates how ridiculous economic practices have become in the western world. The economics of most dominant countries have been reduced to achieving the minimum effect with the maximum use of resources. This proves to be a point of critical importance to the future of the world. Many existing economic practices are not only inefficient or uneconomical, but irrational to boot. As the razor blade example aptly illustrates, much more could be accomplished with much less. It is one thing to waste resources when such wastage results from human error or lack of knowledge. However, it is quite another thing to condone public and private policies which sanction wastages that are totally unnecessary. The death blow to the dominant value system will be delivered—as it is now being delivered—as more and more people recognize that their actions and decisions, contrary to what they are encouraged to believe, are actually irrational and lack common sense.

Cultural Policy and the New World Order

Before we proceed to a consideration of the role that cultural policy must play in the evolution of a new world order, it may prove helpful to clear up some misconceptions about different conceptions of culture.

Throughout the world, there are many fascinating differences in the way in which culture is perceived or defined. Rather than attempt yet another definition of culture, it proves infinitely more profitable for present purposes to identify and examine several of the major contextual uses of the notion of culture. A review of the literature reveals four distinctly different contexts of culture. In order, these "cultural contexts" are the artistic, the social, the anthropological, and the ideological. In terms of coverage and general implications, each of these contexts is broader than the one it precedes. This can be depicted most conveniently in pyramidal form.

Cultural Contexts

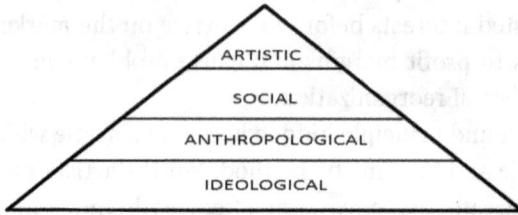

At the apex of this pyramidal structure stands the artistic context of culture. Here, culture is treated as synonymous with the arts, and probably includes the performing arts—music, drama, opera, and dance; the exhibiting arts—painting, sculpting, sketching, and print making; the literary arts—prose, poetry, and creative writing; and possibly the crafts—weaving, embroidery, ceramics, carving, and the like. An examination of public approaches to cultural development and policy reveals that many countries throughout the world used the artistic context of culture as the initial springboard for executing public responsibilities in the cultural domain.

Regardless of what progress has been made using the artistic context of culture, pressure for action in other areas, most notably in sports, recreation, and multiculturalism, has been building rapidly in recent years. In consequence, it is possible to discern a distinct movement beyond the artistic context of culture in most countries in the world today. In many capitalistic countries, there has been an accelerating trend towards defining and placing culture much more in a social context. However, it would be a mistake to assume that this represents a concern with the cultural implications of various social customs, values, mores, and institutions. On the contrary, given the sharp distinction between work and leisure or economic and social time in many of these countries, it is a more restricted concern for all those activities which occupy social or leisure time, such as the arts and crafts, sports, the media, and various recreational and environmental activities.

In the artistic context, the most accepted structure for dealing with the arts and articulating cultural policy is the arts council. Most arts councils operate either as independent or quasi-independent agencies, although they are usually responsible to a governmental department having cultural overtones, such as a ministry of education, a secretary of state, or a ministry of recreation and social services. Faced with the rapidly escalating demand for more cultural development and better coordination of governmental programs, many governments in the western world are now busy drafting legislation to establish ministries of leisure services or the equivalent, thereby reflecting the shift that is taking place from an artistic to a social perception of culture.

In many of the so-called developing countries, culture is perceived to be more anthropological in character. For the anthropologist, culture embraces not only the sociological concern with customs, mores, values, and institutions, but also the whole gamut of human extensions, inventions, and artefacts. Included in such an expansive context of culture would be all the tools of trade and traffic as well as all the accoutrements of life and leisure. In nations relatively untouched by modernization and mechanization, where there still exists no real or firm distinction between work and leisure, industry and craft, it is easier to see and appreciate the sensitive and intimate connection between culture and life. Clearly, one of the central problems of cultural policy in such circumstances is to find effective ways of preserving the beautiful and fragile qualities of these rich cultural traditions in the face of mounting pressure from the dominant countries and vested interests to accept the particular kind of economic growth, technological change, and touristic exploitation which conforms to the norms of the traditional value system.

Finally, culture may be treated in an ideological or almost spiritual way. Whereas the anthropological conception of culture is oriented outward and focuses primarily on human extensions and artefacts, the ideological conception of culture penetrates inward to settle more on human emotions and feelings, ideas and actions. In effect, in this context, culture becomes synonymous with a distinct state of mind or way of life, either in an individual or collective sense.

Given the expansive nature of these anthropological and ideological conceptions of culture, it is understandable that many of the developing nations and communist, or socialist, countries have demonstrated a marked preference for the ministry of culture as the most forceful vehicle for defining priorities and initiating action in the cultural field. The advantages are obvious. On the one hand, it tends to establish a higher priority for cultural concerns in the hierarchy of economic, social, and political values. On the other hand, it tends to draw together, if only for administrative purposes or political expediency, such disjointed cultural pursuits as the arts, the media, sports, and various related cultural activities.

Regardless of variations in governmental structures or cultural contexts, the critical consideration remains the value container within which these structures and contexts are located. There is the ever-present danger that new governmental and administrative structures will get bogged down with the same old set of irrelevant and irrational values of the dominant system. On the one hand, where culture is viewed essentially as leisure time activity, the exercise of cultural policy and development could quickly become one of filling the leisure-time bag with various cultural goodies. Already, the experience suggests that this approach can gather momentum in direct proportion to the traditional economic and political advantages to be derived from it in the form of profits, income, employment, and votes. In effect, the cultural sector becomes an extension of the economic sector, thereby reinforcing the fundamental belief inherent in the dominant value system that the arts, humanities, and any other forms of non-scientific or non-economic activity are basically unproductive and have no real value apart from political and financial opportunism. On the other hand, where culture is conceived anthropologically or ideologically, its ultimate influence can be severely curtailed if it is subordinated to political values, circumscribed by social conventions, exploited by corporate manipulators, or used merely for purposes of collective conditioning or state propaganda.

Whether or not one balks or hesitates at the mention of the word culture depends ultimately on whether culture is conceived as a source of human realization and fulfilment or as a means of collective confinement. The constricting dangers of culture are real enough, have been well documented in the annals of history, and are multiplying rapidly as we plunge ever more deeply into an age characterized by the politics of culture. Nevertheless, with the appropriate precautions, culture may equally prove capable of bringing individuals and nations closer together by creating the conditions for a much more creative and meaningful life.

To achieve this individual and collective aspiration requires nothing short of an ideological perception of culture which is cleansed of the biases of the dominant value system and is vitalized by the essential characteristics of the emerging value system and the new world order. Immediately, the role of cultural policy and the raison d'être for a ministry of culture are drastically transformed and must be viewed in a new light.

At the highest possible level, the role of cultural policy is to scan national and international environments in order to create or strengthen those conceptual values and human practices necessary to usher in the new world order. In effect, cultural policy leads rather than lags; it is much more committed to innovating and shaping than to imitating or reinforcing. To this extent, cultural policy is not a formula for dividing the thin sliver of pie that remains after all the large scientific, economic, political, and educational slices have been removed. On the contrary, it is the recipe for making the pie, the means of determining what ingredients must be combined in what proportions to achieve maximum results.

An example might help to render concrete form to the theoretical shape of the argument. Contemporary developments in the crafts provide an excellent illustration of the conflict that is raging between the two diverse value systems. Combining the functional and aesthetic as well as the human and mechanical aspects of creative process, it is as if the crafts were wedged between a value system in the process of decay and another in the throes of being born.

Looked at from the perspective of leisure-time activity and the dominant value system, the revival of global interest in the crafts acts as little more than an indicator of increased leisure time and affluence. In fact, apologists and authorities in control of the dominant value system are not anxious to have the mass of humanity believe otherwise. And yet, these developments have the most profound and significant implications for the future of humanity. In economic terms, they personify the growing non-cooperation with the existing technological process and technocratic order as well as the resistance against inefficient and irrational industrial practices. In the positive sense, they signal the emergence of new economic structures which strike a better balance between mind and hand, man and machine. Educationally, they manifest the growing disenchantment with traditional teaching and learning methods and reflect the urgent need for pedagogical methods which achieve a better balance between theory and practice, concept and execution. In social terms, they intimate a need for much more effective social contact and communal living. Most of all, in a very human sense, this resurgence of vitality in the crafts is happening on so vast a scale that it can only be interpreted as part of the accumulating evidence that modern man is demanding more opportunity to participate in the making of more imaginative, meaningful, and durable products.

No greater mistake could be made than to ignore the lessons contained in this instructive and incisive example. Why is this? Precisely because once a system is in fundamental disorder, attempts to return to it only serve to create more disarray. Attempts to solve world unemployment, inflation, and resource problems by attempting to induce or coerce a return to the dominant values and conventional theories of the traditional world order only increase public tensions and confuse the populace further.

In the final analysis, it is as imperative for cultural policy to monitor the human environment and global landscape as it is for ministries of culture to act as integrative agencies within governments to bring about necessary change. The real need in government today is not to stand government on its head, but rather to roll it on its side. In other words, the needs are horizontal, not vertical. A ministry of culture should not be concerned with cutting down into the carcass of government in order to cordon off and carry away that part of the carcass which is deemed to be cultural. To work effectively, a ministry of culture must take much more of an ideological stance on culture by cutting across governmental departments in order to link them together in the common search for inventive solutions to perplexing contemporary problems. This is the real cultural challenge facing the world at present. The risks are great. But then, so too are the rewards. A new order always brings with it the joys and mysteries of a new way of life.

CHAPTER THREE

The Cultural Imperative

> *Culture constitutes the topmost phenomenal level yet recognized—or for that matter now imaginable—in the realm of nature.*
>
> —Alfred Kroeber[1]

I believe culture should play a central role in the world. This is not wishful thinking on my part, but rather the result of an objective assessment of the world situation and prospects for the future.

There are many reasons why culture should play a central role in the world. It is needed to transform the relationship between human beings and the natural environment, reduce the amount of tension, violence, terrorism, and conflict in the world, improve relations between the diverse peoples, countries, cultures, religions, and civilizations of the world, decrease income and social inequalities throughout the world, and enhance human welfare and well-being everywhere in the world. It is also needed to reduce the demands human beings are making on the world's scarce resources, create ways of life and lifestyles that are more in keeping with the new global reality, and achieve much more peace, harmony, stability, and unity in the world. Without this, the world is bound to become a more dangerous, demanding, and volatile place—rather than a safer and more secure place—as resources are used up and the carrying capacity of the earth is approached.

If this adverse situation is to be avoided in the future, valuable contributions will have to come from many different disciplines and activities. Economics is important because it is concerned with the

---

[1] Alfred Kroeber and Clyde Kluckhohn, *Culture: A Critical Review of Concepts and Definitions* (New York: Vintage Books, 1952), p. 290.

production, distribution, and consumption of goods and services and creation of material and monetary wealth, and therefore with people's jobs, income, and sources of livelihood. Ecology is important because it focuses attention on the complex connection between human beings, other species, and all of nature, and consequently on the many different ways people interact with the natural environment and the world. Religion and philosophy are important because they are concerned with what is most sacred and profound in life, and hence with what is needed to live life on a higher plane of ethical and moral existence. And science, technology, and education are important because they produce the discoveries, innovations, and inventions that are needed to live happier, healthier, and longer lives, as well as to open up new learning opportunities, educational possibilities, and social developments for the future.

As important as these and other disciplines and activities are—and there is no intention of downplaying or diminishing their importance here—the most important discipline or activity by far is culture. This is because culture possesses numerous qualities and capabilities that are of utmost importance to the world of the future.

Most of these qualities and capabilities derive from the fact that culture can be perceived and defined in many different ways. While some people may see this as a real disadvantage because there is no single definition or understanding of culture on which people can agree, as is the case for many other disciplines and activities, it is actually a great asset because culture can be stretched in many different directions and used to address all sorts of problems, possibilities, and situations.

The best way to expose the many diverse qualities and capabilities that are inherent in culture—and therefore to demonstrate why culture is of utmost importance to the world—is to examine the way culture has evolved "as an idea" over a history spanning some two thousand years. For although culture was initially perceived and defined in very restrictive terms, it has been progressively broadened and deepened over the centuries to the point where it is now perceived and defined in very expansive terms, thereby imbuing it with all sorts of qualities and capabilities that are of quintessential importance to the world of the future. The process whereby this came about is a long and fascinating one—one that sheds a great deal of light on the nature and meaning of culture in general and the role culture is capable of playing in the world in particular.

Although culture "as an idea" has existed for an incredibly long period of time, it has existed for a much longer period of time "as a reality."

Indeed, it can be traced back to the very beginning of human life on earth. Whenever and wherever people came together for the express purpose of living together in the world and working out their complex association with the world, there culture as a reality is to be found. It is to be found, for example, in the cave drawings of the Upper Palaeolithic period some 30,000 years ago, when some of the earliest humans huddled together in caves to keep themselves warm, protect themselves against wild animals and the elements, and attend to their survival.

This is confirmed by the numerous cave drawings that have been discovered in Spain, southeast Asia, and especially the Haute Barone region of France, primarily in such locations as Lascaux, Pech Merle, La Marche, and Altamira. It is also confirmed by all the oldest settlements in the world, most notably in the Tigris-Euphrates region of Mesopotamia, along the Nile River in Egypt, in the Indus River valley in present-day Pakistan, in the Huang He area of China around the Yellow River, on Crete in the Mediterranean, and at Mezo in Central America. It is also confirmed by archaeological explorations of the ancient Sumerian, Hittite, Babylonian, and Assyrian civilizations in present-day Iraq, the Olmec civilization in Mexico, the Minoan civilization at Knossos in Crete, and the excavations undertaken at Ur, Catal Huyuk, Alaca Huyuk, Stonehenge, Carnac, and other historic sites throughout the world.

The Egyptians and the Chinese were probably the first people to recognize the incredible power of culture when it is developed in a systematic, sustained, and conscientious manner. There is ample evidence of this in the cultural achievements of the ancient Egyptians and Chinese, as depicted in the numerous exhibitions, publications, and television programs devoted to Egyptian and Chinese culture throughout the world. One need only marvel at the countless treasures of Egypt and China, some known for millennia, others unearthed only in the past century—including the terra cotta figures discovered at Xian in China, the throne of Sitamon, the funeral mask of Tutankhamen, the pyramids of Giza, the Sphinx, Thebes, Luxor, Abu Simbel, and the tombs of the pharaohs—to realize the lofty heights to which culture can be raised when it is pursued with vigour and cultivated with imagination. It is not surprising in this regard that authorities in the People's Republic of China selected several of China's greatest cultural achievements in an historical sense—the invention of silk, printing, the compass, and drums—when they were confronted with the complex problem of deciding how to depict China to the world at the Olympic Games in 2008.

The tradition that was commenced in Egypt and China was carried on in brilliant style by the Greeks, Persians, and Romans. This is most evident in the case of the Greeks, since Greece is generally regarded as the cradle of western civilization. A great culture flourished there in ancient times, especially in city-states like Athens, Delphi, Corinth, Mycenae, Sparta, and others. This is especially true of Athens, the birthplace of democracy, which is well-known for architectural achievements like the Acropolis, the Parthenon, and the Erectheum, philosophers like Plato, Aristotle, and Socrates, playwrights like Sophocles, Aeschylus, and Euripides, historians like Herodotus and Thucydides, and dramatic venues like the Theatre of Dionysus Eleuthereus, which could seat 17,000 people yet boasted acoustics remarkable even by modern standards.

The Persians also realized many splendid cultural achievements countless centuries ago. A great culture flourished there in ancient times. This culture is equally renowned for its literary masterpieces—the *Shahnameh*, for example—and for its imperial cities at Susa, Persepolis, and Pasargadae. It is a tradition that was carried on in brilliant fashion by the Romans, who also had their superb poets, playwrights, scholars, and literary figures like Horace and Virgil, as well as phenomenal achievements in architecture, philosophy, music, drama, jurisprudence, and so forth.

It was at this time that culture made its appearance in the world as an idea for the first time. For although culture had existed as a reality for thousands of years prior to this, culture as an idea did not come into existence until the Romans used the term *cultura* in public and private discourse in the classical period, thereby making culture one of the oldest ideas known to humankind, with a history (as indicated earlier) dating back some two thousand years. It was an idea that was to evolve progressively and relentlessly in the centuries to follow.

Culture as Cultivation

Initially, the term *cultura* was used in the very limited sense to mean "to till," "to nurture," or "to cultivate," largely because it was derived from the Latin verb *colo* or *colere*. Culture's intimate connection with nature should not be allowed to escape our attention here. Not only does this explain why we have many words in our vocabulary with culture in them that are intimately connected to nature—words like agriculture, silviculture, horti-culture, viticulture, permaculture, and so forth—but also it means that culture possesses the potential to establish a strong bond between human beings and the natural environment. It is a bond that is possessed by very few disciplines, and is very much lacking in the world today. For what other discipline possesses the potential to move laterally across the human species, nature, the natural environment, and other species, as well as to focus on the complex interconnections and interrelationships between them?

Interestingly, the term *cultura*—from which the modern term culture is derived—was also used by the Romans in another sense that was closely associated with the idea of cultivation. When the great Roman scholar and statesman, Cicero, said *"Cultura animi philosophia est"*—thereby linking culture with cultivation of the mind or soul and philosophy—he equated culture with the intellectual and spiritual development of the individual. His intention was not to downplay or disregard the connection between culture and nature, but rather to recognize that culture has an essential role to play in the development of people, largely because it is related to the acquisition of knowledge, wisdom, insight, understanding, growth, and development. It was a captivating idea, but one that had to wait another two thousand years before it was picked up in earnest and developed in depth by two well-known British scholars—Thomas Carlyle and Matthew Arnold—in the middle of the nineteenth century.

Both these scholars had very strong views about what constitutes a "cultured person." This was especially true for Carlyle, who saw culture as the key to becoming "authentic," "true to oneself," and "one of a kind." This is revealed in his "great law of culture," which states that every individual should "become all that he was created capable of being; expand, if possible, to his full growth; resisting all impediments, casting off all foreign, especially all noxious adhesions; and show himself at length in his own shape and stature, be these what they may."[2] But it was also true for Arnold, who saw the cultured person as a person who is refined, sophisticated, well-educated, and knowledgeable about the arts, humanities, and finer things in life.

While most people see culture today as something substantially broader than this, many people continue to think of culture in personal terms and associate culture with knowledge, wisdom, education, learning, and appreciation of the finer things in life. This has important im-

---

[2] Thomas Carlyle quoted in *Home Book of Quotations* (New York: Dodd, Mead and Company, 1967), p. 348.

plications for the future because it means that culture has a great deal to do with the development of people regardless of where they live in the world or what they work at, as well as their quest to live creative, constructive, and fulfilling lives.

Culture as the Arts and Humanities

If the idea of culture was limited to cultivation in classical times, it was deemed to be the arts and humanities in medieval and early modern times. It was largely associated in those days with the Muses of epic and lyric poetry, music, tragedy, sacred song, dance, and comedy. Today, it is more likely to include the performing arts (music, drama, opera, dance, and mime), the literary arts (poetry, literature, and creative writing), the visual arts (painting and sculpting), the environmental arts (architecture, town planning, urban design, and landscaping), the humanities (philosophy, ethics, and history), and often the culinary and heritage arts (food, drink, preservation, conservation, and so forth). Some people even include the "material arts" or crafts in their understanding of culture— weaving, enamelling, engraving, and the like—although there is far less agreement on this because it includes things that are mass-produced and not "one of a kind."

A certain amount of caution should be exercised with respect to what is included in this expanded idea of culture, especially as it relates to the arts. What is considered art in one country may not be considered art in another country. In Japan, for example, tree dwarfing and flower arranging are deemed to be art forms, just as calligraphy is in China and Japan and tattooing is in Tanzania. Then there is Bali, which is rich in the arts and elevates many activities to art forms because everything is done "to the best of people's ability." As discussed earlier, this explains why we use terms like "the art of science," "the art of mathematics," "the art of politics," and so forth in public discourse, since these terms imply that many activities can be raised to the level of art forms and practised accordingly if they are executed with flair and imagination and produced with creativity and excellence.

It is not difficult to determine why culture was expanded to include the arts and humanities in medieval and early modern times. A Renaissance was taking place in Italy at this time—and fanning out to include many other parts of Europe and the world—that was inspired primarily by the arts and humanities. This resulted from the ability artists and humanists possess to change the way we see the world, understand the world, act in the world, and value things in the world. This opened the doors to broader and deeper ways of looking at life, living, reality, the human condition, the world situation, and people's lives.

Eventually, everything was transformed by the Renaissance that commenced in Italy and affected the entire world in the centuries to follow: social and economic arrangements, religious activities, politics, the sciences, education, community development, rural life, government, and virtually everything else. There was a blossoming of creativity and imagination in all these fields—and in the complex interconnections and interrelationships between them—that had a profound effect on people and countries in all parts of the world and the world as a whole for centuries, thereby confirming the incredible power culture possesses when it is viewed in this way.

In the early years, seminal contributions were made to the Renaissance by painters like Giotto, Masaccio, Lippi, Botticelli, Fra Angelico, Mantegna, Raphael, Michelangelo, and da Vinci, sculptors like Pisano, Ghiberti, Donatello, Verrochio, and Cellini, writers like Dante, Petrarch, Machiavelli, Giovanni, and Boccaccio, architects like Brunelleschi, Bramante, and Alberti, and composers like Palestrina, Monteverdi, and Gabrielli. This spawned a cornucopia of contributions from generations of artists and humanists who followed in their footsteps, including Corregio, Titian, Tintoretto, Veronese, Van Eyck, Dürer, Holbein, Grünewald, Riemenschneider, Shakespeare, Marlow, Erasmus, Rabelais, Cervantes, de Vega, de Léon, Vivaldi, Corelli, and others. The whole of Europe and many other parts of the world were caught up in the fervour and excitement of the Renaissance that started in Italy and rapidly spread to other parts of the world.

There is much to be learned from this expanded idea of culture as the arts and humanities that is relevant to the world of the present and the future. This is especially true for the capacity the arts and humanities possess to bring a great deal of fulfillment and happiness into people's lives, bind people, communities, and societies together, develop a much greater sense of awareness and appreciation for nature, the natural environment, and other species, broaden and deepen understanding of countries, cultures, religions, and civilizations as wholes, and enable people to aspire to higher values and ideals and reach for the sublime.

The arts and humanities bring a great deal of fulfillment and happiness into people's lives because they touch and move people in profound and inspirational ways, as well as express strong feelings and emotions. This is because artists and humanists are able to reach into the very depths of our being through the music they create, the pictures they paint, the poems they write, the stories they tell, the acts of kindness they perform, and the thoughts and sentiments they express. As a result, they do a great deal to bind people, communities, and societies together in space and time, primarily by giving them a stronger sense of identity, purpose, belonging, bonding, and self-worth than they would otherwise have.

They also do a great deal to foster our awareness and appreciation of nature, the natural environment, and other species. One need only think of Beethoven's *Pastoral Symphony*, Williams' *Lark Ascending*, Saint-Saëns' *Carnival of the Animals*, Respeghi's *The Birds*, van Gogh's *Starry Night*, and Debussy's *La Mer*—to cite only a few examples drawn from many—to confirm this. What a superb job these and other works do in enhancing our awareness and appreciation of the natural world and everything contained in it. We only have to listen to Beethoven's *Pastoral Symphony* to know how uplifting it is—and how uplifting it was for Beethoven!—to be out in nature enjoying its pristine lakes, babbling brooks, exquisite mountains, and serene calm after the summer storm.

There is another benefit to be derived here. It is the ability to reduce the huge ecological footprint we are making on the natural environment. The arts and humanities do this far better than most other activities because they are primarily labour-intensive rather than capital-intensive or material-intensive in nature, and therefore help to conserve rather than consume resources at a time when severe shortages of resources are manifesting themselves throughout the world. Apart from paints for the painter, paper and computer equipment for the poet, scholar, composer, and author, and raw materials for the craftsperson, the arts do not make excessive demands on the world's scarce resources or globe's fragile ecosystems.

Artists and humanists also do a great deal to expand and enhance our understanding of countries, cultures, religions, and civilizations as wholes. They do this through their ability to create signs, symbols, myths, legends, metaphors, stories, and the like that stand for "the whole" and provide us with a more complete, comprehensive, and compelling understanding of the whole. As a result, they shed a great deal of light on the historical and contemporary character of countries, cultures, religions, and civilizations, as well as what goes on within and between them. This is particularly true for dramatic works. These works are concerned with virtually everything that goes on within and between these human collectivities, from religious customs, educational endeavours, and business practices to political developments, social interactions, and recreational activities.

It is impossible to know or understand any country, culture, religion, or civilization in any depth—be it in Asia, Africa, Latin America, North America, the Caribbean, or the Middle East—without exposure to, and familiarity with, the works of their artists and humanists. Take Russian culture for instance. Think of how much our knowledge and understanding of the historical development and contemporary character of Russian culture is enhanced by exposure to, and familiarity with, such outstanding artistic masterpieces as Tolstoy's *War and Peace* and *Anna Karenina*, Dostoevsky's *Crime and Punishment* and *The Brothers Karamazov*, Chekov's *Uncle Vanya*, *The Seagull*, and *The Cherry Orchard*, Pushkin's *Boris Godunov* and *Eugene Onegin*, Pasternak's *Doctor Zhivago*, and Tchaikovsky's *Symphony Pathétique*. Both the light side and dark side of Russian culture are exposed through these and other artistic and humanistic works, all of which help to provide us with a more complete and comprehensive understanding of one of the most complex and fascinating cultures imaginable.

The same is true for Spanish culture. Exposure to and familiarity with Cervantes' *Don Quixote de la Mancha*, Rodrigo's *Concierto de Aranguez* and *Concierto de Andaluz*, Granados' *Goyescas* and *Danzas españolas*, Albeniz's *Iberia*, de Falla's *Noches en los jardinas de España* and *El amor brujo*, and the paintings of El Greco, Velázquez, Goya, and many other Spanish painters are essential if we want to broaden and deepen our knowledge and understanding of the historical development and contemporary character of Spanish culture. This is largely because these works evoke strong images of hot days, cool nights, splendid architecture in places like Seville, Cordoba, Segovia, Toledo, Madrid, and Barcelona, intoxicating gardens in Granada, flamenco music and dances in the caves of Andalusia, and majestic monuments in all parts of the country. While there is much more to Spanish culture than this, there is no doubt that exposure to and familiarity with these and other works does a great deal to enhance our understanding and appreciation of Spanish culture in the all-encompassing sense.

And this is not all. The arts and humanities also uplift and inspire us, thereby causing us to aspire to higher values and ideals and reach for the sublime. A good example of this is Beethoven's *Ninth Symphony*, and especially its *Ode to Joy*. This symphony is so incredibly beautiful and uplifting and reaches such sublime and lofty heights that the Council of

Europe and European Union recently selected it as "Europe's Anthem," to be played at all official functions because of its inspirational character and ability to represent the whole of Europe and not just specific parts of it. Mahler's *Resurrection Symphony* also uplifts and inspires us in this way, despite the fact that it has not been accorded the same status as Beethoven's *Ninth Symphony* and especially the *Ode to Joy*. Nevertheless, it is a work of monumental proportions and exceptional beauty—a work that likewise uses symphonic music and the human voice to scale herculean heights and inspire us to reach above and beyond ourselves and search for the sublime. And while we are on this subject, how about John Lennon's "Imagine," Louis Armstrong's "What a Wonderful World," and many other equally evocative popular works? Do they not also uplift and inspire us in profound and moving ways, exhorting us to visualize a world filled with harmony, beauty, and hope, where people can "live as one" and experience "the brotherhood of man"?

While the idea of culture as the arts and humanities flourished in medieval and early modern times—and still flourishes today in all parts of the world—a number of substantially broader ideas of culture began to emerge in the nineteenth century. Indeed, the nineteenth century can generally be regarded as a major watershed as far as the idea of culture is concerned. Prior to the nineteenth century, culture as an idea was limited to several very specific activities, most often the arts, humanities, and cultivation. However, since that time, culture has taken on many more expansive and fundamental meanings. It has also acquired numerous other qualities and capabilities that are of utmost importance to the world of the present and the future.

Culture as the Legacy from the Past

Several German authors were in the forefront of the movement to expand the idea of culture beyond the arts, humanities, and cultivation. One of these was Dr. Gustav Klemm, whose first volume of a ten-volume *Cultural History of Mankind* appeared in 1843. It is devoted largely to the study of the gradual development of humankind as a species. This was followed, in 1854 and 1855, by his two-volume *Science of Culture*, which was focused more specifically on the science and history of culture. In these works, Klemm paid great tribute to Voltaire—the renowned French scholar, playwright, and historian—who, Klemm argued, was the first person to set aside kings' lists, dynasties, political events, battles, and so forth in order to study culture *per se*, even if he did not use the term as such. Interestingly, Voltaire also implored people to "plant," "build," and "cultivate," thereby revealing that he was well aware of the idea of culture as cultivation popular in Roman times. For although Voltaire used the idea of culture in a much more expansive way, he was also committed to the idea of culture as cultivation. He saw it as the best antidote against vice and boredom, as well as the most effective vehicle for ensuring civility, order, refinement, manners, and taste.

It was thoughts like those provided by Voltaire, Klemm, and others that paved the way for the idea of culture as "the legacy from the past," or, as it is often called today, "the cultural heritage of humankind." What stands out most clearly when this legacy or heritage is viewed in its totality is its colossal size and universal character. It exists everywhere, and includes virtually everything that has been created by human beings. Not only has it received countless contributions from people, countries, cultures, and civilizations in all parts of the world, but also there is hardly a group, community, region, or country that has not made a strong, lasting, and valuable contribution to it. As the most obvious measure of humanity's collective achievements down through the ages—or "what remains long after everything else is forgotten" as some authors prefer to state it—this incredible treasure-trove of historical and contemporary accomplishments is discernible amidst the rise and fall of different countries, cultures, and civilizations regardless of where they are situated in the world.

In addition to countless other things, this legacy or heritage includes the achievements of the Egyptians, the Mayans, and the Asians; all the cities and historical sites in the world—Venice with its enchanting architecture and enticing canals, Isfahan and Istanbul with their exquisite mosques, Kyoto with its ancient temples, and Buenos Aires, Marrakech, and Savannah, Georgia, with their sumptuous squares and evocative streets; all the music, dances, paintings, and craft objects that have been created in the world; all the most significant accomplishments that have been achieved in economics, science, education, social affairs, politics, human thought, and technology; all the world's great religious teachings and philosophical writings; eastern as well as western medicine; oriental as well as occidental art; written as well as oral history; and cyclical as well as linear concepts of time.

It is all this and much more. It is also the less tangible but equally essential creations of humankind, or what some people prefer to call "the intangible cultural heritage of humankind." This includes the pursuit of knowledge, wisdom, beauty, and truth, the quest for stability, order, justice, unity, and equality, the expression of friendship, compassion, and human love, and all the countless theories, ideas, and concepts that have been created in the world. Presumably this is why the great Swiss cultural historian Jacob Burckhardt—who wrote at length about Italian culture during the Renaissance and Greek culture during classical times—called this precious jewel in humanity's crown "the silent promise" or "thread in the labyrinth" that possesses the potential to transform the entire past and present into a spiritual possession.

Like the less expansive ideas of culture, this substantially broader notion of culture as the legacy from the past or cultural heritage of humankind possesses a number of qualities and capabilities that are of utmost importance to the world of the future. One of these is the ability to create a strong bond between the past, the present, and the future, and therefore enhance people's identity, belonging, solidarity, and ability to move backwards and forwards in time. Another is the ability to speak directly to people about what is most dear to them, and hence about their values, ideals, and rootedness in the world. Still another is the ability to expose people to the mistakes of the past, and consequently the need to correct these mistakes in the future. And yet another—and one that is especially important in the modern world and promises to be even more important in the future—is the ability to focus on the fact that every person, country, culture, and civilization in the world acquires a great deal of cultural baggage over the course of their development that they carry with them in the present, regardless of where they are situated in the world.

While much of this baggage is positive, and is meant to be shared, enjoyed, experienced, and appreciated by all people and all countries, a significant amount of it is negative, and results from hostilities, hatreds, prejudices, and jealousies that are hundreds if not thousands of years old. This produces a great deal of tension, conflict, and confrontation in the world—tension, conflict, and confrontation that emanates from fear, misunderstanding, mistrust, and suspicion of cultural differences. This compels us to be ever watchful and mindful of the baggage we inherit from the past and carry around with us in the present and the future, as well as to ensure that this baggage is used for constructive rather than destructive purposes. We will never create a better world until we come to grips with the negative aspects of this baggage, which is why spiritual leaders like Mahatma Gandhi, Nelson Mandela, Archbishop Desmond Tutu, the Dalai Lama, and others have been so committed to engendering respect and appreciation for all the diverse cultures, religions, civilizations, and peoples of the world. It is also why Nelson Mandela, Archbishop Tutu, the aboriginal peoples, and others have instituted truth and reconciliation commissions—or their equivalent—to come to grips with the causes of hostilities, confrontations, and conflict in the world.

There is one final quality culture possesses when it is viewed as the legacy from the past or cultural heritage of humankind that should not be allowed to escape our attention. It derives from the fact that this legacy or heritage is "shared." It is shared by countless people and countries in the world. It is impossible to be a member of any group—be it a community, race, society, or nation—without sharing many things in common: beliefs, values, ideals, ideas, customs, traditions, and so on. It is this fact that makes it possible to bind people and countries together in space and time when other forces are operating to split them apart, thereby emphasizing the incredible value culture possesses when it is viewed as the legacy from the past or cultural heritage of humankind.

This quality was not lost on the well-known poet, scholar, and Nobel prize-winner T.S. Eliot. In his *Notes Towards the Definition of Culture*, he wrote at length about the need to bind people together and share things in common, as well as how important it is for people to learn from the past and the historical development of their culture and the cultures of others. He also attempted to identify those things that bound people in England and English culture together. These he identified as Derby Day, the Henley Regatta, Cowes, the twelfth of August, a cup final, the dog races, the pin table, the dart board, Wensleydale cheese, boiled cabbage cut into sections, beetroot in vinegar, nineteenth-century Gothic churches, and the music of Elgar.[3] While many people in England may still view English culture in these terms—and listen to the music of Elgar and especially his *Pomp and Circumstances Marches* at highly successful prom concerts at Royal Albert Hall and other venues—it is apparent that English culture has changed substantially since Eliot's day, when these things were shared by the majority of people living in England and were instrumental in binding English culture together, much as the Royal Wedding did quite recently.

This sharing quality is exceedingly important. We need a great deal more sharing in the world if we are to be successful in overcoming one of the biggest problems in the world of all, namely the huge disparities that

[3] T. S. Eliot, *Notes Towards the Definition of Culture* (London: Faber and Faber, 1963), pp. 120, 131.

exist in income, wealth, and resources throughout the world. Needless to say, income, wealth, and resources will have to be shared much more equitably and broadly if we want to eradicate one of the greatest sources of inequality, hostility, and injustice in the world.

While some of the impetus for this will have to come from economics, corporations, and governments, most of it will have to come from culture and people working in the cultural field if it is to come at all. For the impetus to share—like the impetus to bond—comes much more from the arts and culture than it does from economics, politics, and commerce. It is intimately connected with the sharing of feelings and emotions, many different types of artistic, humanistic, and social experiences, the links that bind people, communities, cultures, countries, and civilizations together, and the legacy from the past or the cultural heritage of humankind. It is from things like this that we must find the collective will—as well as the means—to share income, wealth, and resources more equitably and liberally. This will be required on a massive scale if we are to be successful in improving the welfare and well-being of all people and countries throughout the world, especially when so many people and countries throughout the world live close to the level of nadir and despair, with insufficient food, clothing, shelter, fresh water, clean air, health services, and educational and employment opportunities to provide a healthy standard of living and reasonable quality of life.

Culture as a Complex Whole or Total Way of Life
If the idea of culture was expanded significantly in the first half of the nineteenth century, it was expanded much more in the latter part of the nineteenth century. In fact, it was expanded so much that a quantum leap took place in the idea of culture.

Prior to the latter part of the nineteenth century, culture was seen and treated as "a part of the whole," as was the case when it was seen and treated as cultivation, the arts and humanities, and the legacy from the past. However, in the latter part of the nineteenth century, a number of scholars started to see culture as "the total way of life of people" or "a complex whole." This included everything that people were engaged in as they went about the process of meeting their individual and collective needs and working out their complex association with the world.

Several anthropologists were in the vanguard of this development. It evolved naturally and organically when anthropologists started studying culture in general—and cultures in particular—in depth and on the ground.[4] What they discovered was that there were all sorts of words to describe the specific activities in which people were engaged as they went about the process of meeting their individual and collective needs and working out their complex association with the world, but there was no word to describe how all these activities were woven together to form a whole or overall way of life.

Culture was the word they used to designate this phenomenon. It resulted from the fact that there were discernible indications in all parts of the world that all the various activities in which people were engaged— economic, social, political, religious, educational, scientific, artistic, recreational, environmental, and so forth—were woven together in specific combinations and arrangements to form a whole or total way of life that was greater than the parts and the sum of the parts. This is why Sir Edward Burnett Tylor, one of the world's first anthropologists, defined culture formally as "that complex whole which includes knowledge, belief art, morals, law, custom, and any other capabilities and habits acquired by man as a member of society."[5]

Could there be anything more fundamental than this? It includes all activities in society—material and non-material, tangible and intangible, visible and non-visible—and not just some activities. It also includes the ordering process that is used to combine all these activities together to form a whole or total way of life. Surely this is what we mean today when we say we are the "products of our culture." We mean we are the products of everything that exists in our culture, or "our culture as a whole."

Visualized in this way, culture is no longer "the icing on the cake"—as it is when it is seen as the arts and humanities or the legacy from the past. Rather, it is "the cake itself." While economics forms a very important part of this because it is concerned with the production, distribution, and con- sumption of goods and services and creation of material and monetary wealth, it is part of a substantially larger and more all-encompassing pro- cess because it is part of the total way of life of people or a dynamic and organic whole. This makes culture the most important activity in society because it is concerned with all activities in society and not merely some

---

[4] Included in this group were such anthropologists as Sir Edward Burnett Tylor, A. Lane-Fox Pitt-Rivers, Franz Boas, W. H. R. Rivers, Robert Lowie, A. R. Radcliffe-Brown, Bronislaw Malinowski, Alfred Kroeber, Margaret Mead, Ruth Benedict, Ruth Bunzel, Raymond Firth, and many others.

[5] Edward Burnett Tylor, *The Origins of Culture* (New York: Harper and Row, 1958), p. 1.

activities in society, as well as the way in which these activities are woven together to form a whole or total way of life.

What is true for culture is equally true for cultures. Every culture in the world—be it in Africa, Asia, Latin America, North America, the Caribbean, Europe, and the Middle East—is a whole or total way of life composed of many parts. These parts are woven together in specific combinations and arrangements to form wholes or total ways of life that are greater than the parts and the sum of the parts because new properties are brought into existence when the whole or total way of life is created that are not in the parts taken by themselves or separately. This is true regardless of whether we are talking about cultures in the local, regional, national, or inter-national sense, or in the community or ethnic sense. Every culture in the world is a whole or total way of life composed of many different parts. Cultures encompass the gamut of activities when they are visualized in this way, from how people see and interpret the world, organize them-selves, and act in the world to how they conduct their affairs, elevate and embellish life, and position themselves in the world.

This is the **real** *reality that exists in the world and we would be foolish to deny it. At its most fundamental level, the world is made up of many different cultures in the all-encompassing sense—cultures that are constantly changing, evolving, mutating, impacting on one another, and interacting with one another. While these cultures share certain similarities—such as the need for food, clothing, shelter, communications, recreation, renewal, survival, and so forth—they are also very different. This is because the parts of these cultures may be different, or the way the parts are organized and combined to form wholes or total ways of life may be different. This gives rise to the specific identities and unique characters of all the various cultures in the world. It also gives rise to the fact some cultures are best known for their food, clothing, architecture, music, or dance, whereas others are best known for their economic systems, social arrangements, religious beliefs, political practices, communications capabilities, and so forth.*

Like the other ideas of culture examined thus far, this far more all-embracing idea of culture possesses numerous qualities and capabilities that are of vital importance to the world, perhaps the most vital importance of all. Most of these qualities and capabilities emanate from a quality or capability that the ideas of culture considered thus far do not possess, namely the ability to see things in holistic terms. Sight should never be lost of this. Nor should it be underestimated. It is one of humanity's greatest strengths and most fundamental assets, as well as the key to coming to grips with some of the most urgent and pressing requirements of modern times.

In the first place, it makes it possible to see the world and most things in the world as they are, not as we are conditioned to see them due to our penchant for dividing things up into parts in order to study the parts in detail. For the world and the vast majority of things that exist in the world are wholes made up of many parts, not parts taken by themselves or separately. This is true for individuals, groups, institutions, communities, cities, countries, cultures, civilizations, the world, the world system, and many other things. While specialization is very helpful in shedding light on all the various parts of things—and studying the parts in detail—it is not very helpful in terms of understanding that the world, the world system, and most things that exist in the world are wholes made up of an intricate interlacing of many parts, not smorgasbords of independent or disconnected elements.

Nowhere is this more important than with respect to people. Despite the fact that our bodies and our lives are comprised of many different parts, the fact remains that our bodies and our lives are wholes in the comprehensive and all-inclusive sense, not assortments of disconnected and unrelated parts. Failure to recognize this and deal with the consequences of it can cause serious problems for people who are endeavouring to live happy, healthy, and productive lives but are unable to do this because they are unable to combine all the various parts of their bodies and their lives together to form a harmonious and integrated whole. *It is culture, more than any other activity or discipline in society, that enables people to do this, thereby making it possible for them to become "whole people" in the most complete and compelling sense of the term.* We will never become whole people until we recognize that this is a cultural requirement more than it is any other type of requirement.

What is true for people is also true for institutions and groups. Like people, institutions and groups are wholes made up of many different parts. As such, they exude very specific ways of life because the parts are different and the way the parts are combined to form wholes is different. This is what makes it possible to talk about the culture of different groups and institutions, such as "Buddhist culture," "media culture," "police culture," "hospital culture," "corporate culture," and so forth. Each of these terms, and countless others like them, is designed to focus on the fact that these institutions and groups are wholes that manifest very specific ways of life. Terms like this are popular today because they confirm the fact that institutions and groups exhibit very specific ways of life as they go about the process of meeting the individual and collective needs of their members. They are also popular because they indicate that these ways of life must change whenever the shortcomings that exist in them exceed the strengths or become too large for them.

In much the same way that people, groups, and institutions are wholes, so the world and the world system are wholes. They are wholes made up of many different interconnected and interrelated parts. This is becoming increasingly apparent as a result of globalization and numerous developments in transportation, communications, technology, and virtually everything else.

It is impossible to view culture in holistic terms without recognizing that culture provides the "context" or "container" within which virtually everything that exists in the human world is situated. This has great relevance for the world and world system of the future because if we have lost one thing in the modern world, surely it is our ability to see things in context rather than in isolation. We have become so caught up with the *contents* of things that we have lose sight of the *context* in which they are situated.

There are numerous examples of this. Failure to understand that culture provides the context within which corporate activities take place has yielded a situation where many corporate activities are separated from the culture in which they are situated, thereby giving rise to fraudulent accounting practices, numerous financial irregularities, the payment of exorbitant fees and salaries for corporate executives, and the inability to regulate business activities and corporate practices in the public interest. Likewise, failure to understand that culture provides the context within which economic and technological activities take place has yielded a situation where preoccupation with certain types of economic and technological activities is having a deleterious rather than favourable effect on the world situation, especially when undue demands are made on the resources of nature and the lives of people. There is always a price that has to be paid when we get so wrapped up with the parts of things that we lose sight of the whole, just as there is always a price to be paid when we get so fixated with the trees that we lose sight of the forest.

This ability to see things in context rather than in isolation is not the only benefit to be derived from the holistic character of culture as a whole or total way of life. It is also the key to seeing things that are of vital importance to the world. This ability is imperative if we are to come to grips with the environmental crisis and treat the natural environment and other species with the respect and dignity they deserve. Failure to see things in holistic rather than partial or specialized terms has caused us to exploit the natural environment unmercifully and utilize the globe's scarce renewable and non-renewable resources at an alarming rate. Here as well, we have become so preoccupied with the trees that we have lost sight of the forest, thereby leading to environmental excesses and imbalances that are impossible to justify in view of the size and growth of the world's population and the finite carrying capacity of the earth.

Culture also possesses the ability to shed light on the complex inter-connections and interrelationships that exist between and among many human activities when it is seen and treated in holistic terms. This is imperative if we are to be successful in "connecting the dots" and coming to grips with some of the most demanding and debilitating problems of modern times, such as the complex connections and intimate relation-ships that exist but are often ignored between economics and ethics, science and religion, health and education, politics and society, technology and spirituality, and so forth.

Unfortunately, many activities are dealt with independently rather than interdependently due to our penchant for seeing things in specialized and separate rather than holistic and integrated terms. We engage in activities that are high in material inputs, outputs, and resource utilization while simultaneously refusing to admit that these things are intimately connected to the natural environment, climate change, and the frequency of floods, hurricanes, forest fires, tornadoes, and so forth throughout the world. We idolize technological developments while at the same time failing to recognize that many of these developments have an undesirable effect on religious practices and spiritual beliefs. We condone huge expenditures on health care while simultaneously decreasing or eliminating physical education and recreational activity in our schools. While culture may not possess the ability to deal successfully with all of these problems, and many others like them, there is no doubt that it provides the best possible vantage point from which to view these problems, as well as the ability to shed a great deal of light on how to make the necessary changes and embark on the new directions that are required to deal with them.

It is especially imperative for governments and politicians to realize this. Unfortunately, governments and politicians have become so accustomed to taking a partial or specialized approach to problem-solving—largely by creating separate "silos" or independent containers within which various activities and disciplines are situated—that the left hand often does not know what the right hand is doing. What is needed now, and needed more than ever, is a holistic approach to political and governmental decision-making and problem-solving. It is culture, more than any other discipline or activity in society, that makes this possible. As such, it provides the best possible framework for governmental planning, policy, and decision-making, largely by supplying the most effective vehicle for realizing balance and harmony between the various parts of society and public policy as a whole.

There is one final quality culture possesses when it is viewed in holistic terms that has a great deal of relevance to the world of the present and the future. It is the ability to bring things together rather than split them apart. This is desperately needed if the world is to become a safer and more secure place, rather than a more dangerous, demanding, volatile, and fragmented place.

This ability is needed on many fronts. It is needed to unite people, communities, societies, countries, cultures, and civilizations, as well as to establish strong bonds and connections between them. It is needed to create symbiotic links and synergistic relationships between the various disciplines and activities in society, as well as to unify knowledge and understanding of what is fundamental and valuable. It is also needed to eliminate the fragmentation in people's lives—fragmentation that makes it difficult for people to blend all the various activities in which they are engaged together to form a balanced, harmonious, and unitary whole. This is why people in the cultural field have been fighting to educate "the whole person" for more than a century. It is education of the whole person that makes it possible to create an overall way of life that provides fulfillment, happiness, meaning, and contentment in life.

Culture as Values, Beliefs, and Behaviour

About the same time that anthropologists were cultivating the idea of culture as a complex whole or total way of life, sociologists started to evolve the idea of culture as values, beliefs, and behaviour. Over the last century or so, their thoughts and impressions on this subject have congealed to form what is generally regarded as the sociological idea of culture:

Culture, a word of varied meanings, is here used in the more inclusive sociological sense, that is, to designate the artefacts, goods, technical processes, ideas, habits, and values, which are the social heritage of a people. Thus, culture includes all learned behaviour, intellectual knowledge, social organizations and language, systems of value—economic, moral or spiritual. Fundamental to a particular culture are its law, economic structure, magic, religion, art, knowledge and education.[6]

As with all the other ideas of culture, the sociological idea of culture possesses a number of qualities and capabilities that are of utmost importance to the world. Take, for example, the idea of values and beliefs, which is exceedingly germane to the overall understanding of culture in general and cultures in particular. Viewed from this perspective, it is not only the totality of activities that is important—as is the case with the anthropological idea of culture—but also the way in which these activities are assigned weights and priorities. Cultural experiences are configured differently in different cultures, countries, and parts of the world because they are given different weights and priorities, primarily because they are predicated on different perceptions, preferences, convictions, and possibilities.

If values and beliefs play an important role in the sociological idea of culture, so do race, class, gender, identity, identities, customs, traditions, ethnicity, and so forth. It is essential to examine the insights and findings of sociologists in this area very carefully, since race, class, gender, identity, identities, customs, traditions, and ethnicity have assumed great importance in the modern world. The same holds true for language and communication. It is through language and communication that the bonds are created (or not created!) that bind people and cultures together.

In the modern world, it is the media—or the cultural and communications industries as they are often called—that facilitate this act of communication most effectively. It is far from coincidental in this regard that ipods, tablets, BlackBerries, cell phones, the Internet, electronic highways, the computer, and so forth are the lifeblood of modern communication, since they provide the vehicles that are used to transmit images, messages, signals, and symbols that enable people in different parts of a country or culture—or in different countries and cultures—to

---

[6] Paul J. Braisted, *Cultural Cooperation: Keynote of the Coming Age* (New Haven: The Edward W. Hazen Foundation, 1945), p. 6.

share information, ideas, perceptions, values, value systems, patterns, and beliefs. Little wonder there is great concern about who owns, operates, and controls these contemporary vehicles of communication, as well as what messages and ideas are transmitted through them. Failure to exercise adequate control and ownership over the modern means of communication can pose serious problems—and have serious consequences—for countries and cultures in terms of their identity, survival, and sovereignty.

What is of even greater importance as far as the sociological idea of culture is concerned is people's behaviour in general and collective behaviour in particular. Given the state of the world at present and prospects for the future, there is no doubt that people's behaviour is going to have to undergo some profound and fundamental changes if humanity is to go fruitfully into the future.

It is often said that the biggest problem in the world is the environmental problem. But the problem is not with the environment; *it is with us*. We are the ones who are polluting the environment badly, depleting natural resources at an alarming rate, and exerting enormous pressure on the globe's fragile ecosystem and other species. Consequently, we are the ones who must change. It is imperative in this regard that we learn to conserve rather than consume resources whenever and wherever possible, thereby decreasing rather than increasing the huge ecological footprint we are making on the natural environment. This is a cultural requirement more than any other type of requirement because it has to do with values, priorities, and behaviour in general—both individual and collective—as well as changes in values, priorities, and behaviour in particular. We will never deal effectively with the environmental crisis until we alter our individual and collective behaviour and create behavioural patterns, characteristics, and ways of life that do as little damage to nature, the natural environment, and other species as possible.

Culture as the Relationship between
Human Beings and the Natural Environment

Given the need for fundamental changes in individual and collective behaviour and behavioural patterns, priorities, and characteristics, it is fortuitous that two far more expansive ideas of culture have begun to emerge over the last few decades.

The first is the ecological idea of culture. It is predicated on the conviction that culture is concerned with the intimate relationship between human beings and the natural environment. Whereas all the ideas of culture examined thus far have been predicated on the conviction that culture is limited to the human species and is the product of human creation—from the idea of culture as cultivation to the idea of culture as values, beliefs, and behaviour—the ecological idea of culture is predicated on the conviction that culture is concerned with the complex interaction between human beings and nature, the natural environment, and other species. This necessitates another quantum leap in the idea of culture, since it requires opening the doors to nature, the natural environment, and other species as a fundamental dimension of culture.

The ecological idea of culture is an outgrowth of the environmental movement. This movement has made us acutely aware of the fact that human beings do not exist in isolation, but are highly dependent on—and intimately connected to—the natural environment, far more dependent on and connected to than most people think. It has also made us acutely aware of the fact that economics and technology—which are often regarded as the crowning achievement of the human species—have not liberated us from our traditional dependency on the natural environment but rather have increased it. This is manifesting itself in consumption of the world's scarce resources at an astounding rate, rising prices for basic foodstuffs like corn, rice, grain, fish, and so forth, and growing shortages of natural resources such as wood, water, coal, gas, oil, and arable land. As this happens, there is a much greater awareness of the role that the natural environment plays in providing human beings with the sustenance they need for survival, as well as the incredible dependency that human beings have on all forms of plant, animal, vegetable, and mineral life.

Like the other ideas of culture, the ecological idea of culture has a great deal to recommend it, particularly at the present juncture in history. Not only does it focus attention on the relationship between human beings and the natural environment at a time when this is becoming one of the biggest—if not *the* biggest—challenges facing people and countries in all parts of the world, but also it alerts us to the fact that basic changes are required in this area if human survival is to be assured in the future. For the evidence is clear and unmistakable: cultures that do not give sufficient consideration to the intimate relationship that exists between human beings and the natural environment run the risk of overextending themselves, collapsing, and disappearing from the global scene because they are unsustainable. History is full of examples of this, from some of the earliest forms of human settlement on earth to some of the most advanced, particularly in areas around coastlines that are threatened by climate change.

Culture as the Organizational Forms and Structures of Different Species

The ecological idea of culture opened the doors to a much more expansive idea of culture to make its appearance on the scene—quite possibly the most expansive idea of all. It is the biological idea of culture. It is predicated on the conviction that culture is the organizational forms and structures of different species, both human and non-human. This necessitates yet another quantum leap in the idea of culture. It is a leap not unlike the leap that occurred at the end of the nineteenth century to the anthropological idea of culture, as well as at the end the twentieth century to the ecological idea of culture. In this case, it is a leap that emanates from major advances in botany, zoology, and biology generally.

With the introduction of the idea that all species have culture, culture is no longer limited to human beings, but is deemed to exist in the realm of nature as well. This is understandable in view of the fact that other species—like the human species—are living organisms, and as such, obey the laws governing all living things, including birth and death, growth and decay, consumption, digestion, and elimination, gender identification, mixing and borrowing, reproduction, and so forth.

It is this fact that makes it possible to talk about the culture of plants and animals and not just about the culture of human beings. It also explains why we have terms like ant culture, wolf culture, and plant culture in our vocabulary and not merely terms like horticulture, agriculture, silviculture, and permaculture. Whereas the latter refer to activities involving human beings, the former refer to activities involving other species.

Not everyone will agree with the biological idea of culture or feel comfortable about it. Indeed, there may be many who will contend that culture is—and should be—limited to human beings because it is the very thing that separates human beings from other species.

People of this persuasion contend that human beings possess the ability to reason, rationalize, reflect, and engage in various forms of consciousness and reflection that other species do not, or do not possess to the same degree. As a result, they believe that only human beings have culture, while other species do not. Nevertheless, the conviction that culture is not limited to human beings but is evident throughout the realm of nature is rapidly gaining ground and winning converts. This is because more and more people throughout the world are becoming conscious of the fact that countless similarities exist between human beings and other species, despite their obvious differences. Recent research is revealing, for example, that the differences between human beings and other species—which were once thought to be very great—are not as great as was previously assumed.

All that is required to confirm this is to watch other species as they go about the process of meeting their needs and working out their association with the world. Do they not do so in much the same way that human beings do, even if it might be less sophisticated and complex? Like human beings, other species see and interpret the world, even if they see it in their way and not in our way. They also organize themselves into communities and groups, conduct their affairs with a great deal of courage, conviction, and determination, elevate and embellish life by engaging in various forms of play and recreational activity, and position themselves in the world. Anyone who has tuned in to the profusion of television programs made recently about other species will instantly recognize this and accept it. But it can also be confirmed by watching a flock of geese as they stare at us, observing a colony of ants as they prepare for battle or the hunt, studying cats to see how much they enjoy basking in the sun and playing with each other, or observing a pack of wolves as they carve out a prominent place for themselves in nature and the wilderness.

Nor is this all. Many other species bond, mate, and create wholes and total ways of life in much the same way that human beings do. Take bees, for instance. Like human beings, they create cultures that are composed of many component parts, all of which are woven together in specific combinations and arrangements to form wholes or overall ways of life. These wholes or overall ways of life—which include well-defined systems of queen, drone, and worker bees, rigid hierarchies and divisions of labour, finely-tuned communications networks and sensing capabilities, and highly-evolved production, distribution, and consumption mechanisms—act to ensure the survival of bees as a species and attend to their biological and non-biological requirements.

They also guarantee a continuous supply of products. These products, such as honey, wax, the beehive, and the honeycomb, are much in demand in the human realm and have both a functional and aesthetic significance. The beehive and the honeycomb, for example, are intricately designed cultural creations, comparable in their style, design, function, and complexity to many of the cultural artefacts created by human beings. And what is true for bees, the beehive, and the honeycomb is equally true for many other animal and plant species and their creations. Virtually every animal and plant species has its own forms of culture and cultural creation, including its modes of organization, behaviour, procreation, consumption and production activity, and positioning in the environment. In fact, modern advances in the botanical and horticultural sciences are revealing that plants, like people and animals, have feelings and emotions, experience pain, and, what is more, respond very much the way people and animals do when confronted with unpleasantries.

The more scientists learn about the culture of plants and animals, the more is known about the various qualities and capabilities that are inherent in the cultures and ways of life of other species. As with human beings and their creations, this is exceedingly important for the world of the present and the future because it means that there are numerous similarities between human beings and other species despite their apparent differences. Moreover, there is a great deal to be learned from the cultures of other species—and indeed from the entire realm of nature—that is relevant to the development of the human species in general and human beings, human culture, and the world system in particular.

For one thing, there is much to be learned about caring, sharing, bonding, and cooperation. Many animals appear to share much more fully and freely than human beings, and do so far more willingly. Take elephants, for example. It is a well-known fact that elephants care for one another very deeply, are each other's keepers, and pay close attention to what is going on with their fellow companions. They also have phenomenal memories—apparently much more phenomenal than many people—and show an enormous amount of affection, sympathy, and love for one another, especially when they are in trouble. They gather around each other when they are sick, whenever there is work to be done, and when there is a need to rescue their companions from danger or distress. And what is true for elephants is true for many other types and species of animals as well.

It follows from this that one of the best ways to understand and come to grips with the culture, cultures, and the ways of life of human beings may be to study the culture, cultures, and ways of life of other species more intensively. This may prove helpful in determining how human cultures and ways of life can be developed more effectively and fully, anticipating certain events and situations before they happen, preventing others, changing specific patterns and modes of behaviour, and forecasting prospective problems and possibilities. Careful study of the reasons for the survival, thriving, transformation, and extinction of other species and their cultures, for example, may prove helpful in dealing with such life threatening problems as overpopulation, severe shortages of resources, migration, excessive production and consumption activity, and environmental degradation. Many animal species, such as bees, wasps, ants, and so forth, have evolved modes of organization, conservation, and behaviour that reveal an intimate awareness of how large populations can be regulated, managed, and governed most effectively when resources are scarce and space is limited.

These are not the only advantages to be derived from studying the cultures and ways of life of other species more intensively. Another advantage is to improve the relationship between human beings and other species. While many people get an enormous amount of pleasure out of their association with plants and animals (including their pets), there is no doubt that our relations with other species will have to undergo profound change in the future if we want to treat other species with the respect, dignity, and empathy they deserve. Clearly we have only begun to scratch the surface of this situation. There is a great deal to be realized here that will redound to the benefit of all species if human beings are attentive to it and do something concrete and practical about it in the years and decades ahead.

Future Needs and Directions

This completes our examination of the way culture has evolved as an idea over a history spanning two thousand years. While, as noted earlier, culture as a reality has existed for a far longer period of time, culture as an idea came into existence when the Romans used the term *cultura* to mean "cultivation" in classical times, thereby making it one of humanity's oldest ideas.

Since that time, many ideas of culture have been advanced and adopted throughout the world. Included among these ideas are culture as cultivation; the arts and humanities; the legacy from the past or cultural heritage of humankind; a complex whole or total way of life; values, beliefs, and behaviour; the relationship between human beings and the natural environment; and the organizational forms and structures of different species. While these are not the only ideas of culture that have been advanced and embraced throughout the world over the past two thousand years, they are certainly the main ones and without doubt the most essential ones.⁷ These ideas have resulted from contributions from many different individuals, groups, institutions, and disciplines, such as the arts, humanities, history, anthropology, sociology, ecology, botany, zoology, and biology.

Why have so many ideas of culture been advanced and adopted over the last two thousand years? There are many explanations. But most of them boil down to two things in the end: *helping people to understand the world and many different things that exist in the world*; and *helping people to change the world in order to improve their own situation, the human condition, or the world at large.* In order to do this, it has been necessary to enlarge and enhance the idea of culture progressively and substantially over the centuries, from that of culture as cultivation that was popular in classical times to one of culture as the organizational forms and structures of different species that is increasingly popular today.

No other idea in the English language possesses the flexibility, adaptability, and versatility of culture when it is understood and dealt with in these terms. Whereas most ideas are static and unchanging, culture is dynamic and evolutionary. It has been expanded many times over the course of history to remain in tune with the rapidly changing nature of reality and human knowledge and understanding.

In ancient, medieval, and early modern times, culture was seen and treated as "a part of the whole." This was the case when it was seen and treated as cultivation, the arts and humanities, and the legacy from the past or the cultural heritage of humankind. This was necessary to explain many things related to the growth and development of people, the quality of life, and the character of history.

In the late nineteenth and early twentieth centuries, culture began to be seen and treated in substantially broader and more all-embracing terms, often as the whole rather than a part of the whole, and consequently the total way of life of people. This was necessary to explain how people create cultures as wholes or total ways of life as they go about the process of meeting their individual and collective needs and working out their complex association with the world. This is especially true for the anthropological idea of culture, which caused a seismic shift in the nature, meaning, and understanding of culture—both as an idea and as a reality—

---

⁷ See, for example, A. Kroeber and C. Kluckhohn, *Culture: A Critical Review of Concepts and Definitions* (New York: Vintage Books, 1952). Also see D. Paul Schafer, *Culture: Beacon of the Future* (Westport, Conn.: Praeger Publishers, 1998), chapters 2 and 3.

when it was introduced to the world in the late nineteenth century.

In the latter part of the twentieth century and early part of the twenty-first century, culture has been expanded even more, primarily through the biological idea of culture. Here, culture is seen and treated as the organizational forms and structures of different species, both human and non-human. This has been necessary to explain the numerous similarities that exist between human beings and other species, as well as to confirm the fact that what human beings deem to be culture is not limited to themselves but exists throughout the entire realm of nature.

Recognition of these fundamental developments and basic turning points in the evolution of culture as an idea over the centuries has brought us to the present point. How should culture be seen and treated today, as well as in the future? Should it be seen and treated as a part of the whole, a dynamic whole or total way of life of people, the organizational forms and structures of different species, or all of these things? Surely it should be all of these things, since this is the only way it will be consistent with past experience, present realities, and future needs, as well as the many different ideas of culture that have been advanced and embraced throughout the world over the last two thousand years.

The key to coming to grips with this composite understanding of culture is to recognize that there has been a relentless trend throughout history towards an *all-encompassing idea of culture*. This is because the ideas of culture that were advanced in earlier periods of history—such as the artistic, humanistic, and historical ones—are imbedded in the ideas that appeared in later periods of history—most notably the anthropological, ecological, and biological ones—along with a great deal else. This means that the many different ideas of culture that have been advanced and embraced throughout the world over the centuries are not mutually exclusive and competitive but complementary and reinforcing.

Taking our cue from this, we may define culture formally as *the way in which species in general—and the human species in particular—create wholes or total ways of life that are composed of many different parts as they go about the process of meeting their individual and collective needs and working out their complex association with the world.* Among other things, this includes how species see and understand the world, organize themselves, conduct their affairs, elevate and embellish life, and position themselves in the world. This definition capitalizes on the main ideas of culture that have been advanced throughout history and are in active use throughout the world today. It also capitalizes on the fact that culture is not limited to the human species but exists among other species and in the entire domain of nature.

Armed with this all-encompassing understanding of culture, we are in a perfect position to understand why culture is of such vital importance to the world. On the one hand, it embraces virtually everything that exists in the world, thereby making culture not only flexible, adaptable, and versatile but also all-embracing because it includes the human species, other species, and the realm of nature. On the other hand, it affirms the fact that the world is made up of culture in general and countless cultures in particular at its very core and quintessential essence. While economics and economies constitute an extremely important part of this because they are concerned with the creation of material and monetary wealth—and therefore with people's jobs, income, and sources of livelihood—they are part and parcel of a substantially broader, deeper, and more fundamental process. It is culture and cultures in the holistic sense—not economics and economies in the partial or specialized sense—that constitute the real foundations of existence and the "engines that drive the train."

Recognition of this fact should cause us to focus much more attention on the development of culture and cultures in the future. This is the key to realizing viability and sustainability in the world because it means placing the priority on all activities in society and not just certain activities, as well as achieving balanced and harmonious relationships between them. It also makes it possible to capitalize on the many different qualities and capabilities that are inherent in the various ideas of culture that have been advanced and adopted throughout the world over the centuries, and are therefore contained in the all-encompassing idea of culture. *This is especially important with respect to the anthropological, sociological, ecological, and biological ideas of culture, since many of the qualities and capabilities contained in them are indispensable to the realization of a better world of the years and decades ahead.*

Having identified most of the benefits that accrue from culture in general and the various ideas of culture that have been advanced and adopted throughout history in particular, it is now evident why culture is of such fundamental importance to the world. In one form or another, it:

- **Focuses attention on the big picture, the component parts of the big picture, and the complex relationships that exist between the component parts of the big picture.** This is particularly true for the broader anthropological, ecological, and biological ideas of culture and the many qualities and capabilities contained in them. Our penchant for specialization and breaking things up into parts has caused us to lose sight of the big picture, and with it, the ability to see the flaws, deficiencies, and shortcomings that are inherent in the big picture. It is culture that makes us aware of this, and therefore helps us to understand where we have come from in the past, where we stand at present, and where we should be headed in the future. It also makes it possible to see what is most worthwhile and valuable in the world and in life, as well as the damage we are doing to the natural environment, other species, and the world at large.

- **Shifts the priority from a part of the whole to the whole and the need to achieve balanced and harmonious relationships between the parts and the whole.** Culture's capacity for seeing things in holistic terms is of crucial importance here. This is because a number of fundamental imbalances and disharmonies exist in the world—between human beings and the natural environment, materialism and spiritualism, science and religion, the sacred and the secular, and technology and society—that require rectification in the future if human survival and well-being are to be assured. Not only is culture the key to overcoming these imbalances and disharmonies— especially when it is understood and dealt with in the all-encompassing sense—but also it places the priority on the development of the whole person, cohesive communities, countries, cultures, and societies, holistic rather than specialized modes of public and private policy and decision-making, and synergistic relationships between all factors and forces in society.

- **Makes it possible to build strong bonds and connections between human beings, the natural environment, and other species.** This is possible because culture is concerned with all species and not just the human species when it is visualized and dealt with in the all-encompassing sense. No other term in the English language— and presumably other languages—possesses the ability to do this or realize it to the same degree. Since culture is something that all species have in common, it makes it possible to move laterally and horizontally across the human species, nature, the natural environment, and other species because all species share many similarities, manifest certain differences, and are in the same environmental boat. It is this fact that makes it possible to re-establish intimate links and connections between human beings, nature, and other species that have been lost in the modern world due to the separation of human beings from nature and other species.

- **Places more emphasis on conservation than it does on consumption.** Although culture is concerned with all activities in society, much more emphasis is placed on activities that are labour-intensive and low in material inputs and outputs—such as the arts, humanities, social relations, spirituality, and the like—than on activities that are capital-intensive and high in material inputs and outputs, such as many industrial, transportational, and technological activities. This is due to the fact that a strong emphasis is placed in many of the ideas of culture—and certainly in the all-encompassing idea of culture—on the arts, humanities, and related activities. As a result, it is through culture that it is possible to reduce the huge ecological footprint human beings are making on the natural environment by conserving rather than consuming resources at every opportunity and wherever and whenever possible.

- **Possesses the potential to reduce the gap between rich and poor countries and rich and poor people.** Reductions in this gap are far more likely to come through culture than economics because culture in the all-encompassing sense puts a high priority on caring, sharing, cooperation, and matters of the heart, soul, and spirit whereas economics puts a high priority on acquisition, competition, production, consumption, profits, and the pocketbook. While culture is concerned with both matters when it is seen and dealt with in holistic terms, the fact that it places a high priority on the former as opposed to the latter—largely because of its commitment to activities that have to do with feelings, emotions, and the expression of human sensibilities, sensitivities, and sentiments—opens the doors to the realization of more equitable distributions of income and wealth throughout the world.

- **Values history highly and makes humanity aware of the**

cultural baggage that people and countries carry with them from generation to generation and century to century. Unlike many activities that ignore history, culture values history highly because it helps to explain how we arrived at the present point and where we should be headed in the future. It also helps to shed light on the cultural baggage that people and countries carry with them from place to place and time to time, thereby making us conscious of the need to come to grips with the mistakes of the past in order to correct these mistakes and create more effective methods, models, techniques, prototypes, and ideals in the future.

- **Improves intercultural relations and creates more effective communications between the diverse cultures and civilizations of the world.** Culture's capacity to facilitate contact between the diverse cultures and civilizations of the world on a more profound and intense basis is of fundamental importance here. It helps to overcome the fears and suspicions that result from cultural differences and the inability to understand the signs, symbols, values, beliefs, and customs of others, thereby helping to promote peace, harmony, and unity rather than conflict, confrontation, and war in the world.

- **Facilitates changes in behaviour, lifestyles, and ways of life as the key to the survival and well-being of all species.** This is a cultural requirement more than any other kind of requirement because culture is concerned with beliefs, values, behaviour, attitudes, lifestyles, and ways of life much more than any other discipline. Through its ability to deal with generalities and specifics—as well as its ability to see the big picture as well as countless smaller pictures— culture possesses the potential to bring about the fundamental changes in values, behaviour, lifestyles, attitudes, and ways of life that are indispensable for the future. The longer we ignore this, the more adverse the consequences will be. We need strong economies, industries, and corporations, needless to say, but we need them properly contextualized in the broader and deeper domain of culture and informed by cultural, environmental, historical, and spiritual values and not just commercial, financial, industrial, and technological values. Clearly the challenge of the future is to find the right balance between the two.

- **Possesses the potential to help people in all parts of the world to live creative, constructive, and fulfilling lives.** While culture is concerned with money, power, wealth, and prestige when it is visualized in all-encompassing terms, it is far more concerned with helping people to find joy, happiness, and fulfillment in their lives in all parts of the world. The renowned cultural scholar Joseph Campbell—who did so much to expand knowledge and understanding of culture, cultures, and the power of myth—said it best when he said people should "follow their bliss." For Campbell understood that ultimately contentment, fulfillment, and happiness in life come from becoming "whole people" in the most compelling and complete cultural sense of the term.

What is slowly but surely unfolding here is a vision of the world system of the future based on culture. It is a vision that is predicated on living in harmony with the natural environment, other species, and each other, as well as enjoying reasonable standards of living and a decent quality of life without straining the globe's natural resources and fragile ecosystems to the breaking point. While economics has provided the vision on which the world system has been based since the end of the seventeenth century— indeed ever since the publication of Adam Smith's *Wealth of Nations* in 1776—this vision is far too dangerous to carry forward into the future be- cause it is doing a great deal of damage to the natural environment and is producing material demands and expectations that are impossible to fulfill in view of the size and growth of the world's population and the finite carrying capacity of the earth.[8] We must look to culture to create a viable and sustainable vision of the world system of the future, since this is the only way to reduce the huge demands we are making on the natural environment, conserve resources at every opportunity, and achieve peace, harmony, and happiness in the world.

This brings us to the end of a long and fascinating journey as far as culture as an idea is concerned. While we must take full advantage of cul- ture's many strengths and deal effectively with its various shortcomings, what can be said about culture in the final analysis? Surely this. We need culture desperately—both as an idea and as a reality—if the world is to

---

[8] See D. Paul Schafer, *Revolution or Renaissance: Making the Transition from an Economic Age to a Cultural Age* (Ottawa, University of Ottawa Press, 2008).

become a better place and people and countries in all parts of the world are to benefit from culture's numerous qualities and capabilities. Viewed from this perspective, culture is certainly "an idea whose time has come." There is something so vital, vast, and visionary about culture that it is undoubtedly a categorical imperative for the future.

CHAPTER FOUR

The Millennium Challenge:
Making the Transition from an
"Economic Age" to a "Cultural Age"

*If humanity mobilizes all its wisdom, knowledge, beauty, and es-
pecially the all-giving and all-forgiving love or reverence for life and if
a strenuous and sustaining effort of this kind is made by everyone—
then the crisis will certainly be ended and a most magnificent new era
in human history will be ushered in. It is up to mankind to decide what
it will do with its future life course.*

—Pitirim Sorokin[1]

T he third millennium offers a unique opportunity. It is an opportunity to pass out of the present "economic age" and into a
future "cultural age." Shifting from an economic worldview to a
cultural worldview is the key to this.

In the economic age, the emphasis is on economics, economies,
specialization, consumption, commodities, profits, and the marketplace.
In a cultural age, the emphasis would be on culture, cultures, holism,
people, human welfare and well-being, caring, and sharing.

Many may view the contention that it is possible to pass out of the present economic age and into a future cultural age as wishful thinking, or
part of the inevitable sense of frenzy and excitement which accompanies
the conclusion of one millennium and the commencement of another.
However, there is mounting evidence to suggest that it may not be as far-
fetched as many people might think. Already there are signs that the
present economic age is not capable of coming to grips with a host of

[1] P. Sorokin, *Modern Historical and Social Philosophies* (New York: Dover Publications, Inc.,
1963), p. 319.

demanding and debilitating problems—problems as severe and complex as the environmental crisis, the population crisis, increased unemployment, escalating violence and terrorism, growing inequalities between rich and poor countries and rich and poor people, the dehumanization of life, and the division of the world into two unequal parts. Moreover, it is clear that culture is rapidly becoming a potent force in community, regional, national, and international affairs.[2]

It is evident why shifting from an "economic worldview" to a "cultural worldview" represents the key to passing out of an economic age and into a cultural age. Since worldviews affect every aspect and dimension of the human condition—including how people visualize and interpret the world, how they relate to each other and the world around them, how they act in the world and value things in the world—worldviews play a decisive role in determining what human life on earth is about.

Given the impact worldviews have on everything people do, see, create, and think, the lack of attention given to worldviews in the many debates, discussions, reports, and publications devoted to an examination of the state of the world at present and the nature of things to come is disturbing. Clearly the longer worldviews are ignored, the more dire the consequences will be.

The Triumph of the Economic Worldview

There can be little doubt that the present worldview is an economic worldview. It is a worldview which visualizes the world and all that is contained in it primarily, if not exclusively, in economic terms.

This worldview did not suddenly vault into a position of prominence on the world scene. It took several centuries, and the efforts of countless individuals and institutions, to shape the economic worldview into the powerful force it is today. The story of how this worldview evolved is an informative one, especially as it sheds a great deal of light on the nature of the world system at present, as well as the types of problems humanity could encounter in the future if it persists in this practice.

While the origins of the economic worldview are buried deep in history, the Judeo-Christian tradition, and the western experience, it is clear that the geographical explorations of the sixteenth, seventeenth, and

---

[2] This was confirmed most recently by the creation of the World Decade for Cultural Development (1988–1997) and the World Commission on Culture and Development (1993–1995) by the United Nations and UNESCO.

eighteenth centuries, the rise of nation states, and the wealth-oriented policies of the mercantilists played a seminal role.

The geographical explorations of the sixteenth, seventeenth, and eighteenth centuries had the effect of orienting European countries outward rather than inward, more committed to tapping wealth and resources abroad than taxing wealth and resources at home. The rise of nation states had the effect of making power and prestige in the world the principal objective and main concern of national and international development. And the wealth-oriented policies of the mercantilists placed the emphasis squarely on building up the economic and material resources of countries, since goods had to be produced at home before they could be exported and exchanged for products, resources, and materials abroad. The object was to increase exports and decrease imports, since this would cause more gold, silver, and precious metals to flow into a country than out of a country.

The collective impact of these three interlocking developments was nothing short of phenomenal. Not only did it focus attention on the development of the material and financial resources of countries and the acquisition of power, prestige, and wealth in the world, but also it opened the doors on a long and sustained period of colonialism and imperialism from which the world is still struggling to recover.

If these three interlocking developments had the effect of shining the spotlight directly on the development of the material resources of countries and the acquisition of wealth, power, and prestige, Adam Smith showed how it is really possible to increase "the wealth of nations."[3] He did so by focusing attention on economics and economies in general and specialization and the marketplace in particular.

If the objective was to increase material and monetary wealth, specialization—or the division of labour as Smith called it—was the solution. Through his famous example of the pin factory, Smith demonstrated empirically that many more pins could be produced each day if people "specialized" on one or two production functions than if they "generalized" on many production functions. As it was for pins, so it was for all products. Economic output could be enormously enhanced through specialization or the division of labour. If countries wanted to increase their wealth, power, and prestige in the world, therefore, the answer lay in

[3] Adam Smith, *An Inquiry into the Nature and Causes of the Wealth of Nations* (New York: The Modern Library/Random House, Inc., 1937).

training people to perform very specific production functions, as well as increasing the size of the market. For specialization is only limited by "the extent of the market" according to Smith. The larger the market, the greater the potential for specialization. As a result, specialization and market expansion spread like wildfire throughout the western world.

By the middle of the nineteenth century, most if not all of the prerequisites were in place for the triumph of the economic worldview. Not only was the industrial revolution in full swing by this time, but also economics and economies had become the principal preoccupations of national and international concern. Specialization, production, consumption, technology, and the marketplace were seen as the best vehicles to achieve this. It mattered little that economics was becoming known as "the dismal science" because classical economists like Smith, Ricardo, Malthus, and others believed the law of diminishing returns would eventually spell disaster for countries and the arrival of "the stationary state."[4] What mattered most was the development of the economies of countries, industrialization, and the creation of material wealth. Besides, the law of diminishing returns could always be postponed in the short run—even if it was inevitable in the long run according to the classical economists— through advances in technology and elimination of the fixity of land provision at home through exploitation of land and resources abroad.

While Smith and the other classical economists played a seminal role in the evolution of the economic worldview, it was Marx who turned this worldview into the powerful force it represents today. He did so by contending that economics is the "cause" or "basis" of everything else.

According to Marx, all societies are divided into an "economic base" and a "non-economic superstructure." The base is economic because it is concerned with the material conditions of life, and therefore with the "productive forces" in life. Everything else—the arts, ethics, education, religion, philosophy, spirituality, and the like—is superstructure because it is dependent on the economic base, from which it springs and to which it owes its existence. There is a unilateral relationship between the base and the superstructure according to Marx. Changes which occur in the economic base can cause changes in the superstructure, but not the

---

[4] While most classical economists feared the stationary state because it meant a static rather than dynamic economy and no growth in capital, labour, and population, John Stuart Mill saw the stationary state as an opportunity to focus attention on other essential aspects of life and living, such as development of "mental culture," matters of "moral and social progress," and "the art of living." As a result, his writings are very relevant to the subject matter of this chapter.

reverse. In effect, economics is "cause"; everything else is "effect."

The economic base theory quickly gave rise to the theory of the economic surplus. Since superstructural activities owe their existence to the economic base, they can only be expanded when the economic base is expanded, and must be cut back the moment the economic base is jeopardized. In other words, the economic base is the power generator in society. This is where the "productive labour" takes place and a surplus is created between production and consumption. It is this surplus, according to the argument, which makes superstructural activities possible.

Despite the impact these theories had on all parts of the world and not just the communist world, it is really the economic interpretation of history which explains why economics, economies, and the economic worldview have become the powerful forces they are today. Here again, Marx played a crucial role. In a series of incisive statements, he laid bare the economic interpretation of history in no uncertain terms:

> Men . . . begin to distinguish themselves from animals as soon as they begin to *produce* their means of subsistence, a step which is determined by their physical constitution. . . . What individuals are, therefore, depends on the material conditions of their production. . . .
>
> In the social production which men carry on they enter into definite relations that are indispensable and independent of their will; these relations of production correspond to a definite stage of development of their material powers of production. The totality of these relations of production constitutes the economic structure of society—the real foundation, on which legal and political structures arise and to which definite forms of social consciousness correspond. The mode of production of material life determines the general character of the social, political and spiritual process of life. . . .
>
> Morality, religion, metaphysics, and other ideologies, and their corresponding forms of consciousness, no longer retain therefore their appearance of autonomous existence. They have no history, no development; it is men, who, in developing their material production and their material intercourse, change, along with this their real existence, their thinking and the products of their thinking. Life is not determined by consciousness, but consciousness by life.[5]

[5] Patrick Gardiner, ed., *Theories of History* (Glencoe, Ill.: The Free Press, 1959), pp. 126–132.

According to proponents of the economic interpretation of history, the economic base and economic surplus theories are not just true at a particular moment in time. They are always true, they always have been true, and they always will be true. By cleverly mixing the idea that economics and economies should take precedence over everything else because they are "the cause" of everything else with evocative theories like the theory of the class struggle and the overthrow of the bourgeois by the proletariat, Marx and the Marxists were able to create an ideology about the centrality of economics and economies which is the most powerful ideology in existence today. It is an ideology based on the belief that economics and economies constitute "the whole," and everything else is a component part of the whole. In one form or another, this ideology has become the axiom of the age, the cornerstone on which everything else is erected. It is assumed that as economics and economies go, so goes the world.

A very specific theory of individual and institutional behaviour is buried deep in this ideology. It is a theory based on the conviction that individuals and institutions are concerned primarily, if not exclusively, with satisfaction of their economic interests. During the latter part of the nineteenth and early part of the twentieth centuries, neo-classical economists like Marshall and Jevons gave practical shape and theoretical substance to this conviction. They did so by marrying up the principles of maximization and optimization with the principles of hedonism or pleasure and pain. The two fitted neatly together to form the concepts of "the economic man" and "the economic organization." Both are concerned with pursuing their economic interests and getting as much fulfillment as possible from participation in the marketplace and the economy. This had the effect for a time of shifting the focus of attention in economics from "macro economics" to "micro economics." The two are closely related, however, since behaviour of individuals and institutions in the marketplace is intimately linked to the development of economies and economic policy generally.

Ever since they were first propounded, the conviction that economics and economies should constitute the centrepiece of society, the contention that the economic interpretation of history is the most accurate rendering of history possible, and the concepts of economic man and economic organization have steadily gained prominence and momentum in the world. Not only have most governments, corporations, and national and international organizations adopted this as their central premise, but also many educational institutions and media agencies have embraced this practice as well.

By the middle of the twentieth century, the economic worldview was fortified by another powerful force—"development."

How was development perceived and defined? Following the urgings of Truman and the experience of the Marshall Plan,[6] largely in terms of building up the economies of countries, maximizing or optimizing economic growth, asserting the centrality of economics in national and international affairs, and ensuring commitment to the economic interpretation of history. This was consistent with most models, theories, and policies being advocated by developmental theorists, practitioners, and institutions at the time, as well as with the appearance of Rostow's *Stages of Economic Growth.*[7] Here at last was a capitalist manifesto to rival the communist one.

For Rostow, countries had to pass through five well-defined stages if they wanted to achieve development and realize their economic potential. These five stages were: the traditional society; the pre-conditions to take-off; the take-off; the drive to maturity; and the age of mass consumption.[8] Each stage—with the exception of the traditional society, which was seen as an obstacle to development because many traditional beliefs and customs had to be overcome, and possibly a "sixth stage" which Rostow labelled "beyond consumption" because it was so difficult to define—required the realization of very specific economic goals and objectives. For example, in order to "take-off," investment had to be increased substantially as a percent of national income, new industries had to be created and old industries expanded, profits had to be reinvested, and agriculture had to be commercialized, modernized, and revitalized. What emerges overall, then, is a portrait of societies which increasingly focus attention on the development of their economies and concentrate their energies on achieving high performance in key economic indicators. Although this theory contrasts sharply with the Marxian theory in that it carves out a prominent place for capital rather than labour, it still resorts to the economic interpretation of history and the centrality of economics and economies to make its case.

Prompted by such theories and the actions of many national and inter-

[6] Wolfgang Sachs, "The Archaeology of the Development Idea," *Interculture* 23: 4 (Fall 1990). Also see Sachs, ed., *The Development Dictionary* (London: Zed Books, 1992).
[7] W. W. Rostow, *Stages of Economic Growth: A Non-Communist Manifesto*, 3rd ed. (Cambridge: Cambridge University Press, 1991).
[8] *Ibid.*, pp. 4–6.

national organizations, the notion of development spread like wildfire throughout the world. By the late 1970s and early 1980s, many countries and governments in the world had adopted development as their central premise and modus operandi, despite the fact that it was the product of the western experience and the western imagination.

Meanwhile governments had grown rapidly in most parts of the world. And just as it was economists like Smith, Ricardo, Marx, Marshall, Jevons, Rostow, and others who provided the theoretical foundation for the economic orientation of societies and the focus on economics, economies, specialization, growth, and development, so it was an economist who provided the theoretical foundation for governments to play a major economic role in society. The economist was John Maynard Keynes.

Prior to Keynes, governments focused attention largely on political issues such as law-giving, legislation, regulation, and public policy. Keynes changed that. He did so by contending that governments can—and should—play a powerful economic role in society through their ability to collect taxes, spend public funds, influence the level of aggregate demand, control monetary and fiscal policy, and deal with cycles in business activity.[9] Coupled with other developments taking place at the time, most notably the demand for public services and control of commercial and industrial activity, the stage was set for a dramatic expansion of governments everywhere in the world. Only now, as governments are confronted with severe fiscal problems and appear to have grown beyond acceptable limits, are questions being raised about the extent to which governments should be involved in the economic as opposed to the political affairs of nations.

What stands out most clearly when the world system is looked at in totality, then, is the economic worldview on which it is based. It is a worldview which treats economics and economies as the centrepiece of society and extols the values of production, consumption, profits, specialization, growth, development, technology, the marketplace, and human control over nature. Not only are relations between individuals, institutions, governments, countries, and continents conducted largely in terms of these forces, but also the world system is governed primarily by these forces.

Nowhere is this more apparent than at the international level. Countries are ranked primarily on the basis of their gross national product,

---

[9] John Maynard Keynes, *The General Theory of Employment, Interest and Money* (London: Papermac, 1963).

level of capital formation, state of economic development, and rate of economic growth—despite the fact that the United Nations and other international organizations have endeavoured in recent years to use "human development indexes" rather than "economic development indexes" to measure performance and assess progress. Moreover, the world is still divided into "a developed component" and "a developing component" according to criteria which are largely economic in character. Countries which have achieved high levels of income per capita or economic development are deemed to be "developed"; countries which have failed to achieve these levels are deemed to be "developing." This produces a world subdivided into two unequal parts, as well as a pecking order which keeps some nations in a state of subordination and dependence while others enjoy a state of superiority and independence.

Clearly the economic worldview would never have achieved the prominence it has today had it not been for the vision on which it is based. It is a vision predicated on the conviction that eventually it will be possible for people and countries in all parts of the world to live life at high levels of material abundance and leisure time.

While numerous commercial, financial, technological, social, medical, artistic, and scientific benefits have been experienced as a result of the economic worldview and the vision on which it is based—particularly for those who have had the good fortune, resources, socio-economic circumstances, and geographical location to enjoy them—there are a number of reasons why this worldview and its underlying vision should not constitute the driving force of the world system of the future. The costs, consequences, and dangers are just too great.

First of all, there is the very real possibility that the global ecosystem will collapse under the colossal weight which is being imposed on it. The reason for this is not difficult to detect. The economic worldview and its vision of a material Utopia on earth are yielding consumer demands and expectations which are impossible to fulfill, given the size and growth of the world's population and the carrying capacity of the earth. Surely acute shortages of renewable and nonrenewable resources, resource wars, more and more holes in the ozone layer, increased pollution, and environmental degeneration will be humanity's lot if it persists in this practice.

Second, it is apparent that the basic divisions that exist in the world will not be mitigated by the economic worldview. In fact, if anything, they will be exacerbated and enlarged. This is especially true for the division of the world into two unequal parts, as well as the growing gap between rich and poor countries and rich and poor people. This could easily result in a great deal more violence, terrorism, conflict, and confrontation in the world. It is a frightening prospect in view of the high level of these atrocities today.

Third, the world is increasingly becoming a callous, dehumanized, and impersonal place. While it would be a mistake to blame the economic worldview entirely for this, there can be no doubt that it has been a major contributor to it. It has failed to produce the social and human bonds which are necessary to keep people, countries, and continents together when economic, commercial, technological, and financial forces are operating to split them apart.

Fourth, there is less and less likelihood that people will be able to find jobs and secure a decent source of livelihood if the economic worldview is sustained in the future. As companies engage in downsizing, profit maximization, capital movements, globalization, and promotion of their economic and financial interests, this will accentuate even more the basic divisions that exist in the world between rich and poor countries and rich and poor people, as well as the division of the world into two unequal parts.

Finally, and perhaps most symbolically, the vision on which the economic worldview is based cannot possibly be realized when consideration is given to the fact that the world's population is already at seven billion and growing rapidly and the carrying capacity of the earth is severely limited. Even the most impressive gains in technology will not be sufficient to produce more leisure time and material abundance for all. In fact, many of the statistics and trends point squarely in the opposite direction.

Given this situation, it is clear that a new worldview is needed if humanity is to be successful in coming to grips with the severe problems with which the world is confronted at present and could face to an even greater degree in the future. Such a worldview must prove capable of dealing with the intimate connection that exists between human beings, nature, and the natural environment, as well as provide a ray of hope and optimism for the future.

Naturally there are many views and opinions with respect to what kind of worldview this should be. For some, it should be an environmental worldview, one capable of addressing the fundamental relationship between human beings, nature, and other species, the ecological crisis, and the spread of pollution and toxic substances. For others, it should be a technological worldview, one capable of understanding the complex connection that exists between human beings and technology, as well as harnessing the resources of outer space, capitalizing on the computer revolution and phenomenal changes taking place in contemporary communications, and disseminating information and knowledge more broadly. And for still others, it should be a social, political, aesthetic, or spiritual worldview, one capable of improving health care systems, orchestrating complex political processes, realizing artistic ideals, revitalizing religious institutions, and deepening the intimate connection that exists between people, the sublime, and the divine.

To date, little consideration has been given to a "cultural worldview." This is surprising in view of the fact that the world is going through a profound cultural transformation and culture is becoming a powerful force in global development and world affairs. One evidence of this was the creation in 1988 of the World Decade for Cultural Development by the United Nations and UNESCO.[10] A second evidence was the creation by the same two organizations of the World Commission on Culture and Development in 1993.[11] A third evidence, and perhaps the most persuasive evidence of all, is the contention of a number of scholars and statesmen that the world is entering a period of profound conflict and confrontation characterized by the assertion of ethnic and cultural identities and "the clash of cultures and civilizations."[12]

Viewed from this perspective, any worldview which fails to take culture

[10] The World Decade for Cultural Development had four principal objectives. These objectives were to ensure that the cultural dimension is taken into account in all developmental planning; to assist in the preservation and enrichment of cultural identity, including promotion of the arts and safeguarding of the national heritage; to broaden participation in cultural activity; and to foster international cultural cooperation. See Canadian Commission for UNESCO, *World Decade for Cultural Development* (Ottawa: Canadian Commission for UNESCO, 1988).

[11] The World Commission on Culture and Development was regarded generally as a follow-up to the World Commission on Environment and Development (the Brundtland Commission). It was mandated to examine a variety of issues and problems related to culture and cultures and their role in the future—issues and problems ranging all the way from how to define culture and cultures to the influence of culture and cultures on cultural development, groups, communities, regions, nations, and the world as a whole. See World Commission on Culture and Development, *Our Creative Diversity: Report of the World Commission on Culture and Development* (France: World Commission on Culture and Development/EGOPRIM, 1995).

[12] See, for example, Samuel Huntington, "The Clash of Civilizations," *Foreign Affairs* (Summer 1993), pp. 22–49. The fact that this article spawned a debate in international circles not unlike the debate following Thomas Kuhn's contention with respect to "paradigm shifts" (Kuhn, *The Structure of Scientific Revolutions* [Chicago: University of Chicago Press, 1970]) suggests that there may be a great deal of substance to the argument that the world has entered a period of profound cultural conflict and confrontation characterized by the assertion of ethnic and cultural identities and the clash of cultures and civilizations.

and cultures fully and forcefully into account may be doomed to failure from the outset. This is especially true when consideration is given to the fact that development doesn't appear to work when it is not rooted in culture and cultures and fails to take the cultural needs of people, the natural environment, other species, and future generations into account.[13]

Since a cultural worldview contains many of the elements and ingredients which are needed to address the shortcomings of the economic worldview as well as the concerns of other worldviews, it is to this worldview that attention can now be directed. As will be discovered momentarily, this worldview not only possesses the potential to lay the foundation for a new world system—a system which flows from a different set of perceptions, principles, policies, priorities, and practices—it also possesses the potential to open the doors to a cultural age.

The Evolution of a Cultural Worldview

If a cultural worldview is to become a reality, there must be no mistaking the use of the term "culture" in this context. Failure to come to grips with the nature and meaning of culture could have an adverse effect on any attempt to see the world from a cultural rather than economic perspective.

In the economic age, culture is marginalized and trivialized. The means whereby this is accomplished is instructive. First, economics is treated as "the whole" and "cause" of everything else. This makes it possible to treat culture as a component part of the whole, or part of the superstructure of society as Marx would say. Next, culture is perceived and defined in narrow and often elitist terms, usually as "the arts, heritage, finer things of life, and 'cultural industries' of publishing, radio, television, film, video, and sound recording."[14] Since very little money is spent on culture when it is defined in this way and it generates little income, investment, and expenditure activity, this makes it possible to treat culture as a secondary rather than primary sector of society, a form of entertainment, and an instrument of economic policy.

Recent developments throughout the world suggest that culture is breaking out of the straitjacket which has been assigned to it in the

---

[13] See, for example, United Nations/UNESCO, *Rethinking Development: World Decade for Cultural Development 1988–1997* (Paris: UNESCO, 1994). Also see D. Paul Schafer, *The Challenge of Cultural Development* (Markham, Ont.: World Culture Project, 1995).

[14] This is the way most governments and public institutions define culture. See Pekka Gronow, "The Definition of the Sphere of Cultural Development" in *Planning for Cultural Development; Methods and Objectives* (Documents of the Expert Meeting at Hanasaari, Espoo, Finland, 17–19 March 1976). Cultural Development: Documentary Dossier 9-10 (Paris: UNESCO, 1978).

economic age. For example, when people talk about being "the products of their culture" today, they tend to mean they are the products of "everything that exists in their society" or "their culture as a whole."

This is the way Sir Edward Burnett Tylor, the British anthropologist, used the term culture more than a century ago when he said, "Culture or Civilization, taken in its wide ethnographic sense, is that *complex whole* which includes knowledge, belief, art, morals, law, custom, and any other capabilities and habits acquired by man as a member of society."[15] Clearly culture includes economic systems, political ideologies, social conventions, technological innovations, educational endeavours, recreational activities, religious and spiritual beliefs, and interactions with the natural environment as well as art forms, heritage activities, the finer things in life, and the cultural industries when it is defined in this way. Perhaps this is why Wole Soyinka, the distinguished African Nobel laureate, prefers to view culture as "source"—source from which all things flow and to which all things return.[16]

This much more comprehensive way of perceiving and defining culture was confirmed when the member states of UNESCO adopted the following definition of culture at the second World Conference on Cultural Policies in Mexico City in 1982:

> Culture is the whole collection of distinctive traits, spiritual and material, intellectual and affective, which characterize a society or social group. It includes, besides arts and letters, modes of life, human rights, value systems, traditions and beliefs.[17]

Viewed from this perspective, culture is a "dynamic and organic whole" which is concerned with the way people "visualize and interpret the world, organize themselves, conduct their affairs, elevate and enrich life, and position themselves in the world."[18] Not only is this comprehensive understanding of culture consistent with the relentless trend which has manifested itself over the last two thousand years towards a "holistic con-

---

[15] Sir Edward Burnett Tylor, *The Origins of Culture* (New York: Harper Torchbooks, 1958), p. 1 (emphasis mine). Also see World Commission on Culture and Development, *Our Creative Diversity*, pp. 21–31.
[16] Wole Soyinka, "Culture, Memory and Development," *International Conference on Culture and Development, April 2-3, 1992* (Washington: The World Bank, 1992), p. 21.
[17] UNESCO, *Mexico City Declaration on Cultural Policies* (Paris: UNESCO, 1982).
[18] Schafer, *The Challenge of Cultural Development*, pp. 19–26.

cept of culture,"[19] but also it is consistent with the direction culture appears to be headed in the future.[20]

Each component part of this comprehensive concept of culture contributes a great deal to broadening and deepening understanding of the nature, scope, subject matter, characteristics, and capabilities of culture in general and cultures in particular.

How human beings visualize and interpret the world deals with the deeper cosmological, theological, mythological, aesthetic, and ethical beliefs and convictions which people possess. These beliefs and convictions constitute the cornerstone of culture and cultures because they provide the axioms and assumptions on which culture and cultures are based. As such, they determine the way people perceive, interpret, and understand the world—thereby giving rise to such notions as "the whole," "the complex whole" and "the ordered whole"—as well as interact with the natural environment and each other. In consequence, they are intimately connected to nature, the global situation, the world system, the human condition, theories of development, and concepts of space, time, life, death, and the universe.

How people organize themselves deals with all the decisions people make with respect to economic systems, social and political structures, technological and scientific policies, and ecological practices. Included here are all types of human settlement—towns, cities, neighbourhoods, regions, countries, and the world system as a whole. These are undergoing profound change at the present time as a result of shifting trading practices, globalization, rapidly-changing demographic patterns, and new economic, political, social, environmental, and technological realities.

How people conduct their affairs deals with the character of people's lives, and with it, decisions about consumer expenditures and behaviour, living arrangements, child rearing, family life, and personal preferences and practices.

How people elevate and enrich life deals with people's education and training, artistic and scientific preferences, spiritual practices, moral values, and all those things which make life deeper, richer, and more meaningful. This is where the signs, symbols, myths, legends, stories,

---

[19] D. Paul Schafer, "The Evolution and Character of the Concept of Culture," *World Futures: The Journal of General Evolution* 38: 4 (1993), pp. 225–254.
[20] D. Paul Schafer, "Towards a New World System: A Cultural Perspective," *Futures: The Journal of Forecasting, Planning and Policy* 28: 3 (1996), pp. 285–299.

rituals, similes, and metaphors are created which help people understand their cultures and the cultures of others.

And how people position themselves in the world deals with people's geographical location, geopolitical situation, and territorial maneuvering in the world. These factors play a crucial role in determining the way in which people relate to each other and the world around them as members of groups, communities, societies, countries, and cultures.

When culture is perceived and defined in this way, it can be visualized as a gigantic tree with roots, trunk, branches, leaves, flowers, and fruit. Metaphorically speaking, myths, religion, ethics, aesthetics, philosophy, cosmology, and the like constitute the roots; economic systems, technological practices, political ideologies, social structures, environmental policies, and consumer practices constitute the trunk and branches; and educational endeavours, artistic works, moral values, architectural edifices, and spiritual practices constitute the leaves, flowers and fruit.[21]

This metaphor contributes a great deal to understanding culture and cultures as *contexts* and *contents*. For just as trees are dynamic and organic wholes composed of many interdependent and interrelated parts, so are culture and cultures. And just as all the component parts of trees play an indispensable role in the effective functioning of trees as dynamic and organic wholes, so all the component parts of culture and cultures play an indispensable role in the effective functioning of culture and cultures as dynamic and organic wholes.

This metaphor sheds a great deal of light on the fact that culture and cultures exist in breadth as well as in depth. In breadth, they are concerned with all groups, classes, institutions, and activities, and not just certain groups, classes, institutions, and activities. Viewed from this perspective, culture and cultures are everybody's business—everybody has a fundamental stake in them as well as a basic responsibility for them. In depth, they are concerned with all that is most valuable in life, especially the arts, sciences, humanities, ethics, education, caring, sharing, and human love. This ensures that culture and cultures are not dragged down to the lowest common denominator and robbed of their ability to reach for the highest, wisest, and most enduring humanity has to offer.

A number of advantages flow from viewing culture and cultures in this comprehensive, holistic way.

---

[21] This metaphor was set out in a letter the author received from Dr. Min Jiayin of the Institute of Philosophy, Chinese Academy of Social Sciences, Beijing, China.

In the first place, attention is focused on "the whole," as well as the need to situate the parts properly in the whole. This is consistent with the age-old philosophical truth that "the whole is greater than the parts" by virtue of the fact that something has been added which is not in the parts. It is this "extra something" which makes the whole greater than the sum of the parts. Focusing attention on the whole in this way is imperative in a world where sight is often lost of "the whole" and the parts often take precedence over the whole. Nowhere is this more apparent than with respect to the natural environment and the relationship human beings have with it. Failure to give sufficient consideration to the natural environment as a whole has led to consumer practices and policies which now threaten the entire global ecology and life on earth.

Second, and closely related to the first, the emphasis is on activities which bring people, countries, and continents together rather than set them apart. The reason for this is apparent. Since culture and cultures are dynamic and organic wholes, much more emphasis is placed on activities which promote unity, harmony, synergy, and synthesis than on activities which promote division, discord, conflict, and confrontation. This is essential in a world where fragmentation, polarization, and the division of all things into opposites is all too apparent.

Finally, the emphasis is on people and human welfare and well-being rather than on commodities, profits, and the marketplace. This is because culture and cultures are concerned first and foremost with "the human factor in development" and ensuring that development has "a human face."[22] This is imperative in an age where material objects and monetary interests receive more attention than human beings and matters of human welfare and well-being.

With the holistic concept of culture and cultures in place, it is possible to proceed with the process of piecing together a cultural worldview. While many elements and ingredients make up this worldview, among the most essential are: the centrality of culture and cultures; a cultural interpretation of history; affirmation of culture's highest, wisest, and most enduring values; creation of a global federation of "world cultures"; and collective sharing of the cultural heritage of humankind. Since these elements and ingredients contain the secrets which are needed to step over the threshold to a cultural age, it pays to examine them in some detail.

[22] United Nations/UNESCO, *Rethinking Development*.

The Centrality of Culture and Cultures. Making culture and cultures rather than economics and economies the centrepiece of society and principal preoccupation of development would have a profound effect on the future courses of planetary civilization.[23] On the one hand, it would make it possible to mount an all-out assault on human needs, since a much higher priority would be placed on people and human welfare and well-being than on commodities, profits, and the marketplace. Such an assault is urgently needed if people in all parts of the world are to live life at a reasonable level of physiological and psychological comfort and human decency. On the other hand, it would reduce the drain and strain on scarce renewable and non-renewable resources, since the emphasis would be on the qualitative as opposed to the quantitative side of development, and hence on activities like the arts, ethics, education, learning, social interaction, and spiritual renewal which make fewer demands on nature's precious resource legacy and fragile ecosystem.

Nor would these be the only benefits to be derived from making culture and cultures the centrepiece of society and principal preoccupation of development. In terms of the complex relationship that exists between the parts and the whole, it would make it possible to ensure that the parts of the whole are properly contexted in the whole. In the case of economics and economies, for example, this would mean that the more specific goals and objectives of economics and economies—production, consumption, investment, productivity, growth, and profits—would be brought into line with, and constrained by, the broader and deeper goals and objectives of culture and cultures—pursuit of knowledge, wisdom, beauty, and truth; commitment to excellence, creativity, access, participation, and equality; acceptance of cultural identities; promotion of cultural diversity; respect for the rights and traditions of others; and safeguarding of the cultural heritage.[24] Not only would this help to assert the importance of income,

---

[23] D. Paul Schafer, "Cultures and Economies: Irresistible Forces Encounter Immovable Objects," *Futures: The Journal of Forecasting, Planning and Policy* 26: 8 (1994), pp. 830–845.
[24] There is ample evidence of these goals and objectives in the publications of cultural institutions such as UNESCO, the national commissions for UNESCO, the Council of Europe, and others, as well as in the works of cultural scholars such as Kroeber, Sorokin, Burckhardt, Braisted, Huizinga, Alisjahbana, and others. See, for example: Alfred Kroeber, *Configurations of Culture Growth* (Berkeley and Los Angeles: University of California Press, 1969); Pitirim Sorokin, *Social and Cultural Dynamics: A Study of Change in Major Systems of Art, Truth, Ethics, Law and Social Relationships* (Boston: Extending Horizon Books—Porter Sargent Publisher, 1957); Jacob Burckhardt, *The Civilization of the Renaissance in Italy* (Washington, D.C.: Washington Square Press, 1966); Paul J. Braisted, *Towards a New*

employment, resource sharing, conservation, education, training, pursuit of perfection, and promotion of cooperation over competition, consumption, hoarding, homogenization, and survival of the fittest, but also it would help to ensure that economies are pointed in a positive direction in the future.

While economics and economies will always occupy a prominent position in people's lives because they are concerned with jobs, employment, and securing a decent source of livelihood, shifting priority from economics and economies to culture and cultures would transform the entire purpose and practice of development.[25] For to be effective and in tune with people's needs and circumstances, cultures would have to be *comprehensive, coherent, cohesive, humane,* and *contexted.* They would have to be comprehensive in the sense that they are concerned with all the resources of society and not just economic, material, and technological resources; coherent in the sense that harmonious relationships exist among the determinants and component parts of development; cohesive in the sense that the component parts of development are bound together properly; humane in the sense that attention is centred on people's needs and concern for human welfare and well-being; and contexted in the sense that they are situated effectively in the natural, historical, and global environment.

It is impossible to talk about the centrality of culture and cultures without addressing the thorny problem of culture, cultures, and politics. For politics, like culture and cultures, is also concerned with "the whole," albeit from a different perspective. As a result, political concerns, like cultural concerns, are holistic and egalitarian rather than specialized and elitist.

Despite the intimate connection that exists between politics, culture, and cultures, people fear political involvement in culture and cultures for

Humanism: Some Value Perspectives in Emerging Cultural Relations (New Haven: The Hazen Foundation, 1975); Johan Huizinga, *The Waning of the Middle Ages* (London: Penguin Books,1969); S. Takdir Alisjahbana, *Socio-Cultural Creativity in the Converging and Restructuring Process of the New Emerging World* (Pulo Gadung: P. T. Diam Rakyat, 1983); and S. Takdir Alisjahbana, *Values as Integrating Forces in Personality, Society and Culture* (Kuala Lumpur: University of Malaya Press, 1966).

[25] See, for example: UNESCO, *The Futures of Cultures* (Paris: UNESCO Publishing, 1994); Eleonora Barbieri Masini and Yogesh Atal, eds., *The Futures of Asian Cultures: Perspectives on Asia's Futures III* (Bangkok: UNESCO Principal Regional Office for Asia and the Pacific, 1993); Eleonora Barbieri Masini, coordinator, *The Futures of Culture: Volume I: Meeting of the Working Group on the Futures of Culture, Paris, 9–10 January 1990* (Paris: UNESCO, 1991); and Eleonora Barbieri Masini, coordinator, *The Futures of Culture: Volume II: The Prospects for Africa and Latin America* (Paris: UNESCO, 1992).

good reason. For history confirms that culture and cultures can easily be manipulated for political purposes, as encounters with Nazism, fascism, imperialism, colonialism, the Holocaust, and "cultural revolutions" throughout the world readily reveal.

How can culture and cultures become the centrepiece of society and principal preoccupation of public and private concern without increasing the risk of political manipulation of cultural life? The answer lies in establishing numerous safeguards, precautions, and countervailing measures. What are these safeguards, precautions, and countervailing measures? As history and experience confirm time and again, they include: the democratization of institutions and activities; the decentralization of opportunities and resources; and the establishment of institutions and agencies at arm's length from government and the political process. With such measures in place, cultural initiatives and programs should be free to evolve in a manner that best suits people's needs, rights, responsibilities, and circumstances. Without them, there is a need to remain ever watchful and mindful of the political uses and abuses of culture and cultures.

With the necessary countervailing measures in place, what can be said about the complex connection between culture, cultures and politics? Surely this. It is the first and foremost responsibility of governments, politicians, and the political process to develop culture in general and cultures in particular. In order to realize this, governments and politicians will have to abandon their penchant for thinking about culture and cultures in narrow and specialized terms and start thinking about culture and cultures as the very essence and raison d'être of their existence. In order to achieve this, parliaments and cabinets will have to spend much more time discussing and planning the development of culture and cultures; cultural departments will have to replace economic departments as the key departments in government; cultural models will have to replace economic models as the principal means of government action and decision-making; and cultural policy will have to be accorded the highest status and stature in public policy. For this is what it takes to make the development of culture and cultures the principal priority of governments, politics, and the political process.

A Cultural Interpretation of History. If culture and cultures are to provide the lenses through which the world of the future is visualized, it will not be sufficient to assert the centrality of culture and cultures. It will also be necessary to interpret history from a cultural perspective. For interpretations of history deal with many of humanity's most profound and pressing questions: What are the origins of life? Why have human beings evolved the way they have? What has brought humanity to the present point? Where does humanity go from here?

According to the economic interpretation of history, people are concerned first and foremost with economics and economies. Regardless of how important economics and economies are or have been—and there is no intention of deprecating their importance here—the problem is that this is not backed up by the evidence. Surely what stands out most clearly when an objective eye is cast back over the past or around the world at present is the fact that people in all parts of the world are and have been concerned first and foremost with culture and cultures. The reason for this is apparent. Since people have a variety of needs which must be attended to simultaneously rather than sequentially—to breathe, think, bond, eat, communicate, procreate, love, and believe—they have been compelled to build culture and cultures in the holistic sense in which the terms are used here as the first and foremost act of human activity if they are to survive and function effectively in society. These needs give rise to a complex constellation of interdependent environmental, social, economic, political, technological, educational, recreational, and aesthetic requirements—all of which are and have been much in evidence from the outset of human history.

To illustrate this point, take as an example the hunt culture, one of the earliest cultures known to humankind, although any other culture could be used to prove the same point. From everything that is known about the hunt culture, the social, aesthetic, environmental, and spiritual aspects of the hunt were as essential as the economic aspect and as much in evidence as the economic aspect from the outset. In other words, the hunt was a "cultural event" par excellence. In order to hunt successfully, people had to band together in groups; hence there was a social and human dimension to the hunt. In order to prepare properly for the hunt, people had to mythologize it; hence there was an aesthetic and spiritual dimension to the hunt. And in order to eat, people had to catch and consume their prey; hence there was an economic and technological dimension to the hunt. Regardless of whether these activities took place before, during, or after the hunt, they were integral and indispensable aspects of the hunt, as the rock paintings at Ardèche, Altamira, Lascaux, and Addaura and the earliest petroglyphs constantly remind us. Presumably this is why all the earliest societies are referred to as "cultures" rather than "economies." For close inspection of them reveals that all human needs and activities have been much in evidence from the very beginning.

What is true for the hunt culture is true for all cultures. It is difficult to point to a culture anywhere in the world, or at any time in history, which has preoccupied itself initially—or exclusively—with the development of its economy and only later turned to the development of other activities. Regardless of how destitute people are or have been, they have never neglected the need for social bonding, artistic expression, mythology, community organization, recreation, spiritual renewal, and just plain idling. To contend that societies develop their economic bases first and only later turn to development of their non-economic superstructures is not only misleading, it also represents a gross simplification of reality and is inconsistent with the facts of the matter. For the facts of the matter indicate that the creation and development of culture and cultures has been the principal preoccupation of people everywhere in the world from the commencement of history right up to the present day.

This is where a cultural interpretation of history proves infinitely superior to an economic interpretation of history. Predicated on a holistic rather than specialized way of looking at the human condition and human development over the centuries, it provides a much more authentic and accurate way of interpreting the past, assessing the present, and confronting the future. It does so by confirming the fact that people in all parts of the world have been preoccupied with building cultures in a very specific spatial and temporal sense. These cultures have been "dynamic and organic wholes" in the sense that they are concerned with all human activities and not just certain human activities. Whether these cultures pass through springs, summers, falls, and winters as Spengler contended, or are confronted with more and more complex challenges to which they must respond as Toynbee argued, there is no doubt that the development of cultures has been at the very heart of human history down through the centuries.

For Johan Huizinga, the central task of cultural history is the morphological understanding and description of the actual, specific courses of cultures and civilizations.[26] Spengler reinforced this view when he said history is "a picture of endless formations and transformation, of

---

[26] Johan Huizinga, *Men and Ideas: History, the Middle Ages, the Renaissance: Essays by Johan Huizinga*, translated by James S. Holmes and Hans Van Marie (London: Eyre and Spottiswoode, 1960), p. 51.

The Age of Culture

the marvellous waxing and waning of organic forms."[27] Presumably this is why Karl Weintraub contends that the principal task of cultural history and cultural historians is to shed light on the development of cultures as wholes.[28]

Next to the development of cultures as wholes, what stands out most clearly when an objective eye is cast back over the past or around the world at present is the fact that culture and cultures can be used for positive or negative purposes.

On the positive side, they can be used to enhance the human condition and propel humanity to higher and higher levels of accomplishment. Viewed from this perspective, there is not a culture anywhere in the world or at any level—group, community, regional, national, or international—which has not made a valuable contribution to global development and world affairs. Not only is it possible to find the most outstanding cultures in all parts of the world—Africa, Asia, Latin America, the Caribbean, and the Middle East as well as North America and Europe—but also it is difficult to think of a culture in any part of the world which has not made a substantial contribution to the cultural heritage of humankind. *It is on this undeniable historical and contemporary fact that humanity should seek to build a more just and equitable world system in the future.*

On the negative side, what shows up with equal clarity is the fact that culture and cultures can be used to commit incredible acts of bestiality, brutality, violence, and oppression. Moreover, they can result in a great deal of pain and suffering. This makes it imperative to ensure that there are numerous checks and balances on the exercise of cultural power, as well as countless opportunities for cultural communication, understanding, education, dialogue, and exchange.

Recognition of the fact that culture and cultures can be used for negative as well as positive purposes helps to open the doors to more accurate and authentic interpretations of history. Such interpretations are desperately needed if the injustices which have been and continue to be done to African, Asian, and Latin American nations, aboriginal groups, and ethnic minorities as a result of one-sided and distorted interpretations of history are to be corrected. Regardless of how difficult and painful this process is, it simply must be undertaken if a more equitable and effective foundation

[27] Oswald Spengler, *The Decline of the West* (New York: The Modern Library, 1962), p. 18.
[28] Karl J. Weintraub, *Visions of Culture: Voltaire, Guizot, Burckhardt, Lamprecht, Huizinga, Ortega y Gasset* (Chicago: University of Chicago Press, 1966), p. 3. (The introduction is very germane to the discussion of cultures as wholes and the role of cultural historians and cultural history.)

is to be laid for the world of the future. A cultural interpretation of history could prove exceedingly valuable here, as it would help to counteract the many injustices which exist at present, as well as recognize the contributions which all peoples, countries, and cultures have made and are making to global development and world affairs.

Affirmation of Culture's Highest, Wisest, and Most Enduring Values. When culture and cultures are perceived and defined in holistic terms, all values are cultural values. Economic, social, political, and religious values are cultural values every bit as much as artistic, humanistic, scientific, and educational values because they make specific cultural statements and express precise cultural relationships and priorities.

The ability to treat all values as cultural values places culture in an ideal position to make a constructive contribution to value theory. For it makes it possible to create a common framework or container within which values can be situated, analyzed, discussed, and compared. Without this, values merely exist in different domains of experience and it is impossible to make intelligent choices and meaningful comparisons among them.

If culture's only asset in the field of value theory was its ability to provide a common framework or container within which values can be compared and evaluated before a final course of action is taken, it might be dismissed more readily as a force to be reckoned with in the future. But fortunately culture has a great deal to say about those particular values which are most germane to the human condition. It does so by singling out those values which have been accorded humanity's highest accolades and withstood the test of time.

What are these values? As stressed repeatedly throughout the text, they include: the thirst for knowledge, wisdom, beauty, and truth; the pursuit of excellence, perfection, and creativity; the importance of justice, equality, and diversity; the necessity of caring, sharing, and human love; the need for order, stability, and identity; respect for the rights, traditions, and beliefs of others; and the search for the sublime. While these are not the only values with which culture is concerned, adherence to these values is essential because it is values such as these which tend to take the needs of human beings, other species, the natural environment, and future generations into account.

Adherence to cultural values is of vital importance if humanity is to go fruitfully into the future. While wisdom may be required to make sensible and informed choices about future courses in planetary civilization, and creativity may be required to bring about the new cultural forms and structures which are needed to build a more viable and effective world system in the future, it is culture's highest, wisest, and most enduring values which represent humanity's greatest hope for the future. Without the ability to reach for the very best humanity has to offer, it is difficult to see how humanity will be able to realize its full potential and avoid falling into an abyss of skepticism, cynicism, fatalism, and despair. Takdir Alisjahbana expressed this sentiment best when he said: "Culture in the last analysis represents the human aspiration to realize the highest form of life."[29] Perhaps this is why successive generations of cultural scholars, from Voltaire, Klemm, Arnold, and Burckhardt to Hall, Kothari, Kroeber, Girard, Braisted, Nettleford, Nandi, Soedjatmoko, Senghor, Paz, and Masini, have been so committed to the development of the intellectual, artistic, social, scientific, educational, and spiritual resources of society. Not only do developments in these areas provide the perfect comple-ment—and counterpoise—to the development of economic, technological, commercial, and material resources, but also they provide strong indicators of the nature of things to come.[30] Pitirim Sorokin stated this conviction most effectively when he talked about the need to shift from "sensate cultures" to "ideational, idealistic, and mixed cultures."[31]

Creation of a Global Federation of "World Cultures." Viewed from the perspective provided by economics and economies, the challenge of the future is to create a "global economy" and "global culture." Viewed from the perspective provided by culture and cultures, the challenge is to create a global federation of "world cultures." The two are as different as night and day.

The arguments in favour of a global economy and global culture are compelling. According to those who advocate it, there has been a relent-less trend throughout history towards the creation of larger and larger economic and cultural units. Pushed to its logical conclusion, it is clear where this trend ends up. It ends up with the creation of a global economy and global culture, with a world court, financial system, commercial net-

[29] Alisjahbana, *Values as Integrating Forces*, p. 228.
[30] See, for example: Sorokin, *Social and Cultural Dynamics*; Kroeber, *Configurations of Culture Growth*; and W. M. Flinders Petrie, *The Revolutions of Civilisation* (New York: Harper and Brothers, 1971).
[31] Sorokin, *Social and Cultural Dynamics*, pp. 20–39.

work, language, judicial system, police force, and possibly government. Proponents of this view cite the progressive movement from small groups to city states to countries to global trading zones, as well as the creation of international institutions like the United Nations, the World Bank, and the International Monetary Fund, adoption of English as a universal lingua franca, the ubiquitous spread of American films, television programs, and popular music, the emergence of a global communications system, and the appearance of a "world without frontiers," to support the case that a global economy and global culture are in the making and rapidly taking shape.

For proponents of this line of thinking, a global economy and global culture are not only inevitable. They are also desirable. According to the argument, they will open up unlimited opportunities for understanding, cooperation, communication, and exchange among all the peoples and countries of the world, largely because all people and countries will share a common worldview and set of values. This will dramatically reduce the potential for violence, conflict, confrontation, and unrest in the world—at least according to the argument—because economic and cultural differences will be eliminated and peace, harmony, stability, and security will be established in the world.

Those opposed to a global economy and global culture are quick to counter these arguments. They contend that every movement towards the realization of larger economic and cultural units has spawned a dialectical reaction towards smaller economic and cultural units. The reason for this is easy to detect. Since people derive their sense of identity and belonging from economic and cultural units which are significantly smaller, less abstract, and more tangible than a global economy and global culture—clubs, families, groups, subcultures, minorities, neighbourhoods, communities, and the like—proponents of this view contend that smaller and more manageable economic and cultural units are equally inevitable and predictable. Moreover, the world is already subdivided into so many different economic and cultural units, they contend, that it is highly unlikely these units will disappear. They are far too ingrained in the human condition and the need for ecological and cultural diversity.

Is it possible to reconcile these contradictory views? Is it possible, for example, to experience the benefits which might accrue from a global economy and global culture while simultaneously experiencing the benefits which derive from many diverse and discrete economies and cultures? The answer appears to lie in the creation of a global federation of world cultures.

Regardless of where cultures are situated in the world or how small or remote they might be, all cultures are rapidly becoming "world cultures" in the sense that they are products of the global village and the colossal changes which are taking place in contemporary communications. This makes it imperative for cultures everywhere in the world to maintain their identity, independence, and sovereignty while simultaneously adapting to a world that is in perpetual motion and changing rapidly. In order to achieve this, they will have to grow organically from their own roots, traditions, values, and circumstances—especially as endogenous rather than exogenous development is the key to survival, sustainability, and sovereignty in a dynamic and unpredictable world—while at the same time incorporating many of the changes which are taking place in demographics, technology, communications, and commerce throughout the world.

Creating a global federation of world cultures where all cultures address a common set of causes and concerns while simultaneously maintaining their identity, integrity, and autonomy could provide the key to this. What are these common causes and concerns? In one form or another they all relate to improvements in the quality of life, the natural environment, and the human condition for all members of the global family. Realization of these causes and concerns will not be possible without a great deal more cooperation, communication, and exchange among all the cultures and peoples of the world. Rabindranath Tagore, the great Indian poet and sage, foresaw this day when he said, "Only that will suffice which is basically consonant with the good of all men. We must prepare the field for the cooperation of all the cultures of the world where all will give and take from others. This is the keynote of the coming age."[32]

If cooperation, communication, and exchange is essential among all the cultures and peoples of the world, so is achieving unity in diversity. It is impossible to realize this without sharing certain similarities, since unity requires the cultivation of basic bonds and commonalties of experience between peoples, countries, and cultures. Likewise, it is impossible to achieve unity in diversity without preserving differences, for too much sameness can kill the creative spark which is needed to make people, countries, and cultures different and unique. Thus unity in diversity is achieved—and maintained—by walking the tightrope between

[32] Paul J. Braisted, *Cultural Cooperation: Keynote of the Coming Age* (New Haven: The Edward W. Hazen Foundation, 1945), p. 5.

similarities and differences. It is a balancing act that is fraught with difficulties. A slip in the direction of too much sameness can cause people to rebel, if only to protect themselves from the numbing effects of standardization, homogenization, and uniformity. A slip in the direction of too many differences can be equally disastrous, since people fear and mistrust what they are unable to understand. This makes finding the right admixture of sameness and distinctiveness one of the greatest challenges confronting humanity.

Collective Sharing of the Cultural Heritage of Humankind. If there is one area where people and cultures must learn to achieve unity in diversity, surely it is in the area of collective sharing of the cultural heritage of humankind. As the crowning achievement of humanity's relentless quest down through the ages to reach for the highest, wisest, and most enduring culture has to offer, this precious heritage of hope possesses the potential to bring the whole of humanity into intimate contact.

It is this heritage of hope which needs to be turned to humanity's collective advantage in the future. Nowhere is this more essential, or more pressing, than in terms of addressing human needs. For if the world is to become a happier, healthier, and safer place, it is essential that people in all parts of the world are able to live life at an acceptable level of physiological comfort and human decency. This necessitates having sufficient food, clothing, shelter, fresh water, clean air, sanitation, and health care to ensure survival, as well as enough environmental, artistic, social, recreational, and spiritual amenities to live creative and fulfilling lives.

While collective sharing of the cultural heritage of humankind is essential in all areas, it is particularly essential in such areas as sharing renewable and non-renewable resources, income, employment, and educational opportunities, and appropriate technologies. Until those who own and control these possibilities share them with all members of the human family—not as a moral duty but as a fundamental necessity—the world will be saddled with an international system which is unjust, unfair, and inimical to global harmony and world peace.

Given the need to share the cultural heritage of humankind more liberally and broadly, a great deal of energy will have to go into determining how this can be accomplished most effectively in fact. This is what makes contemporary technology like computers, smartphones, iPads, virtual reality, satellite radio and television, electronic superhighways, web sites, social media, and the like so timely. While there are countless problems to be worked out in connection with the ownership, use, content, and control of these devices and systems, they provide a ray of hope in what would otherwise be a bleak and depressing situation. For through their ability to store, retrieve, and transmit knowledge, information, and ideas from one end of the earth to another in the flash of a second, they make it possible for people and countries in all parts of the world to share the common fruits of humanity in a spirit of generosity and altruism. It is an opportunity that is far too important to be missed.

If humanity is to be successful in making the shift from an economic worldview to a cultural worldview, two additional requirements are imperative. The first is the need to capitalize on culture's capacity for links, and the second is the need to capitalize on culture's capacity for synthesis. For along with the other elements and ingredients which comprise a cultural worldview, these also form part of the millennium challenge of making the transition from an economic age to a cultural age.

Of all the links which are required in the world of the future, two stand head and shoulders above the rest. The first has to do with the links that are necessary between people, cultures, races, and groups. The second has to do with the links that are necessary between human beings, other species, and the natural environment.

More effective links between people, cultures, races, and groups are imperative in a world characterized by a great deal of multicultural and multiracial mixing, the assertion of ethnic and cultural identities, and the fact that more conflicts now take place within countries than between countries—as the pain, suffering, and anguish endured by people in Burundi, Rwanda, Sri Lanka, the former Yugoslavia, the former USSR, Ireland, and elsewhere in the world readily reveals. While there are no easy answers to these problems and they are buried deep in history and the human condition, it is difficult to see how these problems can be solved without a great deal more *intercultural* and *cross-cultural* education, training, communication, and exchange. This is what makes the arts, education, ethics, spirituality, and social affairs so crucial to the world of the future. Without activities such as these to broaden and deepen cultural understanding and build partnerships and bridges among the diverse peoples, countries, and cultures of the world—activities which are best epitomized in recent years by the universal response to Beethoven's *Ninth Symphony* and particularly the *Ode to Joy*—it is impossible to see how peace and harmony will be achieved and maintained in the world.

If it is essential to establish effective links between peoples, cultures, races, and ethnic groups, it is equally essential to establish effective links between human beings, other species, and the natural environment. Such links bear on the intimate ecological association that all people have with various forms of animal and plant life. Without these links, human life will be severely challenged, if not ultimately curtailed, in the future.

If it is essential to build on culture's capacity for links, it is equally essential to build on culture's capacity for synthesis.

Clearly no greater mistake could be made in the world than to fall into the trap of polarization. For regardless of what types of problems have been encountered as a result of excessive preoccupation with economics, economies, economic growth, development, technology, specialization, and the marketplace, rejecting these forces out of hand will result in the same kind of overloaded and imbalanced system with which the world is saddled at present.

Culture's capacity for synthesis provides a way out of this dilemma. For when culture and cultures are defined and dealt with in holistic terms, they possess the potential to combine all the parts of the whole in a more effective ordering and orchestration of the whole. Here the challenge lies not in dismissing or downplaying the powerful forces contained in the economic worldview, but rather in situating these forces in context and blending them with other forces like the arts, humanities, philosophy, religion, education, science, and spirituality in the creation of a more comprehensive and compelling worldview. Johan Huizinga, the distinguished Dutch cultural historian, provided a glimpse of what this worldview might look like when he said, "The realities of economic life, of power, of technology, of everything conducive to man's material well-being must be balanced by strongly developed spiritual, intellectual, moral, and aesthetic values."[33]

Attending to matters as quintessential as these could prove valuable and timely as humanity braces to confront one of the most difficult and demanding periods in its history. For it could place humanity in a much stronger position to address the complex problems and limitless opportunities of the new millennium. Ultimately that is what the millennium challenge and making the transition from an economic age to a cultural age are all about.

[33] Weintraub, *Visions of* Culture, p. 216.

Part Two

FUNDAMENTALS OF A CULTURAL AGE

CHAPTER FIVE

Functioning of a Cultural Age

The systematic interpretation of culture brings us close to the thesis that global development is in reality the development of cultures and civilizations.

—Nada Švob-Đokić[1]

Now that firm prerequisites have been established for a cultural age, it is possible to turn our attention to how a cultural age would function in fact. What worldview would underlie it, what model of development would drive it, and what concerns would dominate it?

A Cultural Worldview

One of the biggest challenges for a cultural age will be piecing together, making known, and using a cultural worldview to replace the economic worldview, which has the advantage of being reasonably well-known and

---

[1] Nada Švob-Đokić, "Culture as a System: Identity, Development, and Communications," *Razvoj/Development International* 6: 2–3, p. 299.

accepted throughout the world. Since there are many different concepts and definitions of culture in use throughout the world today, the most promising approach in piecing together this cultural worldview may be to examine what individuals and institutions working in the cultural field have been most concerned about.

While construction of this worldview from ideas and practices across such a wide range of disciplines is fraught with difficulties, and is subject to numerous qualifications and generalizations, it simply must be done if we are to ascertain the way in which the world would be viewed from a cultural perspective.

From anthropology, sociology, history, and philosophy there is the concern with the whole, discussed earlier. From the arts there is the concern with excellence, creativity, beauty, diversity, and the search for the sublime, as well as the ways in which knowledge and understanding of cultures are enhanced through signs, symbols, and stories that stand for the whole. From the humanities there is the concern with people, cooperation, equality, and the connection between spiritualism and materialism. From ecology, biology, and other disciplines that have a close historical and contemporary affinity with culture there is the concern with the natural environment, other species, and the relationships, including the similarities and differences, between these and human beings. While none of these concerns is exclusive to any of the disciplines cited, it is these disciplines that tend to place a relatively high priority on them.

When these concerns are looked at in totality, they provide the basis for the construction of a cultural worldview. In contrast to the economic worldview, a cultural worldview would be predicated on the conviction that the best way to view the world and everything in it is through the prism of culture. The priority would be placed on the whole, not just on economics or any other part of the whole, and on the need to achieve balanced, harmonious, and equitable relationships between the parts and the whole. This would then be used to address the complex challenges and opportunities involved in making improvements in society, the human condition, and the world system. What would be of the greatest concern for a cultural worldview is the way in which people tie together all the various activities in which they are engaged to form a whole or total way of life.

Concern with space and time would be another crucial aspect of a cultural worldview. In spatial terms, this would mean placing the emphasis on the relationship between human beings and their institutions, on the one hand, and the natural environment, or "the land," as well as specific places, on the other. In temporal terms, it would mean placing the emphasis on the ways in which human institutions have developed over time, as well as where they stand at present and where they are headed in the future. For culture, this would mean focusing attention on the theoretical and practical heritages that the diverse peoples and countries of the world have built up, as well as the entire cultural heritage of humankind. For specific cultures, it would mean focusing on the relationships between people and traditions, customs, and identities.

It should be pointed out here that a cultural worldview would not reject the economic worldview. Rather, it would subsume the economic worldview, and a great deal else, in a broader, deeper, and more fundamental way of looking at the world. Further, just as the economic worldview is a collective worldview, so too would a cultural worldview be. It may differ substantially from the individual worldviews of people and institutions working in the cultural field, just as the economic worldview may differ substantially from the individual worldviews of people and institutions working in the field of economics. However, this does not alter the fact that it is possible to talk about a cultural worldview in the collective sense.

The development and use of a cultural worldview in this collective sense could prove valuable and timely at the present juncture in history. In the first place, it would place humanity in a much stronger position to make sensible and sustainable decisions about future courses and directions in planetary civilization. In the second place, it would provide an opportunity to make a breakthrough in environmental matters because a high priority would be placed on the relationship between people and the natural environment. In the third place, it would render a better perspective on the numerous conflicts between groups of people, countries, and cultures. The large majority of these conflicts are far more than economic conflicts, even though many economic factors may be involved, such as control and ownership of land, or access to natural resources and wealth. Rather, they are cultural conflicts to the extent that they also involve such factors as differences in worldviews, values, or traditions, as, for example, in the Middle East, Afghanistan, Iraq, and elsewhere in the world. A cultural worldview would place the priority on unity, synthesis, inclusion, and holism, rather than division, separation, exclusion, and polarization.

Development of Culture and Cultures

Since the development of culture and cultures would be the major consequence of adopting a cultural worldview, it is necessary to examine what this means in practice.

Developing culture in depth means placing the priority on the quest for knowledge, wisdom, beauty, and truth; the importance of creativity, excellence, compassion, caring, and sharing; the need for equality, diversity, identity, and unity; respect for the needs and rights of others; appreciation of the cultural heritage of humankind; and the search for the sublime. These are ideals that people and countries in every part of the world value a great deal, despite significant differences in their worldviews. It also means placing a great deal of emphasis on the arts, humanities, education, learning, spirituality, philosophy, ethics, anthropology, sociology, ecology, and biology, since these activities and disciplines have very close connections with culture. This would help to ensure that culture's highest, wisest, and most enduring ideals would be located at the core of the development process.

Developing culture in breadth means ensuring that people have access to as many cultural options and opportunities as possible, and are able to participate as actively and fully as possible in all aspects and dimensions of cultural life. Every individual and every ethnic group has a great deal to give to the development of culture, as well as a great deal to receive in return. Governments, corporations, foundations, and local, regional, national, and international organizations would have to play forceful and proactive roles in cultural development and policy here, and remove as many barriers to access and participation as possible.

Specific cultures would also have to be developed in depth and breadth. Such development would be comprehensive, involving the development of all activities in society, and not just certain activities.

Development would also be coherent, so that all the component parts of cultures are properly situated. Given the innumerable difficulties involved, this may well turn out to be one of the greatest challenges in the development of cultures. Situating the component parts of cultures properly is most essential in the case of economics, if it is to serve human, social, and environmental interests, and not merely commercial, industrial, financial, and corporate interests. The specific goals of economics, such as production, consumption, investment, growth, and so on, would have to be brought into line with, and constrained by, the broader and deeper cultural goals of access, creativity, equality, compassion, cooperation, and the safeguarding of the natural environment and cultural heritage of humankind.

Positioning economies properly within cultures would reduce the strain on scarce resources, because much more emphasis would be placed on activities that make fewer demands on them. It would also humanize economies by placing a higher priority on income and resource sharing, job creation, training and retraining, diversity, distribution, cooperation, and inclusion than on consumption, exploitation, uniformity, profits, competition, exclusion, and the market. Clearly, strong economies are needed to deliver the improvements and investments in technology, capital accumulation, and material living that are required to eliminate poverty and hunger, but strong economies must be positioned properly within cultures if economic excesses and imbalances are to be prevented. Technology, communications, the arts, education, health, the sciences, religion, politics, and all the other component parts of cultures must also be properly positioned. There are always problems when priority is given to any part over the whole, regardless of what part it may be.

Developing cultures that are cohesive is equally important. This would necessitate creating strong connections between activities, ethnic groups, geographical regions, and so on. Where such connections exist, cultures are likely to remain intact, and soar to higher and higher levels of accomplishment. Where they do not exist, cultures can become unglued and split apart. Cultures can easily fall prey to complex communications problems, particularly where geographical size or formidable terrain makes staying in touch difficult or impossible. They can also succumb to tribal divisions or ethnic unrest when ethnic or linguistic groups visualize their futures in terms of isolation, exclusion, and separation, rather than integration, togetherness, and inclusion. It is here that artists, arts organizations, and the creative industries have a key role to play through their ability to create parts of the whole that stand for the whole.

Another key requirement would be the development of cultures that are civilized, meaning that resources are shared equally, there are no major disparities in income or wealth, and discrimination and violence are eliminated, or at least reduced. The objective here would be to create a level playing field on which all citizens and groups can find a place. This should go a long way towards ensuring that cultures have a human face, and that people's needs, rights, and responsibilities can be dealt with in a fair, equitable, open, and compassionate manner.

Finally, having adequate control over decision-making processes, and development policies and practices, is essential. Regardless of whether cultures are local, regional, national, or international, possessing adequate control over internal affairs and external relations is mandatory if cultures are not to become the victims of standardization, imperialism, globalization, or commercialization. Governments, citizens, and community groups will have to work to ensure that decision-making processes and development practices are in domestic rather than foreign hands, and that a reasonable amount of cultural programming is indigenous, rather than imported or imposed. What is at stake here is the survival of cultures into the future.

A Cultural Model of Development

There are many different ways to perceive and define development, but most would agree that development is concerned with the fulfillment of human needs. If human needs are to be dealt with effectively in the future, it will be necessary to evolve models of development that are equal to the task. They must be capable of doing justice to all human needs, and not just certain human needs. They must also be capable of coming to grips with the many different problems associated with people's needs, as previously discussed. A cultural model of development would be capable of dealing effectively with the shortcomings of the economic model of development, as well as with the needs of people and countries in every part of the world.

While the diagram of the cultural model of development that follows has been greatly simplified, it displays the main features of the model and illustrates why it is essential to take a cultural rather than economic approach to development. It is clear from the diagram that, when development is viewed from a cultural perspective, its scope and subject matter are enormous, comprising six fundamental matters:

(1)   culture as a whole and cultures as wholes;
(2)   the component parts of culture and cultures;
(3)   the relationships between the component parts of culture and cultures;
(4)   the interactions between the component parts and the whole of culture or cultures;
(5)   the relationship between the quantitative and qualitative dimensions of culture and cultures; and
(6)   the relationship between culture and cultures, on the one hand, and the natural, historical, and global environment, on the other.

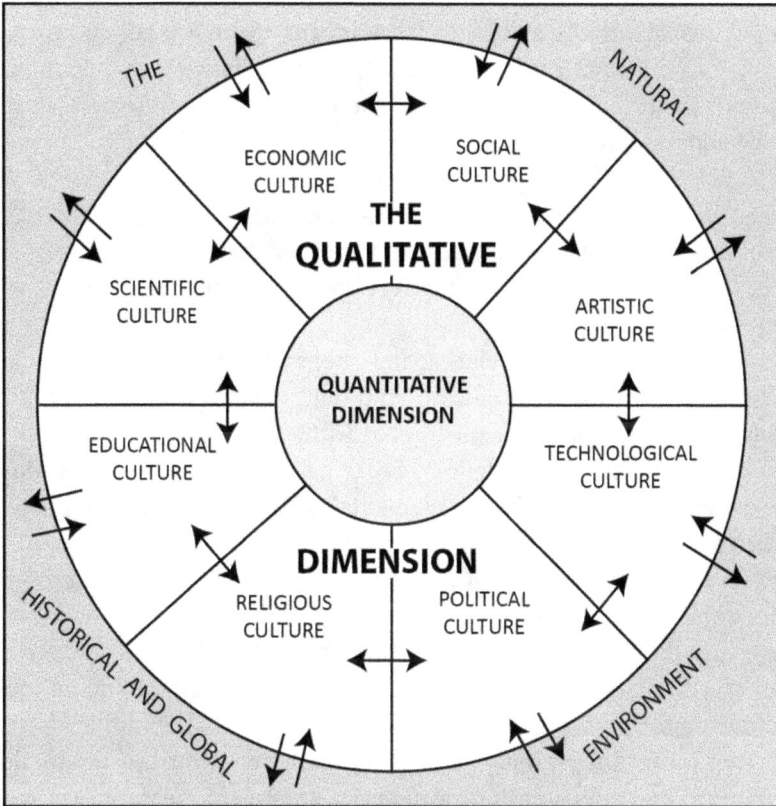

The Cultural Model of Development

The most important priority is to develop culture as a whole and cultures as wholes (the complete circle), but a very important aspect of this is developing the component parts of culture and cultures in their own right. These component parts are depicted in the diagram as the "economic culture," the "social culture," the "political culture," and so on, since they all share culture in common. Each can be developed most effectively when it is developed in terms of the uniqueness, creativity, excellence, integrity, and diversity inherent within it. Given the highly specialized nature of the modern world, a great deal is known about each of these component parts and how to develop them most effectively, even if the resources are not always available to achieve this.

Far less is known about how to deal with the complex relationships between and among the component parts. What, for example, is the relationship between the economic culture and the social culture, and how can this relationship be dealt with most effectively? Or to cite another example, what is the relationship between the technological culture and the religious culture? Understanding these relationships and coming to grips with them looms ever larger in the overall matrix of concerns that must be addressed.

It is also imperative to examine very carefully the dynamic interplay between the component parts of culture and cultures, on the one hand, and culture and cultures as wholes, on the other. A larger and larger price will be paid if these relationships are not understood and dealt with effectively.

Turning now to the relationship between the quantitative and qualitative dimensions of culture and cultures, it is the qualitative dimension that is more difficult to deal with, because it is so difficult to measure and define. Nevertheless, breaking culture and cultures down into quantitative and qualitative elements serves the very useful purpose of focusing attention on the material and non-material dimensions. This in turn helps to draw attention to the natural environment, consumption of renewable and non-renewable resources, the rapid rate of population growth, and the finite carrying capacity of the earth. It is obvious from the model that the larger the quantitative dimension of culture and cultures, the more pressure is exerted outwards on the qualitative dimension. In effect, the more time, money, and energy are spent on the production, distribution, and consumption of material goods and services, the more pressure is exerted on the natural environment, resources, and other species, and the less time, money, and energy are available for social interaction, spiritual renewal, friendship, human love, family, recreation, the arts, and other things that make life richer, fuller, and more meaningful.

This leads us to the most important relationship in the cultural model of development, namely the relationship between culture and cultures and the natural, historical, and global environment. History confirms time and again that when culture and cultures are not positioned properly in their environment, the consequences are devastating in terms of environmental exhaustion, cultural conflict and confrontation, and repetition of the mistakes of the past. There may be nothing more important to the world of the future than situating culture in general and specific cultures in particular effectively in their environment. On the one hand, this means ensuring that all the diverse cultures of the world are predicated on values, policies, and practices that ensure environmental sustainability, human well-being, and harmony between all people and countries of the world. On the other hand, it means ensuring that all the diverse cultures of the world are based on understandings of the past that are as accurate as possible.

It is imperative to examine very carefully the impact that culture and cultures have on the natural environment. Rather than taking the natural environment as a given or taking it for granted, as the economic model of development tends to do, the cultural model opens up a commanding place for the natural environment at the very core of the development process and in every aspect of development activity. Since all human activities are composed of material and non-material elements, it is essential to examine in great detail the material draws and ecological impacts that different types of human activities have. For example, manufacturing, commercial, transportation, and technological activities draw and impact heavily on the natural environment, because the material component of these activities is high and the potential for damage is great. Conversely, many artistic, educational, social, and spiritual activities draw and impact lightly on the natural environment, because their material component is low and the potential for damage is significantly reduced.

The implications of this for local, regional, national, and international development are clear and unequivocal. As world population increases and more pressure is exerted on the natural environment, a great deal more emphasis will have to be placed on activities that draw less on the natural and global environment, and do as little environmental and global damage as possible. In the economic model, human needs with a high degree of material input and output are given a high priority because they produce higher levels of material living and more rapid rates of economic growth. This puts a great deal of strain on the environment. In the cultural model, in contrast, the satisfaction of human needs is much less dangerous and demanding, since the emphasis is placed on achieving a judicious balance between the quantitative and qualitative dimensions of development, and between people's material needs and their non-material needs.

Attention also needs to be focused on the dynamic and reciprocal interplay between the natural environment and culture. Just as culture, and specific cultures, affect the natural environment by constantly pressing outwards, so the natural environment affects culture and cultures by constantly pressing inwards. There are many examples of this. Scientists, for example, are concerned with expanding knowledge and understanding of everything that exists from the outer reaches of the cosmos to the smallest forms of plant and animal life. Artists have been concerned with expanding human awareness of the natural environment for centuries, primarily by enhancing our appreciation of its beauty and grandeur. The natural environment also has an uncanny way of striking back when it is exploited and abused, by way of hurricanes, floods, tornadoes, earthquakes, droughts, global warming, and the collapse of cultures that have failed to take the natural environment fully into account.

Culture and cultures must also be properly positioned in the global environment. As recent developments indicate, every culture is situated in the world and interacts with other cultures in very specific ways. As globalization increases and cultures interact more frequently and extensively with one another, a great deal of thought and attention will have to be given to how cultures are positioned in the world, and what threats and dangers they may pose to other cultures. Without the creation of many more connections between the diverse cultures of the world, conflict and confrontation will be inevitable, and harmony and peace will not be achieved. This requires a dramatic increase in international cultural relations, as well as many more opportunities for intercultural communications and exchange. These are the real keys to solidarity, friendship, and understanding.

Culture and cultures must also be situated properly in the historical environment. This means protecting the legacy of artefacts, ideas, ideals, values, traditions, monuments, and beliefs that has been built up over the course of history. This legacy provides people and countries with connections that create a continuous bond between past, present, and future generations, as well as the means of differentiating between right and wrong, good and evil, valuable and valueless, meaningful and meaningless. Without protection of the cultural legacy of humankind from the ravages of time, people and countries will be unable to learn from the past, maintain their distinctive identities and diversities, and preserve their cherished ways of life. However, this also means coming to grips with the cultural baggage that people and countries inherit from the past, particularly where this baggage is negative, since it creates hostilities and resentments that stand in the way of achieving peace and harmony. The "truth and reconciliation" initiatives instituted in South Africa and other countries offer a ray of hope in this regard, indicating a willingness on the part of specific groups to admit the wrongs of the past, and to seek reconciliation and forgiveness. Another set of examples concerns the attempts now being made to right the wrongs that have been done to aboriginal peoples, in New Zealand, Australia, Canada, the United States, Mexico, and other countries, through the resolution of land claims, the provision of greater control over the development of indigenous activities, the preservation of distinctive cultural traditions, and the installation of self-government for aboriginal peoples.

This completes our analysis of the cultural model of development, which provides the contextual, conceptual, and practical framework required to make sensible and sustainable decisions about a variety of community, regional, national, international, and planetary matters. It does so by incorporating the natural, historical, and global environment fully into the development equation, as well as by recognizing that development is an interactive, egalitarian, inclusive, and holistic activity. It also addresses two of the greatest shortcomings of the economic model of development: failure to take the natural environment into account in planning and decision-making; and the tendency to treat development as an economic activity rather than a multi-dimensional and comprehensive cultural activity.

Key Cultural Concerns

Just as the economic age is driven by a number of powerful forces, so a cultural age would be dominated by a number of fundamental concerns. It is important to identify and examine these concerns, since they flow inevitably from the conviction that culture and cultures should be made the centrepiece of society, and the principal preoccupation of municipal, regional, national, and international development.

It is essential to emphasize, once again, that the dominant forces of the economic age would not disappear in a cultural age. Rather, they would be incorporated into it, along with much else. It simply is not possible to create material resources without these forces, as they provide the wherewithal required to fuel economic growth, drive economic development, and propel countries to higher and higher levels of commercial attainment. Moreover, they are so deeply ingrained in the world system, people's lives, and development that it seems unlikely that they could ever disappear. They would, however, be constrained by the key concerns of a cultural age.

To illustrate this point, take the questions of specialization and holism.

What specialization is to the economic age, *holism* is to a cultural age. Specialization would not disappear, because it will always be required to increase knowledge and understanding of the component parts of culture and cultures, as well as to increase production, productivity, and efficiency in all areas of life. Nevertheless, holism would be a cultural age's central principle. Holism does not reject the need for knowledge and understanding of specific parts of the whole, but incorporates this into the quest to broaden and deepen knowledge and understanding of what is more fundamental: the total way of life of people, and the need to achieve harmonious relationships between material and non-material requirements.

This would not be the only benefit to be derived from making holism a key concern. Many individuals, institutions, groups, and countries have become so caught up with, and dependent on, specialization that their futures are in jeopardy. As long as the demand for their particular specialization is strong there is no real problem, but as soon as the demand diminishes there are serious problems indeed. While this has been going on steadily since the industrial revolution, and has been a basic concern for a long time, it is assuming alarming proportions today as a result of globalization, the liberalization of trade, rapid changes in technology, and new environmental and ecological realities. More and more individuals, institutions, groups, and countries are discovering that excessive dependence on a highly specialized skill, profession, production function, or handful of products can lead to unemployment, under-employment, and obsolescence. Holism could prove valuable here as it puts the emphasis on the cultivation of many diverse skills and the ability to function in a variety of contexts, rather than the cultivation of a single skill within a single context.

What makes *human well-being* a key concern of a cultural age is the fact that it has been pushed into the background over the past two hundred years or so, while concern for products, profits, and the market has been pushed into the foreground. Do people have enough food, clothing, shelter, security, education, recreation, and social, artistic, health, and spiritual amenities? Are they able to participate actively, freely, and fully in the life of the community, region, country, and culture in which they live? Are social, religious, linguistic, economic, and financial barriers to access and participation breaking down or building up? Are these and other obstacles preventing people from improving their lot, and expanding their range of opportunities and choices? These are the questions that must be asked and answered if human well-being is to be a key concern, making it possible to address people's needs and requirements in a sustained, systematic, proactive, and egalitarian manner.

This fact has been brought home with striking clarity in recent years as a result of the violent reactions of some groups of people to free trade and globalization. They claim that these arrangements do not place the priority on human well-being, but rather on corporate profits, excessive rates of economic growth, exploitation of the natural environment and labour, and promotion of the interests of powerful institutions such as the World Trade Organization, the World Bank, or the International Monetary Fund. To this must be added the fact that some free trade agreements have been negotiated in secret, with little or no input from the public, civil society, or social and environmental organizations.

Distribution would also be a key concern in a cultural age. Despite the advances in production, productivity, and productive capacity over the past fifty years, the distribution problem has yet to be solved and, if anything, it is worse than ever. Not only are there substantial disparities in income, wealth, power, and resources, but these disparities are getting more conspicuous. If this problem is to be dealt with successfully in the future, distribution will have to become a mainstream concern rather than a marginal one. If as much progress can be made in the area of distribution over the next one hundred years as has been made in the area of production over the past one hundred years, the greatest single obstacle to global harmony, peace, and stability will have been overcome.

Sharing and compassion are also essential to ensure human survival and well-being, and to make it possible for all people and countries to live with dignity and respect. This would go a long way towards addressing some of the most obvious causes of hostility and resentment in the world. If the focus is on giving rather than taking, dispersion rather than accumulation, it will become possible to shift from looking after oneself to concern for others, from survival of the fittest to concern for the plight and well-being of the majority of people and countries in the world.

A great deal of emphasis will have to be placed on *altruism* if this is to be achieved. Not only is the world in need of individuals who can make commitments to causes that are greater than themselves, altruism is also needed to address the world's most difficult, demanding, and debilitating problems.

Regrettably, the world seems to be moving farther away from altruism rather than closer to it. The erosion of religious beliefs and practices in many parts of the world has brought with it a significant loss of interest in things that are greater than the self. Then there is the increase in affluence and materialism throughout the world, and the effect this is having in freeing people from dependence on others while at the same time fostering a preoccupation with the self and self-sufficiency. To these trends against altruism should also be added the tendency to develop concern for rights without a commensurate concern for responsibilities, and the need to give something back to community and society in return for the safeguarding and promotion of human rights.

It would, then, be beneficial if more people took President John F. Kennedy's advice: "Ask not what your country can do for you, but what you can do for your country." But this advice does not apply simply within any one country. Without a revival and diffusion of altruism, it is difficult to see how or why rich countries would increase their aid and assistance to poor countries, reduce or eliminate their oppressive debt loads, or help them to deal effectively with poverty and address the needs of the disadvantaged.

The arts have long had concerns that are fundamentally linked to culture, and would therefore be key concerns of a cultural age. Foremost among these concerns are *excellence, creativity, beauty,* and *the search for the sublime.* The challenge is to aspire to the best that can be achieved, regardless of the audience for which it is intended or the field in which it is created, and to emphasize the role of creativity in all areas of life, so that discovering new and better ways of doing things with fewer resources, and more effective and efficient results, becomes standard practice in science, business, industry, government, medicine, welfare, and education as much as in the arts.

There would also be much to be gained from making the creation, conveyance, and cultivation of beauty a key concern in a cultural age. Everybody appreciates beauty and derives a great deal of satisfaction and inspiration from it, whether in songs, paintings, poems, landscapes, or thoughts, and every culture, country, and civilization in the world possesses a profuse legacy of beautiful works. These legacies need to be much better known and used throughout the world, for beauty knows no bounds and requires little or no knowledge, commentary, or interpretation. People everywhere in the world need beauty in their lives on a daily and full-time basis if they are to achieve meaning, fulfillment, and happiness.

Finally, there is the contribution that the arts can make to the search for the sublime, as they inspire people to reach above and beyond themselves in the quest for the unattainable. Scientists also display this ability when they make major breakthroughs in research and exploration, but it is an ability that artists possess in abundance. Through their expression of profound thoughts and feelings in simple, straightforward, and compelling ways, artists are responsible for much of the inspiration that is needed to propel people, communities, countries, and cultures to higher and higher levels of accomplishment.

What makes *democratization* and *decentralization* key concerns of a cultural age is the fact that they expand the range of options and opportunities available to people by making it possible for them to engage in all aspects and dimensions of cultural life. This is why it is imperative to break down the barriers to participation. Aggressive action will be required on the part of governments against those barriers that prevent the realization of human rights or contravene the need to treat all people equally, as well as those that impede particular groups from playing an active role in society and gaining access to the resources they need. This is the message underlying UNESCO's "Recommendation on Participation by the People at Large in Cultural Life and Their Contribution to It," adopted in Nairobi in 1976. Without democratization and decentralization, cultural development becomes static, pedantic, sterile, and elitist rather than dynamic, fluid, flexible, and egalitarian. In the words of Augustin Girard, a French authority on cultural development and policy:

> decentralization of activities . . . is at once the first step in the direction of cultural democracy and, at the same time, essential to cultural creativity, vitality and freedom. Thus decentralization is necessarily the guiding principle of cultural democracy.[2]

Democratization is needed to provide full access to existing institutions and resources, as well as to provide opportunities to create new institutions and resources. However, all institutions and resources are controlled by powerful elites, who have a vested interest in maintaining the status quo, in which they exercise control. Democratization can only be achieved through a great deal of struggle, and may well result in harassment, intimidation, and even imprisonment. Further, creating new institutions and resources often involves very great risks. Even so, experience shows

[2] Augustin Girard, *Cultural Development: Experience and Policies* (Paris: UNESCO, 1972), p. 137.

---

that when artists, craftspeople, scientists, and scholars have been provided with funds to create new institutions and resources, those funds are seldom wasted or squandered and the returns are usually far greater than the funds expended. It does not take a great leap of imagination to visualize the numerous benefits that could accrue from a comprehensive programme of assistance to talented individuals to create alternative institutions and resources. Ultimately, this may be the litmus test for democratization.

Like democratization, decentralization is necessary if people's needs, rights, and responsibilities are to be attended to properly. Unlike economic development, which tends to be centralized in nature, and national and international in character, cultural development tends to be decentralized in nature, and local, regional, or "grassroots" in nature. Biserka Cvjetičanin, director of Culturelink and a former Deputy Minister of Culture in Croatia, put her finger on the crux of the problem when she pointed out that:

> The trend towards globalization has favoured the establishment of planetary networks, but at the same time it has triggered an opposite process, that of "localization," with different cultures asserting cultural pluralism and diversity rooted in local cultural traditions. In contradistinction to cultural universalism, we now witness a return to individual cultures, traditions, and values. There is a constant tension between these two phenomena, universal and particular.[3]

More and more people throughout the world are recognizing that it is "localization" in general, and the quality of life in neighbourhoods, communities, cities, and regions in particular, that is the decisive factor in life. If these fundamental human collectivities lack a diversified array of cultural institutions and amenities, and reasonable access to them, and if people lack control over the decision-making processes and planning structures governing their lives, no amount of national or international development will make up the difference. It is through localized activities and institutions that people learn to cope with the centralizing, standardizing, and homogenizing effects of economic, political, commercial, and technological development. It is little wonder that in recent years

[3] Biserka Cvjetičanin, ed., *Directory of Institutions and Databases in the Field of Cultural Development* (Zagreb, Croatia: IRMO/Culturelink, 1995), p. 1.

there has been a rapid proliferation of "grassroots" organizations aimed at restoring people's sense of identity, solidarity, belonging, and control over the decision-making processes affecting their lives. Their appearance is part and parcel of the reaction to globalization, the creation of larger and larger trading blocs, the growth of multinational corporations, and the concentration of financial and commercial power in fewer hands.

If problems as fundamental as these are to be dealt with successfully, a great deal of emphasis will have to be placed on cultural development at the local, municipal, and regional level. This will require, among other things, a dramatic increase in the funds available for cultural development at this level; the creation of plans and policies capable of expanding localized resources and institutions; the broadening of participation in planning and decision-making; the commissioning of creative people to enhance the aesthetic state of neighbourhoods, communities, cities, and regions; and the employment of "cultural animators" to act as catalysts for change by helping to take culture out of the hands of narrow elites and special interest groups, and to place it under the control of society as a whole. Without this, it is difficult to see how municipal and regional authorities will be able to respond to the needs and demands of their citizens, especially now that, as we have seen, more than half of the world's population lives in urban environments.

Alongside democratization and decentralization there is a dire need for *cooperation*. Indeed, cooperation should become so contagious in a cultural age that it spreads to all people, institutions, governments, countries, and cultures in the world. At present, however, competition is valued far more highly than cooperation is. People have been competing for such basic necessities as food, clothing, shelter, income, and employment for so long that competition has come to seem normal or even "natural," as the widespread belief in slogans such as "the survival of the fittest" confirms. Moreover, competition is deemed by the proponents of the prevailing ideology to be the key to a healthy and vigorous economy, because it is deemed to yield the best possible situation for producers, consumers, and society as a whole. Competition also plays a major role in motivating people to higher levels of accomplishment. Yet cooperation will be needed far more than competition in the future. It will simply not be possible to come to grips with the complex problems confronting humanity through competition, which would aggravate these problems more than alleviate them.

It is obvious why *conservation* should also be a key concern in a cultural age, given the size and growth of the world's population, and the limited carrying capacity of the earth. There are many ways in which conservation can be achieved: by eliminating duplication and waste whenever and wherever they are encountered; by placing much more emphasis on permanence, recycling, and repair, rather than on obsolescence, acquisition, and new purchases; and by trying to realize E. F. Schumacher's dictum that "small is beautiful." The arts can be used to good advantage here, for what lies at the root of many artistic activities is the desire to achieve a great deal with the utmost simplicity.

This brings us to what would be the final major concern of a cultural age: *spirituality*. Spirituality is not an alternative to materialism, just as holism is not an alternative to specialization. Spirituality recognizes that material needs exist and constitute a very essential part of life, but goes beyond materialism by placing the emphasis on the need to achieve harmony and balance between the material and non-material dimensions of life. It is through culture that this harmony and balance is achieved most effectively. This means deriving maximum fulfilment from all the physical, emotional, and intellectual experiences that constitute life, as well as combining all these experiences to form an integral consciousness. In the words of Duane Elgin and Colleen LeDrew:

> An integral culture and consciousness involves a new way of looking at the world. It seeks to integrate all the parts of our lives: inner and outer, masculine and feminine, personal and global, intuitive and rational, and many more. The hallmark of the integral culture is an intention to integrate, to consciously bridge differences, connect people, celebrate diversity, harmonize efforts, and discover higher common ground. With its inclusive and reconciling nature, an integral culture takes a whole-systems approach, and offers hope in a world facing deep ecological, social and spiritual crises.[4]

A Cultural World System

The present world system undoubtedly yields numerous benefits for people and countries in every part of the world, and for the world as a whole, but it is not without its problems. In the first place, it is divided into two unequal parts, developing and developed, and income, resources,

---

[4] Duane Elgin and Colleen LeDrew, "Global Paradigm Report: Tracking the Shift Underway," *YES! A Journal of Positive Futures,* Winter 1997, p. 19.

wealth, and power are not shared equally. The destructive and dangerous effects of this division have already been discussed.

In the second place, the system is unbalanced in the sense that priority is given to the development of all the municipal, regional, and national economies of the world, as well as the global economy. This gives rise to the vast panorama of bilateral and multilateral relationships among the diverse economies, countries, governments, and international institutions of the world, relationships that are intended to facilitate the movement of goods, services, resources, capital, information, technology, and people at speeds and in volumes hitherto unknown. Since the central purpose is to build up the commercial, industrial, financial, agricultural, and techno-logical capabilities of countries, priority is given to these relationships in international development and global affairs. Since bilateral and multi-lateral relationships are much more difficult between countries than within them, because of differences in worldviews, values, customs, languages, and so on, ways have to be found to overcome these difficulties, and these are provided by international artistic, educational, social, athletic, and spiritual relationships. The result is that these latter types of relationships are seen as marginal and supportive, rather than valued in their own right, and little time, energy, attention, or funding is devoted to them.

In the third place, as we have seen, the human element is missing from most international relationships, since much more emphasis is placed on products, profits, finance, and so on. This above all makes it imperative to develop a world system that is capable of coming to grips with all the problems facing humankind, not just the economic ones. In order to de-velop this new system, a great deal more attention will have to be given to how culture in general, and all the various cultures of the world in par-ticular, can be developed most effectively and interact most efficiently.

By far the most important priority in this regard is building up artistic, social, athletic, educational, humanistic, and spiritual relationships be-tween countries to the point where a reasonable measure of equality and parity is also achieved between these and commercial, industrial, fi-nancial, agricultural, and technological relationships. This would make it possible to put the emphasis on human well-being rather than on prod-ucts, profits, and the marketplace, and also to enhance communication across ethnic, linguistic, geographical, and political boundaries.

Despite the vast importance of commercial, industrial, agricultural, financial, and technological relationships, they tend to be cold and impersonal, largely because they deal with profits and products rather than people. Thus the potential for war, aggression, conflict, violence, and terrorism is always present. This is precisely where the arts, humanities, education, social affairs, and spirituality come in. Human feelings and expression are their very essence. Equally important is the fact that relationships in these areas could provide a strong stabilizing force when commercial, military, political, financial, industrial, and technological relations are in flux. They help to cushion the shocks that result from erratic swings in the pendulums of political, economic, and military power. Comprehensive programs of exchanges involving musicians, composers, writers, painters, theatre and dance companies, symphony orchestras, scholars, athletes, social, spiritual, and religious leaders, and development workers could provide the cement that would keep people, countries, and cultures together when other forces are operating to split them apart. In this way, peace, stability, security, and friendship would be more readily achieved and maintained in the world.

To this should be added the fact that relationships in the arts, social affairs, sports, education, the humanities, and spiritual affairs can do more than anything else to eradicate the fear, suspicion, misunderstanding, and mistrust that result from inability to understand the signs, worldviews, or values of others. The communications revolution and the steady emergence of an interdependent world make it possible to reduce these negative factors in human affairs through a massive build-up of such positive and humane relationships, predicated on in-depth encounters with the creative accomplishments of all cultures, peoples, and countries. Thus the whole world could be brought into intimate, personal contact. This is an opportunity that is far too important to the future of the world to be passed up.

Achieving a reasonable measure of parity among all the diverse economic and non-economic relationships between people, countries, and cultures is also the key to evolving a world system that is unified, balanced, equitable, and integrated. In such a system, decisions would be made on the basis of what is in a country's or a culture's best cultural interests, not merely its best economic interests. The relevant question should always be whether a relationship with other countries and other cultures contributes to a country's or a culture's cultural interests as a dynamic and organic whole, regardless of the economic, commercial, financial, or technological implications. In the words of Verner Bickley and John Philip Puthenparampil:

If all national cultures, quintessentially, are considered as representing, as they do, "ways of life," values and "symbolic systems" which are significant and meaningful in the lives of particular peoples, it should be possible to conceive of ways in which intercultural relations could be perceived and evaluated. Firstly, it will be agreed that transactions which have an adverse impact on the dignity and wholeness of cultures cannot, for that reason, be defended. Secondly, in any organization of purposes intended to be served by intercultural transactions a high place has to be given for purposes which serve to enhance the dignity and vitality of cultures. Thirdly, good cultural relations are those which have a positive impact on cultures and contribute to their "autonomous development." Fourthly, a fundamental aim of intercultural relations/transactions will be the development of a scheme of shared values and "mutual consequentiality" among cultures.[5]

Placing the emphasis on what is in the best cultural interests of countries and cultures would change the ways in which countries and cultures interact with and relate to one another, causing new patterns to form and new possibilities to emerge. This is particularly important in a world where cultures and countries are becoming increasingly multicultural and multiethnic in nature, with a great deal more intercultural mixing, and a greater emphasis on cultural identities, diversities, and differences. Mahatma Gandhi put the case well:

> I do not want my house to be walled in on all sides and my windows to be stuffed. I want the culture of all lands to be blown about my house as freely as possible. But I refuse to be blown off my feet by any.[6]

What makes Gandhi's counsel particularly wise is the fact that he warns against being blown off one's feet by any culture, thereby signalling the dangers that result when countries and cultures become closed, homogeneous, and chauvinistic, rather than open, diverse, and responsive to

---

[5] Verner Bickley and John Philip Puthenparampil, eds., *Cultural Relations in the Global Community: Problems and Prospects* (New Delhi: Abhinav, 1981), p. 9.

[6] Quoted in World Commission on Culture and Development, *Our Creative Diversity* (Paris: UNESCO, 1995), p. 73.

outside influences. As the Romanian scholar Mircea Malitza has pointed out:

> Cultures in watertight compartments are doomed to oblivion. Dialogue is essential. The choice between the development of a national culture and an increase in exchanges with the outside world is a false one. Interdependence cannot be denied. The cultures which have blossomed are those which have had the advantage of innumerable influences, received and transmitted in accordance with a process of unceasing enrichment.[7]

The poet T. S. Eliot expressed similar sentiments when he wrote in his *Notes Towards the Definition of Culture* (1948) that the development of culture depends on two interrelated factors: the ability to go back and learn from domestic sources and the past; and the ability to receive and assimilate influences from abroad. Both capacities are imperative if cultures are to develop properly and interact effectively across the total spectrum of cultural achievements. Interaction with other countries and cultures, and international scrutiny and evaluation, are the best defences against ossification, parochialism, and chauvinism.

One of the biggest problems in the development of the world system of the future is the need for cultures to retain their distinctive identity and traditions while simultaneously being able to absorb and integrate influences from other parts of the world. In the past, cultures have been able to cut themselves off from other parts of the world, but as a result of the phenomenal changes in communications, technology, and trade this is now exceedingly difficult, if not impossible. Virtually all cultures in the world are now compelled to deal with all the dynamic developments going on in the world, and to open up to external influences while struggling to retain their identities. The solution to this problem lies in creating a global federation of world cultures, in which all cultures would benefit from, and contribute to, developments taking place in other parts of the world, while maintaining their distinctiveness. Just as culture in general and specific cultures in particular are wholes composed of many interconnected parts, so too is the world system. As a result, there is much to be learned from the functioning and development of cultures as dynamic and organic

[7] Mircea Malitza, "Culture and the New Order: A Pattern of Integration," *Cultures* 3: 4 (1976), p. 102.

wholes that is relevant to the development and functioning of the world system. In the first place, attention should be focused on the development of worldviews and values that are consistent with the world system as a whole, not just particular parts of this system. Otherwise excesses, imbalances, and deficiencies are experienced that are not in the best interests either of particular cultures or of the world as a whole. The best example of this is the environmental crisis, as we have seen throughout this book so far.

Putting the emphasis on the world system as a whole also shines the spotlight on the need to achieve unity and harmony in the world system as a holistic entity, not just selective parts of it. This is imperative if people, countries, and cultures in every part of the world are to live in peace and harmony rather than conflict and confrontation. What is desperately needed here is a global system that breaks down the barriers separating the developed and the developing parts of the world.

Finally, emphasis should be placed on the need to achieve synthesis rather than polarization and separation in the world system. As free trade protests, anti-globalization movements, and terrorist attacks suggest, it is easy for the world system to become subdivided into opposing camps when commitment to finding an effective synthesis is absent or deficient. If polarization and separation are to be eliminated from the world system, and a real synthesis is to be achieved, governments, countries, and cultures will have to give much more consideration to practices and policies that unite rather than divide, and promote consolidation rather than divergence.

It is equally important to focus attention on the realization of harmonious relationships between the component parts of the world system. Where it is not possible to do this it may be necessary to cut back on certain activities. The Dutch historian Johan Huizinga wrote the following with reference to particular cultures, but it is equally applicable to the world system as a whole:

> A culture which no longer can integrate . . . diverse pursuits . . . into a whole . . . has lost its centre and has lost its style. It is threatened by the exuberant overgrowth of its separate components. It then needs a pruning knife, a human decision to focus once again on the essentials of culture and cut back the luxuriant but dispensable.[8]

[8] Quoted in Weintraub, *Visions of Culture*, pp. 219–20.

As far as the cultural world system of the future is concerned, the "essentials" would be conservation, cooperation, education, the arts, learning, friendship, human love, spirituality, the need for free expression, and the quest for excellence, beauty, creativity, and equality. The "luxuriant but dispensable" elements would be *excessive* consumption, production, profits, competition, obsolescence, pollution, consumerism, materialism, and waste.

What is required is what Pitirim Sorokin advocated, a shift from "sensate cultures" to "idealistic, ideational, and mixed cultures." Sorokin believed that what is needed more than anything else is a commitment to playing down activities that consume excessive amounts of natural resources, and to playing up activities that conserve resources, and achieve harmony and synergy in the world. The key to this shift lies in creating many more connections between the component parts of the world system, and therefore between countries and cultures. The British theatre and film director Peter Brook had this foremost in mind when he wrote that "the culture of the individual" and "the culture of the state" would be followed by "the culture of links":

> It is the force that can counterbalance the fragmentation of our world. It is to do with the discovery of relationships where such relationships have become submerged and lost—between man and society, between one race and another, between the microcosm and the macrocosm, between humanity and machinery, between the visible and the invisible, between categories, languages, genres. What are these relationships? Only cultural acts can explore and reveal these vital truths.[9]

In a world characterized by a great deal of multicultural and multiethnic mixing, the assertion of ethnic and cultural identities, and increased violence and terrorism, many more connections will be needed between the diverse countries and cultures of the world if the world system is to function effectively in the years ahead. While there are no easy answers to these problems, since they are buried deep in history and the human condition, it is difficult to see how they can be overcome without many more such connections. Paul J. Braisted had this in mind when he wrote more than sixty years ago:

[9] Peter Brook, "The Three Cultures of Modern Man," *Cultures* 3: 4 (1976), p. 144.

> Cultural cooperation is so directly a national interest that it should furnish the fundamental motivating principle in governmental foreign service, replacing or reordering all lesser motives. It should become the controlling principle in personnel selection and training, in establishment of new standards of service, and fresh criteria of effectiveness.[10]

Indeed, all relationships are cultural relationships when the world system is viewed from a cultural perspective. Economic, political, military, technological, and commercial relationships are included in culture when culture is visualized and defined in holistic terms. They make profound cultural statements in their own right, are integral parts of cultures as dynamic and organic wholes, and have powerful cultural implications and consequences. One need look no further than the impact that the economic, political, military, technological, and commercial relationships of the United States have on all the various cultures and countries of the world to confirm this.

If all international relations are cultural relations when the world system is viewed from a cultural perspective, all countries and cultures are developing countries and cultures. They are struggling to make improvements in the various social, political, economic, artistic, scientific, educational, and spiritual components that comprise them, as well as striving to achieve harmonious, synergistic, and equitable relationships between these components. No country or culture in the world can consider itself to be developed in the cultural sense, as there is always room for improvement.

This represents a significant departure from the present practice, since it breaks with the well-established tradition of making a distinction between developed and developing countries on the basis of a few highly selective economic criteria. It also has major implications for the world system of the future, because it means that no distinction would be made among the different countries and cultures of the world. This, in itself, could remove one of the biggest obstacles to world peace, security, and stability. A much more unified and integrated approach could be taken to the world system, based on the conviction that all the diverse countries

---

[10] Paul J. Braisted, *Cultural Cooperation: Keynote of the Coming Age* (New Haven, Conn.: Edward W. Hazen Foundation, 1944), p. 25.

and cultures of the world have different assets and abilities to contribute to global development and progress.

CHAPTER SIX
Priorities for a Cultural Age

Will humans make the choices that need to be made to bring about a future world at peace?

—Elise Boulding[1]

While many priorities may be identified for a cultural age, among the most essential are a new environmental reality; an all-out assault on the barriers to the fulfillment of human needs; new meanings of wealth; a new corporate ideology; a new political system; a cultural approach to citizenship; a breakthrough in education; the creation of liveable and sustainable cities; and a united world. Coming to grips with these priorities is imperative if peace, harmony, and progress are to be achieved.

A New Environmental Reality
Given the size and growth of the world's population, and the finite carrying capacity of the earth, a new environmental reality is mandatory if human survival and global well-being are to be assured. As Greenpeace, the Sierra Club, Friends of the Earth, and many other organizations have advocated for years, a new environmental reality must be based on three fundamental prerequisites: cleaning up the natural environment whenever and wherever necessary; conserving resources, arresting climate change, stopping the loss of other species, and preventing the spread of greenhouse gases, pollution, and toxic substances; and increasing awareness of the fragility of the natural environment. The first prerequisite requires environmental action after the fact; the second requires environmental

---

[1] Elise Boulding, *Cultures of Peace: The Hidden Side of History* (Syracuse, N.Y.: Syracuse University Press, 2000), p. 256.

safeguards and precautions before the fact; and the third requires an entirely new association between people, the natural environment, and other species.

A great deal of progress has been achieved in recent years by taking environmental action after the fact. While these measures do not provide a total solution to the environmental crisis, cleaning up oil spills after they happen, burying nuclear materials and toxic substances, and dealing with colossal accumulations of waste have accomplished a great deal in terms of sound environmental management and effective ecological practices. Much of the progress that is needed in this area will have to come from North America and Europe, as well as Japan and other developed countries, since they are among the world's most significant polluters.

While environmental action after the fact has been and remains essential, it pales by comparison to the need for environmental safeguards and precautions before the fact. A battery of initiatives is required, both preventative and precautionary.

On the preventative side, the most urgent initiatives are reducing the use of fossil fuels (oil, gas, and coal); developing new technologies and alternative sources of energy such as wind, geothermal, solar, hydrogen, and tidal power; instituting and enforcing rigorous standards with respect to emissions from trucks, vans, and cars; preventing the use of toxic substances such as chlorofluorocarbons and pesticides; purifying water and air; and protecting endangered species. Since these preventative measures are unlikely to occur on their own, governments will have to play a proactive role if real progress is to be achieved. This is a cause for concern because most governments have not demonstrated a capacity to deal with these problems effectively. This is particularly important with respect to establishing and enforcing rigorous standards for emissions and preventing the spread of toxic substances, since these practices represent the greatest of all threats to environmental well-being.

On the precautionary side, the most important initiatives include increasing the time scale of products so that they last longer, do not wear out so easily, and are recycled at every opportunity; reducing the spatial scale of products so that they take up less room and do not use up as many resources to begin with; recycling and repairing products rather than throwing them out; and shifting from products and activities that are high in material input and output to products and activities that are low in material input and output. Such initiatives would go a long way towards conserving resources and reducing the demands that human beings are making on the global ecosystem. Much could be accomplished in this area if, as discussed in an earlier chapter, more emphasis was placed on products and activities that are labour-intensive rather than capital- or material-intensive.

While action is urgently required on all these fronts, what is required more than anything else is an entirely new association between people, the natural environment, and other species. Unfortunately, the prevailing attitude in many parts of the world is that the natural environment owes people a living, and that humanity will eventually tame the natural environment and bring it under its control. These convictions are deeply rooted in technological beliefs and religious practices, particularly in the Western world. Unfortunately, they also underlie the world system. It is believed that humanity will ultimately be able to change weather patterns, control or prevent natural disasters, and regulate the ebb and flow of nature through advances in science and technology. The progressive deterioration of the natural environment and the destruction of the ecosystem are the best indicators of the fallacy of this line of thinking. The forces of nature are too powerful and pervasive to be controlled. Instead, the focus should be on the need to see the natural world in a totally new way, as well as on renewing, revitalizing, and respecting it at every opportunity.

The arts have a crucial role to play in this regard, since they have the capacity to broaden and deepen people's awareness with respect to nature and other species, make fewer demands on resources, and help to protect the natural environment from excessive consumption and production. As the late Jane Jacobs argued:

> Evidence of aesthetic appreciation accompanies early evidences of Homo sapiens. Nobody who has seen reproductions of the most ancient cave paintings can doubt the aesthetic sensibility infusing them, no matter what other purposes they may or may not have served. Foragers have decorated themselves and their possessions, danced, and made music, all of which must have kept them from doing excessive foraging. Practicing and appreciating art is seldom environmentally harmful. It's especially significant, I think, that aesthetic appreciation includes admiration for the rest of nature: flowers, ocean waves, rocks, seashells, vines, human faces and figures, birds and other animals, the sun, the moon, stars, grasses, butterflies—recurring motifs in art, sometimes rendered literally, some-

times abstractly or formalized—and, in due course, art that shows appreciation of cultivated farmland, wild landscapes, seascapes, streetscapes, monuments, and domestic scenes.[2]

Artistic, environmental, and spiritual works are far more than interesting forms of aesthetic, ecological, and spiritual expression, or devices for popular entertainment. They are forays into what ecologists and environmentalists call "deep ecology," ways of getting to know the natural world as an aesthetic and spiritual entity. Recognition of this fact is essential if humanity is to be successful in evolving the values, lifestyles, and worldviews that are necessary to realize a new environmental reality. It is a reality that hinges on never taking more from the natural environment than is necessary, renewing the environment at every opportunity, and respecting other species, natural resources, and fragile local, regional, national, and international ecosystems.

This is why crossing over the threshold from the present economic age to a future cultural age is essential. There has been an intimate connection between culture and nature stretching back thousands of years—the very word "culture" derives from the Latin verb *colere* meaning "to till" or "to cultivate"—meaning cultural scholars have been concerned about the relationship between human beings and the natural environment for almost as long a period. It is through culture that the development policies and practices can be created to counteract adverse contemporary developments, confirm the Kyoto Protocol and other international instruments, increase human knowledge and understanding of the fragility of the natural environment, and reduce unreasonable environmental demands and expectations.

Fulfilling Human Needs

While a new environmental reality is necessary to ensure the survival of human beings as a species, an all-out assault on the barriers to the fulfilment of human needs is needed to improve the well-being of the majority of people in the world. When a substantial percentage of the world's population is living on less than two U.S. dollars a day, it is not possible to claim that their welfare is being properly attended to.

Accordingly, it is necessary to institute powerful measures to improve the quality of life for all people, but particularly for those living in sub-

[2] Jane Jacobs, *The Nature of Economies* (Toronto: Random House Canada, 2000), p. 127.

Saharan Africa, Asia, Latin America, the Caribbean, and the Middle East. At the most fundamental physiological level, this means ensuring that they have sufficient food, clothing, and shelter to ensure survival. There is a great deal that developed countries can do towards this goal, through increasing foreign aid and assistance, both in absolute terms and as a proportion of their gross domestic product; opening up markets for, and reducing or eliminating tariffs on, agricultural and industrial products from these regions; training many more development workers and expanding development opportunities; reducing the debt loads of the poorest countries; promoting gender equality and helping to reduce mortality rates; and supporting the elimination of hunger and homelessness.

The changes that are needed to achieve the fulfilment of human needs also include improving governance, ending corruption, enforcing the rule of law, expanding educational opportunities, and promoting participation in planning and decision-making, not only in the developing countries but in the developed countries as well. This too would make a major contribution to ensuring that people have sufficient amenities in all areas, from fresh water and clean air to education and health care, as well as social, recreational, artistic, and spiritual amenities, to be able to live decent and dignified lives. Clearly, humanity now possesses enough productive capacity to satisfy the elementary needs of citizens in all areas of life and in every part of the world, provided only that it is properly directed. What is lacking is, primarily, the public and private will, and secondarily, the necessary distributive mechanisms and procedures, to make this dream a reality. When large quantities of foodstuffs, clothing, and other basic necessities are destroyed every year to keep prices high, and when production systems are operating at far less than full capacity, it is difficult to contend that humanity lacks the ability to solve this most endemic of all human problems.

Shifting attention away from products and profits, and towards people and their well-being, is imperative for this purpose. If the United Nations, the World Bank, the International Monetary Fund, the G8, and other international organizations stepped up their financial commitments in this area, and pressured other organizations and institutions to do likewise, the results could be substantial. These efforts could and should be supplemented by other measures to address people's elementary needs, such as more effective distribution of surplus food, clothing, books, computers, and medicine; increased commitments from governments, corporations, and foundations to distribute income and wealth more equitably; transfers of appropriate technology to enhance sustainable development; fundamental changes in education and training; and, especially, increasing the capacity of poor people and poor countries to gain access to the credit, capital, real estate, and entrepreneurial skills they need to take control of their own lives.

When human needs are visualized from a cultural rather than an economic perspective, they extend far beyond such economic issues to encompass social, aesthetic, recreational, scientific, health, and spiritual needs as well. A group of scholars and statesmen assembled by the Kapur Surya Foundation in India in 1995 examined crucial issues in global development and human affairs, and concluded:

> Development must assure the satisfaction of the minimum basic needs for food, habitat, health, education, and employment, and the quest for inner peace and self-realization. This can only be achieved if we can cultivate need-based, as against desire-based, lifestyles, which are not superficial or self-indulgent, and are non-destructive of the environment and other cultures. These must be frugal in means and rich in ends, and not beyond the reach of increasing numbers of citizens. While being equitable, development must not sacrifice initiative and excellence, but be ecologically responsible, economically viable, cumulative, life-enhancing, culture-specific, and culturally sensitive.[3]

Such a transformation in understanding with respect to the nature of people's basic material and non-material needs has fundamental implications for public and private policy and decision-making processes, as well as for the way in which human needs and their fulfillment are visualized and dealt with. It means, for example, that human needs are no longer seen as a hierarchy or ladder, with economic, material, and quantitative needs spread out across the lowest rung. Rather, they are seen as a holistic constellation, with economic and non-economic, material and non-material, and quantitative and qualitative needs constantly impinging on one another and interacting with one another. This could bring an end to the assumption that, once people's economic,

---

[3] Kapur Surya Foundation, *Culture and Development: Abbreviation of a Three-Day Dialogue on Culture and Development* (New Delhi: Kapur Surya Foundation, 1995), p. 1.

material, and quantitative needs have been met, everything else will fall naturally and inevitably into place. It could also give rise to the realization that a broad spectrum of resources must be put in place if people's choices and opportunities are to be enlarged, and development with a human face is to be achieved. This will require development policies and practices that are capable of addressing people's needs simultaneously rather than sequentially.

It will not be sufficient to address people's needs in all areas of life. It will also be necessary to change attitudes with respect to the contributions that people make to production and productivity, since this affects income distribution, access to resources, people's value to society, and people's sense of identity and self-worth. In the economic age, all these things are viewed largely in material and financial terms, which explains the high priority awarded to economic, industrial, commercial, business, and technological production and productivity in the overall scheme of things, since the material, quantitative, and monetary component of these activities is very high. This is what most governments, corporations, international organizations, and labour organizations have in mind when they talk about the importance of production and productivity, as well as the need to increase production and productivity if living standards are to be improved. It is a way of thinking about and dealing with production and productivity that can be traced back to the classical economists, and the distinction they made between "productive" and "unproductive" labour. It is this attitude that must be changed if people's needs are to be addressed satisfactorily. It is necessary to recognize that all labour is pro-ductive and makes a significant contribution to the fulfillment of human needs, regardless of whether it takes the form of mental, emotional, spiritual, aesthetic, or physical activity. The "output" of artists, scientists, scholars, philosophers, social workers, homemakers, teachers, health care workers, and spiritual leaders is every bit as essential, and makes as significant a contribution to development, as material output.

In much the same way as a new understanding of production is needed, so too is there a need for a new understanding of what development is. When development is viewed from a holistic and comprehensive cultural perspective it becomes necessary to include all the factors that contribute to development: the artistic, scientific, social, educational, political, environmental, and spiritual alongside, and interacting with, the economic, industrial, commercial, and technological. Culture constitutes the essence of development because it is concerned with the totality of human needs, and the ways in which human needs may be addressed most effectively in different countries and cultures.

New Meanings of Wealth

It is commonplace to view wealth today in material, monetary, and financial terms. This has a long history. The mercantilists of the seventeenth and eighteenth centuries viewed wealth as gold, silver, and other precious metals; the classical economists viewed wealth largely in terms of "material products," or, as Adam Smith called them, "the necessaries and conveniences of life"; and the neoclassical, Keynesian, and post-Keynesian economists viewed wealth primarily in terms of "goods and services," which is how most countries, economists, and people view wealth today. To be wealthy is to be a person who either possesses numerous goods and services, or the income and financial resources to acquire them. This has given wealth a highly material, monetary, and financial orientation in the modern era. However, what the world needs now, more than ever, are new meanings of wealth. This is necessary in order to reduce the demands that people make on the natural environment, as well as to describe more accurately what wealth is really all about. More and more people are discovering that possessing, or being able to possess, numerous goods and services is not necessarily a guarantee of satisfaction, happiness, or fulfillment in life, or an assurance that one has "wealth" in a broader, deeper, and more fundamental human sense.

Culture has a crucial contribution to make to realizing new meanings of wealth. When culture is perceived and defined in holistic terms, wealth comes to be seen as qualitative as well as quantitative, non-material as well as material. What is needed to achieve wealth in this sense is the ability to achieve a harmonious balance among all the forces and factors that constitute life. To be wealthy in this sense is to be a person who derives a great deal of fulfillment from many sources, both simple and profound.

If new meanings of wealth are necessary, so too are new measures of wealth. This is especially important in the collective, public sense, since most countries are engaged in efforts to define and measure their wealth, and compare their wealth with that of others. The key to developing these new measures of wealth lies in developing a set of comprehensive cultural indicators capable of measuring wealth in qualitative and quantitative terms. In the development of these indicators three points are essential.

First, indicators from a variety of fields and disciplines—including the arts, the sciences, the humanities, the environment, religion, politics, and health, alongside economics, technology, and business—will have to be brought together and compared. Second, the best indicators from each field and discipline will have to be selected for inclusion in the final set of indicators. Finally, the resulting indicators will have to be refined in order to improve their effectiveness.

While it will take time to develop this set of comprehensive cultural indicators, the most essential of them will probably be environmental indicators, such as the quality of water and air, and levels of toxicity and waste; health indicators, such as longevity, health care, disease control and prevention, and substance abuse; social indicators, such as welfare assistance, participation rates in community, regional, and national development, and levels of violence and crime; educational indicators, such as student-to-teacher ratios, access to elementary, secondary, and post-secondary education, and student dropout rates and debt loads; recreational indicators, such as the availability of parks, conservation areas, and leisure-time activities; economic indicators, such as employment possibilities and income opportunities; and aesthetic, political, and spiritual indicators, such as the quantity and quality of artistic offerings, the stability of political systems, the provision of safety and security measures, and the diversity of religious and spiritual possibilities. While some of these indicators will be difficult to formulate, because they are much more qualitative than quantitative, and therefore less susceptible to concrete forms of measurement, they must be included in the final set of indicators if wealth in the cultural sense is to be understood and measured effectively.[4]

The development of this set of comprehensive cultural indicators will require a great deal of collaboration among policy-makers, planners, statisticians, and scholars from a variety of fields. It will also require a great deal of cooperation on the part of the United Nations, the World Bank, the International Monetary Fund, the World Trade Organization, the Organization for Economic Cooperation and Development, the World Economic Forum, UNESCO, and other such institutions, since they play

---

[4] See, for example, Tony Bennett, *Cultural Policy and Cultural Diversity: Mapping the Policy Domain* (Strasbourg: Council of Europe, 2001); Colin Mercer, *Towards Cultural Citizenship: Tools for Cultural Policy and Development* (Hedemora: Bank of Sweden Tercentenary Foundation, and Sida and Gidlunds Förlag, 2002); and Alvin Toffler, "The Art of Measuring the Arts," *Annals of the American Academy of Political and Social Sciences* (1967).

the pivotal role in the creation and use of indicators throughout the world. Indeed, the role of UNESCO could be paramount in this, given that it is the principal cultural organization in the world. Not only is it involved in monitoring cultural trends and developments on a regular basis, but it is also in an ideal position to bring together the multidisciplinary teams that are required to ensure that the proposed set of indicators is developed effectively.

The development of these indicators could prove timely in creating new understandings and measures of wealth, intimately connected to securing quality of life for people and countries in every part of the world. (There are precedents in, for instance, the efforts by the Canadian Policy Research Networks to develop a "quality of life index."[5]) This is imperative if people are to experience happiness, fulfilment, and security in their lives, and if humanity is to be successful in reducing the demands it makes on scarce resources. Otherwise, the environmental crisis will broaden, deepen, and intensify, the division of the world into two unequal parts will become more pronounced, and disharmony rather than harmony will characterize people's lives and the world system. This will exacerbate even further the gap between rich and poor countries, and between rich and poor people, aggravating a situation that is already too close to the breaking point.

A New Corporate Ideology
In view of the fact that corporations wield an enormous amount of power and influence in the world, a new corporate ideology is imperative.

In the economic age, corporations are expected to maximize their profits and compete as vigorously as possible, because doing so satisfies the dictates of the economic ideology and economic age most effectively. The justification that is usually given is that this yields the best possible situation for producers, consumers, the economy, and society as a whole. Not coincidentally, it also yields the best possible situation for corporations, corporate executives, and shareholders, since it makes it possible for them to earn high rates of return on their efforts and investments, and look forward to even higher rates of return in the future. These convictions contribute substantially to the prevailing corporate ideology or "corporate culture," as it is often called today.

In recent years, however, vigorous attacks have been launched against

5 Carol Goar, "A Measure of Progress," *Toronto Star*, June 6, 2001, p. K6.

this prevailing ideology, as well as against corporations more generally. These attacks have been accompanied by vigorous critiques of "corporate capitalism" on the grounds that it often results in monopoly rather than competition, as well as on sweatshops, branding, outsourcing, labour exploitation, and exorbitant incomes for executives. While these developments have created major problems for corporations, what sustains the corporate ideology and makes it so powerful is the fact that it is substantiated by more than two hundred years' worth of economic theory and practice, the support of the world's most powerful national and international institutions, and the full force of the world system. It is this situation, far more than the greed of individuals, that explains why the existing corporate ideology is perpetuated. This situation will not change until a new corporate ideology is created.

The key to creating this new corporate ideology lies in crossing the threshold from the economic age to a cultural age. In a cultural age, corporations would serve human, social, and environmental functions, as well as economic ones. Clearly, corporations will always be needed to produce the goods and services that are required to satisfy people's needs, fuel economic growth, stimulate consumption and investment activity, and power industrial and technological development. However, in a cultural age they would also be expected to play a major cultural role, through a careful balancing of commercial and cultural objectives, especially in the communities, cities, regions, and countries in which they function. Some will argue that it is impossible to develop this new corporate ideology because corporations are too deeply immersed in the present world system to alter their behaviour to any great extent. Despite this, it is clear that profound changes are required if corporations want to function effectively in the world of the future. They could well profit from Machiavelli's sage advice to rulers, nearly five hundred years ago: that it is in their best interests to attend to people's needs because this will redound to their advantage in the long run. Corporations and corporate executives have a great deal to gain from improving the quality of life in communities, cities, regions, countries, and the world as a whole.

A great deal of emphasis will have to be placed on corporate cultural responsibility if this is to be achieved. This will require three basic commitments on the part of corporations: making realistic rather than excessive profits; increasing corporate giving well beyond its present level; and cooperating more effectively in commercial and industrial affairs.

Earning realistic rather than excessive profits is necessary to reduce the hostility aroused by profit maximization, corporate power, and unreasonable financial benefits for corporate executives. It is also necessary to focus attention on the need to invest in worthwhile causes and undertakings, such as reducing the debt loads of countries in sub-Saharan Africa, Asia, Latin America, the Caribbean, and the Middle East; conducting an all-out campaign to stamp out poverty, unemployment, hunger, and human suffering; redistributing surplus food, clothing, building supplies, and textbooks to needy families and countries; eliminating the exploitation of labour, especially child labour; curtailing human rights abuses, including all forms of gender exploitation; and promoting health care, medical research, and human longevity. Corporate commitment to these and other goals would ensure that corporations are fully engaged in the design, development, and functioning of the world system of the future, rather than remaining aloof from it.

Corporations will also have to increase their giving quite substantially if they want to improve the communities, cities, regions, and countries in which they do business. As matters stand now most corporations devote only small proportions of their profits to these requirements. Despite this, there are examples of corporations that have recognized the short-term and long-term benefits that can be derived from making improvements in this area. In Britain, for example, from the late nineteenth century onwards, the Cadbury company of Bournville went to great lengths to ensure that those who worked in its chocolate and cocoa factories experienced improvements in their working conditions and quality of life. In the United States similar efforts to improve people's lives and advance community interests have come from offshoots of many large corporations, including the Ford Foundation, the Rockefeller Foundation, the Eastman School of Music, and the Hershey High School for underprivileged children.

It would be a mistake to conclude that such corporate cultural responsibility is a thing of the past. During the past twenty years the Turner Broadcasting Corporation, for example, has contributed large amounts of money to the United Nations to improve conditions for the poorest people and countries of the world, as well as to prevent the spread of HIV/AIDS and other debilitating diseases. The Bill and Melinda Gates Foundation and the Microsoft Corporation have contributed millions of dollars to improving literacy rates, immunizing populations against diseases, and transferring computer and library skills to countries in the "developing world." These examples serve as a clarion call to corporations in every part of the world to increase their financial commitments to levels that are consistent with human, environmental, and cultural needs, and not merely their own commercial and financial interests.

The final requirement for the creation of a new corporate ideology is the promotion of cooperation rather than competition. This does not mean that corporate competition would cease in a cultural age. There will always be a need for corporations to compete in order to drive commercial and industrial development, create new inventions, innovations, and technologies, fuel capital accumulation, and increase sales, income, and market share. Yet this would not be the only mode of corporate behaviour in a cultural age, especially as competition itself often leads to monopoly rather than sustained competition. Cooperation would play a much more important role in corporate behaviour. Corporations would spend a great deal more time working with employees, customers, consumers, and other corporations to evolve the decision-making processes and planning structures needed to create a more equitable, viable, and secure world.

Without a new corporate ideology, corporations may well be in for a very rough ride in the future. While their prospects are reasonable at present, their long-term prospects are far less favourable. Rapid rates of technological change, escalating terrorist attacks, anti-globalization protests, outrage over fraudulent corporate accounting procedures and investment practices, and growing scepticism over corporate motives and objectives will probably cause many more bankruptcies, mergers, down-sizing exercises, and assaults on corporations, producing a great deal more instability as well as more unemployment. This could reduce consumers' incomes and thus the funds necessary to purchase corporate products. This situation could be aggravated by adverse reactions from civil society and consumers' associations. In contrast, a new corporate ideology would make it possible to improve the outlook for corporations.

A New Political System

It is impossible to deal with the most pressing priorities for a cultural age without dealing with the need for profound political changes. During the past sixty years governments have become so immersed in economic affairs that their principal role is now economic rather than political. Consistent with the prevailing economic ideology and the basic tenets of the economic age, governments believe that immersion in economic affairs is the key to everything: increases in wealth, income, and standards

143

of living; the generation of consumption, investment, and employment activity; improvements in education and health care; breakthroughs in transportation and technology; advances in the arts and sciences; and the enhancement of human welfare and environmental well-being.

This conviction has its origins in the "political economy" of the classical and neoclassical economists, although it was not until after the Keynesian "revolution" that it became commonplace throughout the world. Since the 1940s, governments have been expected to play a forceful economic role in society by controlling monetary and fiscal policy, stimulating business and industry, promoting economic growth, regulating business cycles, managing debts, deficits, and surpluses, administering complex tax systems, and expending public funds to boost the level of aggregate demand. While this has done a great deal to increase economic growth, it is not without its problems.

In the first place, it has made it impossible for governments to deal effectively with the two most pressing problems of modern times: the environmental crisis; and the need to achieve an effective balance between the material and non-material dimensions of development. Indeed, these problems are generally deemed to stand outside the realm of economics altogether.

In the second place, it has made it difficult for governments to act objectively, impartially, and in the public interest. It is impossible for governments to get deeply immersed in one sector of society, in this case the economy, without impairing their capacity to deal equitably with all sectors of society and society as a whole. The effect is that the tail is forever wagging the dog. The most obvious example of this is the way in which corporations have become so powerful and pervasive that they are often able to dictate to governments what is in the best interests of citizens and society. This makes it possible for corporations to subordinate political interests to their will, often through the creation of large industrial zones and free trade areas that are exempt from governmental regulation and the rule of law. This has caused an erosion of political power, and consequently also a loss of interest in politics and the political process on the part of citizens and community groups.

Governments will have to extricate themselves from this situation if they are to act in the public interest, and deal with pressing local, regional, national, and international problems and issues. First and foremost, they will need to re-establish their ability to play a political role in society. In order to do this they will have to assert control over corporations and put themselves in a much stronger financial position than they are today. This will be exceedingly difficult to achieve, because many governments have mishandled the policies prescribed by economists, particularly Keynesian economists. Keynes himself advocated creating surpluses in times of prosperity, in order to have funds available to be spent on public works and other activities in times of recession, but instead many governments have increased their deficits in good times in their efforts to accelerate economic growth and satisfy the desires of consumers. Not coincidentally, increasing debt loads have increased the dependence of governments on corporations, as significant proportions of government income in many countries are siphoned off to service debts.

This is not to say that governments should abandon their commitments to developing strong economies and dealing with fundamental economic problems, but governments will have to deal with these problems in a totally new way, redistributing income and wealth more fairly, holding corporations accountable for their financial actions and environmental shortcomings, and situating economics properly within the broader cultural context.

Governments will have to use all the policy tools and techniques at their disposal if they are to achieve this. Legislation and regulation will be necessary to impose full control on corporations and to return the political process to citizens, community groups, and other actors in the public realm. Taxation will be necessary to restore the financial health of governments and strengthen their capacity to address key public issues. While care must be taken not to dampen economic growth or stifle consumption, investment, or entrepreneurial activity, a great deal can be achieved through progressive taxation. A new political system would make it possible for governments to achieve balance and harmony between all sectors and segments of society, and to deal equitably and impartially with all citizens and community groups.

Taking a cultural approach to the political process is the key to this new system. When culture is visualized and dealt with in holistic terms, the principal responsibility of governments is to develop culture in general, and cultures in particular, in the all-encompassing sense. There is an intimate connection between culture and politics here, since both are concerned with "the whole," and the need to achieve balanced, harmonious, synergistic, and sustainable relationships between the parts and the whole. Governments, above all, possess the authority and the responsibility to deal with all sectors of society on a sustained and systematic basis. All other institutions and groups deal only with specific parts of the whole.

A new political reality is unfolding in the world and it would be fool-hardy not to admit it. Vast and complex cultural systems are emerging in every part of the world that are constantly changing and evolving as changes take place in their various parts. While some of these changes can be foreseen, many occur with little or no warning and have devastating effects on cultural systems as wholes through interactions between the parts. Examples include: sudden and unexpected catastrophes such as floods, hurricanes, and forest fires; the changes now taking place in many countries in relations between and within the genders, which were not predicted in the days when marriage was generally assumed to be between a man and a woman, and for life; the spread of HIV/AIDS, SARS, mad cow disease, and other infections; and the ongoing occurrence of terrorist attacks in the United States, Britain, Spain, and elsewhere. Governments are thus compelled to deal with abrupt, erratic, and often unpredictable changes in cultural systems.

It is no longer a case of developing local, regional, and national economies, and then assuming that everything will work out for the best. Rather, it is a case of continuously monitoring and guiding complex cultural systems, and ensuring that they are managed effectively. In order to do this, governments will have to know much more about how complex cultural systems actually function, as well as how changes in their parts interact and affect the systems as wholes. This is why it is necessary to take a cultural rather than economic approach to the political process. Parliaments, cabinets, and caucuses will have to devote much more time to discussing and analyzing the development of culture and cultures in breadth and depth. Ministries of cultural development will have to replace ministries of economic development as the key ministries in government. Cultural models will have to replace economic models as the main devices for government planning and decision-making, and cultural development and policy will have to be accorded the highest priority in the political pro-cess. The aim should always be to evolve political policies and practices that include all individuals, institutions, and sectors of society in decision-making, improve the lot of all citizens and community groups, and make it possible for people to live in harmony with the natural environment, each other, other countries, other cultures, other species, and past, present, and future generations.

Ministries of cultural development, as well as specially designed cultural agencies at arm's length from government and the political process, will have particularly important roles to play. They will have to be extremely active inside and outside government. Inside government, they will have to act as integrating mechanisms and coordinating vehicles for all departments and agencies, winning respect for culture's most elevated principles, values, and ideals. They will also have to be involved in promoting understanding of the way in which culture can act as a coalescing force, and as a conceptual framework for public policy and decision-making. Outside government, they will have to become extremely active in sowing the seeds of cultural development in communities, cities, regions, and society as a whole, broadening and deepening participation in the political process, expanding understanding of the vital role that culture can play, and creating a climate conducive to a healthy and vigorous cultural life. Such ministries and agencies will have to possess the powers, and the funding, to execute these responsibilities efficiently, effectively, and in a trustworthy manner. History has shown that such responsibilities are best carried out when they are consistent with the principles of access, participation, equality, democratization, and decentralization.

However, as critics have repeatedly warned, permanent solutions will not be forthcoming without a strong commitment to freedom, independence, and democracy. In particular, when it comes to the political process and its impact on the development of culture, this commitment will require the creation and maintenance of a large and viable private sector, capable of formulating and implementing programmes, initiating activities, providing funds, acting as an effective counterpoise to government, and taking risks.

A Cultural Approach to Citizenship

The signing of the Universal Declaration of Human Rights in 1948 signalled the start of an era in which human rights have become a major political issue. However, it is sometimes forgotten that the Declaration goes beyond the traditional list of civil and political rights, to encompass social and cultural rights as well. Thus, Article 22 of the Declaration asserts that:

> Everyone, as a member of society, has the right to social security and is entitled to realization, through national effort and international cooperation, and in accordance with the organ-

ization and resources of each state, of the economic, social, and cultural rights indispensable for his dignity and the free development of his personality.

Article 27 asserts that:

> Everyone has the right freely to participate in the cultural life of the community, to enjoy the arts, and to share in scientific advancement and its benefits.

While focusing time and attention on human rights has accomplished a great deal over the past sixty years, there is an urgent need to devote time and attention to people's responsibilities, since failure to do so creates a one-sided and distorted view of citizenship. On the one hand, there is what people have a reasonable right to receive from society. On the other hand, there is what people must give in order to receive something in return. It is only when these two requirements are in balance that it is possible to claim that all the requirements of citizenship have been addressed.

Clearly, every person has numerous responsibilities to execute if they want to enjoy certain rights in return. Included among these responsibilities are acquisition of the skills, tools, and techniques that are needed to function effectively in society; participation in the cultural development of the community, the region, and the nation; concern for the plight of people who are less fortunate than oneself; sharing income, wealth, and resources realistically and fairly; recognition of the needs, rights, freedoms, values, and worldviews of others; abstinence from violence and terrorism; and concern for the natural environment, other species, other ethnic groups, and past, present, and future generations. It is thus essential to develop a Universal Declaration of Human Rights and Responsibilities.

This has become steadily more apparent as increasing numbers of citizens have become involved in protest movements aimed at addressing responsibilities as well as rights. Although citizens' involvement in these movements can be disruptive and does not always produce concrete results, it makes a significant contribution to social progress nevertheless. There are numerous examples where citizens' coalitions have altered age-old political and bureaucratic practices, confronted corporate and wealthy elites, and challenged international institutions. It is amazing what can be accomplished when citizens work together for the common good of their fellow citizens, as well as the needs and concerns of society as a whole.

Augustin Girard recognized how essential this is when he wrote that "cultural development is both the ultimate aim of political action and also the means of giving every individual a sense of his responsibility in the common work of mankind."[6]

It is interesting to note in this regard that concerted attempts have been made in recent years to develop "character education" and "character communities," predicated on the collective as well as the personal, the altruistic as well as the egoistic, the other as well as the self, and responsibilities as well as rights. Concerned about the perceived rise in violence, vandalism, and destructiveness in communities and schools, proponents of character education and character communities put a great deal of emphasis on caring, sharing, self-discipline, fairness, honesty, integrity, equality, justice, respect, commitment, and empathy.

They are helping to pave the way for the development of a secular ethics that will be capable of complementing and enriching religious ethics.

Such a secular ethics would answer the call by the World Commission on Culture and Development for "a global ethics," focused on human rights and responsibilities; democracy and the elements of civil society; the protection of minorities; commitment to peaceful conflict-resolution and fair negotiation; and equity within and between generations. While the Commission recognized that this global ethics would constitute the minimum requirements of citizenship and government, it felt that ample room should be left for political creativity, social imagination, and cultural pluralism.[7] This is imperative if a global ethics is not to become oppressive, overbearing, or coercive.

A Breakthrough in Education

At present, very few educational institutions, particularly at the elementary and secondary levels, provide opportunities for people to learn about culture in general and their own cultures in particular. This means that people have to turn instead to personal study, exploration, discovery, general observation, and a variety of learning materials and possibilities. Yet the lack of formal education in the basic rudiments of culture is a cause for concern. If people are to function effectively in the specific cul-

[6] Girard, *Cultural Development*, p. 143.
[7] World Commission on Culture and Development, *Our Creative Diversity*, p. 33–51.

tures in which they live, and if many of the tensions and conflicts that exist throughout the world are to be reduced or overcome, much more will need to be known about the diverse cultures of humankind. The problem is compounded by the fact that it is difficult to learn about culture in the holistic sense when education is broken down into specialized disciplines. In addition, there are barriers to transcending one's cultural conditioning in order to understand other cultures. As the Mexican futurologist Antonio Alonso Concheiro has written:

> [W]e generally assume that cultures are simply different modes of adaptation to nature, different codes for the same funda-mental purposes. . . . We seldom recognize that in this manner we are only studying and classifying cultures which we invent through our own cultural framework, and not the cultures themselves. In other words, we generally reach for and obtain only ethnocentric visions of other cultures.[8]

Despite the difficulties involved in teaching and learning about culture and cultures in the holistic sense, no greater mistake could be made than to abandon the attempt. Although people may never get to know and un-derstand their own culture, or the cultures of others, in some ultimate, metaphysical sense, the very fact that they make the effort enhances the prospects for peace, harmony, tolerance, appreciation, and respect throughout the world.

An ideal cultural education would contain four key ingredients: learn-ing about culture in general; learning about one's own culture in particular; learning about the cultures of others; and learning to live a creative, constructive, and fulfilling cultural life.

Fortunately, there are now many educational materials available to as-sist in learning about culture in general, as well as a rapidly expanding array of articles, reports, and other publications dealing with every specific culture in the world. The emphasis should be on broadening and deepen-ing understanding of the various parts of one's own culture, as well as on how these parts are organized and orchestrated to form a whole. This would require a great deal more emphasis than at present on integrated, holistic, and horizontal approaches to education. Yet, clearly, everybody is involved in many different cultures simultaneously, since they are

---

[8] In Eleonora Barbieri Masini, coordinator, *The Futures of Culture* (Paris: UNESCO, 1991), Vol. 2, p. 65.

involved in local, regional, and national cultures, and may also possess a variety of ethnic origins and cultural backgrounds.

Learning about the cultures of others would be equally important, but, unfortunately, this is the most neglected area of education in every part of the world. Not only is the education of most people limited to their own culture, there are very few opportunities to learn about the cultures of others. The upshot of this is the rise in violence, terrorism, racism, and xenophobia throughout the world, as fear, misunderstanding, and mistrust increase, and the potential for cultural conflict and confrontation is heightened. It is therefore essential to ensure that people's education in this vital domain of human life is broadened and deepened as much as possible. There are many organizations that provide valuable services and learning opportunities in this regard, including UNESCO and its regional centres, as well as the Council of Europe, the Maison des Cultures du Monde, Culturelink, the Transnational Network for Appropriate/Alternative Technologies (Tranet), the Intercultural Institute of Montreal, the Zentrum fur Kulturforschung, the Cultural Information and Research Centres Liaison in Europe (Circle), CultureGrams, the Austrian Cultural Documentation Centre and International Archives for Cultural Analysis, and various publishing companies.

The world of the future will be characterized by a great deal more interaction and mixing among its diverse peoples and cultures. Not only will this help people to become aware of the strengths and the shortcomings of their own cultures, it will also increase respect for the cultures of others and the reality of cultural differences. This development is already being foreshadowed, as, for example, in the discussions, exhibitions, and arts events at the First Universal Forum of Cultures in Barcelona in 2004.

The ideal cultural education concerns, above all, learning to live a creative, constructive, and fulfilling cultural life. That will require skills and understanding that extend well beyond what is needed to function effectively in the economy, to include the capacity to develop one's own identity, and to make a contribution to those aspects of cultural life that require improvement; respect for other people, countries, ethnic groups, cultures, and species, and the natural environment; and development of the sensitivities that are required for responsible citizenship. There is much to be learned from the way in which cultures have developed that is relevant to this goal. Just as the challenge in developing cultures is to develop all their parts, and achieve balance among them, so the challenge in personal development is to develop all the human faculties and achieve harmony among them. If, as Ruth Benedict contended, cultures are "personalities writ large," then people are "cultures writ small." Here lies the secret of leading a creative, constructive, and fulfilling cultural life. It is culture, not economics, that provides the wherewithal to knit all the diverse parts of people's lives together to form a coherent whole. It does so by placing the priority on the whole, as well as the need to achieve synergistic and sustainable relationships between the parts and the whole. This is why people in the cultural field are so concerned with the education of "the whole person," in order to help people to live integrated lives and realize their full potential.

It is difficult to see how education of "the whole person" can be attended to effectively without a comprehensive and integrated education in the arts. As Walter Pitman argues in his book *Learning the Arts in an Age of Uncertainty* (1998), arts education provides the key to developing all the various facets of the human personality in concert by focusing attention on the development of the cognitive and affective abilities of the individual. Through comprehensive and integrated education in the arts, people learn to develop the creative capabilities that are needed to function effectively in society, as well as to apply their creative capabilities to problem-solving and all the various challenges they encounter in life. This in turn is not possible without life-long learning, or education for life, beginning in the earliest years of childhood, strongly influenced by the family, and deeply rooted in the educational system. It is education filled with the joys and rewards of creativity and discovery, and fuelled by the desire to make improvements in all domains of life.

It is culture that best facilitates this process, because culture provides the breadth of vision and the depth of understanding needed to illuminate a clear and viable path to the future. In the final analysis, it is through culture in general and cultural education in particular that vast new vistas and fertile avenues are opened up for exploration and discovery, bringing people into contact with the finest accomplishments of all the different cultures of the world and the very best that humanity has to offer. Cultural education is far more than a vocation, it is a way of life.

Liveable and Sustainable Cities

Of all the changes taking place in the world today, none is more evident than the growth of cities, in size, scope, density, and complexity, in every part of the planet. More and more people are looking to cities to solve their problems, and to provide higher standards of living, greater safety and security, economic and ecological sustainability, and improvements in the quality of life. If cities lack the prerequisites that are needed for happy, healthy and secure living, no amount of development at the regional, national, or international level will make up the difference.

With the growth of cities have come attempts to determine what makes cities "liveable," and prevents them from becoming degrading and depressing. One factor is the provision of stimulating work and strong social programs. Another is the maintenance and enhancement of urban infrastructure, from educational institutions and libraries to health services, effective transit systems, a variety of housing styles and types, and ample and attractive public spaces. To this list should be added the diversity of artistic, athletic, culinary, commercial, and shopping opportunities that cities offer at their best, as well as the features that vary from city to city, such as historical sites, open-air markets, and captivating ways to idle away leisure time.

The arts have a crucial role to play in enhancing the urban environment. They provide fulfillment and happiness to millions of city dwellers, through art galleries and museums, theatre and dance companies, orchestras and art centres, concerts and poetry readings. They contribute to the attractiveness of cities, not only through the activities of professional organizations but also through community arts centres and festivals, murals, buskers, landscaping, and the artistic expressions of young people and children. They contribute to social cohesion by engaging large numbers of people in the artistic process, both as participants and as members of audiences. They contribute to the economies of cities by generating investment and expenditure on facilities, hotels, restaurants, tickets, clothing, transport, and tourism, as well as by attracting businesses and skilled workers. They also make an important contribution to cross-cultural communication by bringing people together in peaceful rather than violent ways, making it possible for them to communicate effectively across ethnic and linguistic divides. This will be increasingly important in cities where populations are becoming more diverse and multiethnic.

The arts also contribute to the liveability of cities through the creative energy and synergy that they inject into all aspects and dimensions of city life. By creating many of the concepts, styles, and techniques that are needed to institute change, artists and arts organizations help to pave the way for many other types of development. It is not surprising that many planners, policy-makers, and researchers are focusing on the role that "the creative industries" play in urban development by producing "clustering effects" and "convergent capabilities" that link different sectors of cities together. Equally important is the contribution that the arts can make to the revitalization of cities. In recent years dynamic creative activities have injected new life into cities, after years of neglect, often by stimulating concentrations of artistic resources in downtown cores or other key locations. Inspired by corporate executives, arts administrators, planners, educators, and other citizens, such districts do a great deal to rejuvenate cities that are dying from the inside out.

Given all these contributions, the role of the arts must be seen in a new light. Rather than being the icing on the cake of urban living, the arts should be seen as the centrepieces that are needed to create liveable cities. Governments and corporations need to recognize this and do something concrete about it. Too often, they are anxious to squeeze all the economic and tourist potential out of the arts without providing a great deal in return.

Creating liveable cities should go a long way towards creating sustainable cities, but much more will be required. Water supplies will have to be more dependable and reliable, as well as free from contaminants and imperfections. Air quality will have to be substantially improved. Gridlock will have to be overcome, and transit systems will have to be upgraded and enhanced. Waste disposal and urban sprawl will have to be curtailed. Streets and neighbourhoods will have to be safe to walk in, day and night, and free from sexual predators. Programs will have to be created to help immigrants and other newcomers to become fully integrated into urban life. Much more attention will have to be given to emergency preparedness, affordable housing, safety and security, crumbling infrastructure, ecological management, crime prevention, and programs for young people. Policies will have to be predicated on taking a holistic and egalitarian approach to municipal planning and decision-making, in order to build cities that are comprehensive and creative rather than segmented and imitative. The focus should be on providing stores, workplaces, and schools that are close at hand rather than miles away, so that people can walk to them rather than drive, and enjoy the urban experience rather than merely tolerate it. In her many writings on the "death and life" of cities, the late Jane Jacobs emphasized the need to provide a balanced and diversified array of amenities at the neighbourhood or local level, so that cities can become liveable and sustainable.

Unfortunately, the approach that has often been taken to municipal planning and decision-making in the past has been piecemeal and exclusive, rather than systematic or inclusive. Yet, like cultures, cities are cultural wholes composed of many diverse and interdependent parts. Not only do these parts vary greatly from one another, but they also vary greatly in the way they are combined to form wholes. These parts must be successfully integrated into the whole, and harmonious relationships must be established between and among them, if cities are to function effectively. Here culture enters into urban development in a very different way than other factors do. Culture is the cement that binds the parts together to form the whole. This is what makes it possible to talk about the "culture of cities" and mean something profound and fundamental by the phrase. It is also what makes culture *the* most important factor in urban development. Without culture in general and cultural cohesiveness in particular, cities are merely smorgasbords of disconnected and unrelated parts, rather than integrated, coherent, dynamic, and organic wholes.

Radical change will also be needed in the ways in which cities are financed. Without the ability to raise revenues, address pressing fiscal problems, and negotiate effectively with other levels of government, municipal governments will not be able to deal effectively with environmental degeneration, gridlock, declining medical facilities, deteriorating infrastructure, out-of-date social programs, inadequate transit systems, insufficient housing, or the effects of homelessness, unemployment, and poverty. The short-term solution requires making it possible for municipal governments to increase their revenues, for example through increased property taxes, gasoline taxes, user fees on publicly owned and operated facilities, lotteries, licensing charges for garbage collection and other services, cost-sharing arrangements with other levels of government, and taxes on hotels, restaurants, and other commercial establishments that profit greatly from municipal development but pay little of the cost of providing services. The experience with these types of taxes in the United States and many European countries suggests that when municipal governments possess the authority to impose taxes of this type everyone benefits. In the long term, however, what will be required is a change in constitutional arrangements, and a redistribution of powers among national, regional, and municipal governments. The beneficiaries of these changes will be people, who, as Charles Landry has pointed out, are the most valuable and precious resources of any city. Seen from this perspective, every individual and every institution has a crucial contribution to make to the development and enrichment of cities.

A United World

The world is deeply divided today along economic, political, military, religious, technological, and cultural lines, but the cultural divisions are the most crucial. At least this is the opinion of the U.S. political scientist Samuel P. Huntington:

> World politics is entering a new phase, and intellectuals have not hesitated to proliferate visions of what it will be—the end of history, the return of traditional rivalries between nation states, and the decline of the nation state from the conflicting pulls of tribalism and globalism, among others. Each of these visions catches aspects of the emerging reality. Yet they all miss a crucial, indeed a central, aspect of what global politics is likely to be in the coming years. It is my hypothesis that the fundamental source of conflict in this new world will not be primarily ideological or primarily economic. The great divisions among humankind and the dominating source of conflict will be cultural. Nation states will remain the most powerful actors in world affairs, but the principal conflicts of global politics will occur between nations and groups of different civilizations. The clash of civilizations will dominate global politics. The fault lines between civilizations will be the battle lines of the future.[9]

Huntington subscribes here to the understanding of cultures and civilizations as "total ways of life." It is his view that it is impossible to understand many of the most difficult problems confronting the world today, such as in Afghanistan, Iraq, Israel and Palestine, or the Islamic world in general, without having recourse to broader and deeper notions of culture. While countless economic, political, and military factors are involved, particularly ownership of land and other resources, the assertion of military might, access to production, distribution, and consumption opportunities, and control of technology, resources, and technological capabilities, these factors do not begin to account for the numerous tensions and conflicts in the world.

[9] Samuel P. Huntington, "The Clash of Civilizations?" *Foreign Affairs*, Summer 1993, p. 23.

Cultures can affect people, countries, and the world in positive and negative ways as indicated earlier. On the one hand, they can be sources of fulfillment and happiness, highlighting all that is most desirable and worthwhile in the world. On the other hand, they can be sources of brutality and oppression, bringing to the fore all that is most troublesome and despicable. This makes it imperative, as noted previously, to be ever watchful and mindful of the various uses and abuses of culture, as well as develop safeguards to ensure that these human collectivities are used in constructive rather than destructive ways. In order to do this, it is essential to build strong bonds among the diverse cultures and peoples of the world. In the words of Verner Bickley and John Philip Puthenparampil:

> If culture, fundamentally, is the "depth dimension" of a people or nation, then the ideal of intercultural transactions is seen as the effectuation of an "interior bond" between peoples, which has a greater value and significance than other kinds of relationships, of a political or economic nature only. Because culture, basically, is value- and worldview-oriented, intercultural transactions are capable of performing a critical and educative function. . . . Cultural interchanges bring the insights and perspectives of the participating cultures to one another, and thus help to modify narrow monocultural views to produce alternative and more flexible approaches and responses to human problems.[10]

The arts and education have a vital role to play here. Music, drama, painting, literature, dance, philosophy, ethics, and learning expose the real heart, soul, and spirit of countries and cultures. Performances by African dance troupes, Asian acrobatic groups, Latin American pop stars, and European musical ensembles have captivated large audiences across the world. Think, for example, of how the song "Amazing Grace" has touched imaginations beyond the confines of religious services, because its message that spirituality can "save a poor wretch like me" has touched a nerve.

It is not difficult to visualize the kind of world that could result from building strong bonds between countries, cultures, and peoples, particularly those that have little or no contact with each other at present. Humanity should not rest until people in North America, Europe, Australia, New Zealand, and Japan have much more knowledge and

---

[10] Bickley and Puthenparampil, eds., *Cultural Relations in the Global Community*, p. 8.

understanding of the worldviews, values, and traditions of people in Asia, Latin America, sub-Saharan Africa, and the Middle East, and vice versa. Intimate connections at "cultural contact points" are imperative if the many tensions throughout the world are to be lessened or overcome.

It is also essential to get at the root causes of tensions, most of which have to do with the fact that the world is divided into two unequal parts, and income, wealth, resources, and power are not shared equally. If problems as complex and debilitating as this are to be overcome in the future, it will be necessary to create a world characterized by justice, equality, and opportunity for all people and all countries. When culture is perceived and defined in holistic terms, the emphasis is on unity and synthesis rather than division and separation, so the potential exists within culture to create the conditions for a united world. What is needed, now more than ever, is the public and professional will to create a united world in which economic criteria such as gross domestic product would no longer be used to separate countries, and less and less attention is paid to the stereotyping that results from labelling certain countries and cultures as backward or underdeveloped.

There are numerous examples in business, industry, medicine, the arts, the sciences, education, politics, and the mass media where cooperation among individuals, institutions, countries, cultures, and civilizations has produced results that could not have been realized in any other way. Such results thrive on the creative energy and synergy that derives from bringing people together, even where they have vastly different worldviews and ideas. Paul J. Braisted summed it all up as long ago as 1944: "Cultural cooperation is described as the way in which the world's peoples can work together, voluntarily, constructively, and to mutual advantage, in building a progressive, orderly and more kindly society."[11]

As we have seen in this chapter, many new commitments will be needed if cultural cooperation is to be achieved. Most of these commitments will require dramatic changes in attitudes and behaviour on the part of the richer, more powerful, and more privileged nations of the world. Until those who possess and control income, investment, employment, capital, technology, and resources commit themselves to cultural cooperation and sharing, not as a vague moral duty but as a fundamental necessity, humanity will be saddled with a world system that

---

[11] Braisted, *Cultural Cooperation,* p. 28.

is unjust, unfair, and inimical to global harmony and world peace. As Braisted and his co-authors later emphasized: "Mankind is faced with problems which, if not dealt with, could in a very few years develop into crises worldwide in scope. Interdependence is the reality; worldwide problems the prospect; and worldwide cooperation the only solution."[12]

With this plea for worldwide cooperation and sharing, our discussion of the priorities that would be essential for a cultural age is complete.

---

[12] Paul J. Braisted, Soedjatmoko, and Kenneth W. Thompson, eds., *Reconstituting the Human Community* (New Haven, Conn.: Hazen Foundation, 1972), p. 14.

Part Three

GLIMPSES INTO A CULTURAL AGE

CHAPTER SEVEN

The Cultural Personality

The study of culture properly begins with the study of the cultural elements in the individual.
        —James Feibleman, *The Theory of Human Culture*[1]

P rofound changes are taking place in the cultural complexion of the world. Not only is the world in a state of dynamic and evolutionary flux, but also a whole new era is opening up in community, regional, national, and international development.

At the centre of all this activity is the individual. With all the changes going on in economic and political systems, ethical and religious values, ecological and environmental practices, and social and demographic patterns, now is a propitious moment to be enquiring into the role, nature, functioning, and responsibilities of the individual. For it is clear that more and more people in all parts of the world are having a great deal of difficulty coping with the realities of the present and prospects for the future.

---

[1] James Feibleman, *The Theory of Human Culture* (New York: Humanities Press, 1968), p. 5.

It would be foolhardy to contend that the ideas set out in this chapter are sufficient in themselves to deal with the enormity or complexity of this situation. What the chapter attempts to do, however, is set out a general framework or approach capable of addressing some of the more significant aspects of the situation. It does so by proposing an "ideal prototype" of the human personality against which individuals can measure the reality of their own experience and to which they can look for guidance in times of adversity. It is a prototype that is based on the conviction that when culture is seen in the holistic sense, it provides one of the most promising avenues of all for coming to grips with the problems and possibilities of living in a cultural age and experiencing a great deal of happiness, fulfillment, and contentment in life.

But first let us put some flesh on the bare bones of the captivating idea of the cultural personality. What are its main characteristics, its fundamental attributes? That is my initial focus.

The Characteristics of the Cultural Personality

While there are many characteristics and attributes which give the cultural personality its specific shape and identity, in the final analysis the cultural personality is *holistic, centred, authentic, unique, creative, altruistic*, and last but far from least, *humane*. Let us examine each of these characteristics in turn. In the process, flesh will start to appear on the framework of the cultural personality.

First and foremost, the cultural personality is holistic. By this is meant that the cultural personality is constantly endeavouring to mould all the component parts of being into a single, integrated entity. To achieve this, according to Jan Christiaan Smuts, is to achieve the highest state of personality development:

> Personality then is a new whole, is the highest and completest of all wholes, is the most recent conspicuous mutation in the evolution of Holism. . . . [It is] the supreme embodiment of Holism both in its individual and its universal tenderness. It is the final synthesis of all the operative factors in the universe into unitary wholes, and both in its unity and its complexity it constitutes the great riddle of the universe.[2]

To be holistic, then, is to be constantly striving to see, feel, experience,

---

[2] Jan Christiaan Smuts, *Holism and Evolution* (New York: The Viking Press, 1926), p. 263.

and comprehend the unity or oneness of all things, or, as Goethe expressed it, "to live in the whole." It matters little that holism in some ultimate, metaphysical sense may be unattainable: it is always possible to add new information and insights to the ever-expanding dimensions of the whole. What is important is to be continuously and systematically engaged in the search to achieve this ideal, and to this end, relentlessly acting to fuse the mental, physical, emotional, and spiritual aspects of being to form a seamless web. In the final analysis, this is what the cultural personality is all about. It is about perpetual acts of integration and synthesis aimed at melding all the diverse fragments of being together—the internal and the external, the subjective and the objective, the material and the non-material, and the self and the other—to form a harmonious whole.

Just as the cultural personality is engaged in the constant search to discover the inherent wholeness in the self and in the world, so it is constantly endeavouring to recognize this same wholeness in other people. For the cultural personality, people are not defined by their colour, age, profession, status, geographical location, or any other single characteristic. Rather they are defined in terms of their wholeness, taking all of their diverse attributes, strengths, and frailties into account. In other words, they are defined as total human beings and treated accordingly. If judgements are to be made at all, they are always made on the basis of the whole person and never on the basis of one or two selective traits or distinguishing characteristics.

Since holism is in effect "the tendency in nature to form wholes that are more than the sum of the parts by creative evolution,"[3] it is appropriate to ask what it is that makes the whole greater than the sum of its parts for the cultural personality. This "extra something" has been variously described as a value system, a soul, a spirit, or a philosophy of life. Since it is through this process that the cultural personality becomes centred in the world as well as in the self, it requires a certain amount of explanation.

As with personality development of any type, the starting point for the development of the cultural personality is with life's everyday experiences. These experiences are not only exceedingly diverse, but also largely undifferentiated. They invade the individual at all times, as well as from all directions.

With the passing of time, the cultural personality begins to make

---

[3] E. McIntosh, ed., *The Concise Oxford Dictionary* (Oxford: Oxford University Press, 1965), p. 581.

associations and connections between the myriads upon myriads of experiences which are encountered in everyday life. These associations and connections form the basis of values, since they involve comparisons between one type of experience and another. Here is where assessments are made of life's different encounters, and priorities are established among these encounters, thereby making it possible to rank them differently in the total scheme of things. Just how important culture is in this process of value formation was revealed by Mircea Malitza when he said, "Culture is the crucible from which values emerge, where preferences are formed and the hierarchy among them is established."[4]

According to Albert Kroeber and Clyde Kluckhohn, values are important because they provide "foci for patterns of organization for the materials of culture . . . and give significance to our understanding of cultures." They go on to observe:

> [V]alues provide the only basis for the fully intelligible comprehension of culture, because the actual organization of all cultures is primarily in terms of their values. This becomes apparent as soon as one attempts to present the picture of a culture without reference to its values. . . . The account becomes an unstructured, meaningless assemblage of items having relation to one another only through coexistence in locality and moment . . . a mere laundry list.[5]

What is true for culture is also true for the cultural personality. For just as there are collective values in this larger cultural sense, so there are personal values in a more restricted, individual sense. And it is these values which help to give shape, substance, character, and integrity to the cultural personality.

Without doubt, values make it possible for the cultural personality to sort out what is relevant from what is irrelevant, what is valuable from what is valueless, and what is meaningful from what is meaningless. Without this, as Kroeber and Kluckhohn so rightly observe, life really does become little more than a laundry list, an assemblage of activities bearing little or no relationship to one another, let alone the wider community within which they are situated. Without values, there is no means of

4 Mircea Maltiza, "Culture and the New Order: A Pattern of Integration," *Cultures* 3: 4 (1976), p. 98.
5 Alfred Kroeber and Clyde Kluckhohn, *Culture: A Critical Review of Concepts and Definitions* (New York: Vintage Books, 1952), pp. 340–41.

separating truth from falsehood, good from bad, justice from injustice, morality from immorality.

For the cultural personality, there are three aspects to this question of values which demand reflection and attention. First, there is the conflict between personal and societal values. There are bound to be times when there will be fundamental differences between the personal values of the individual and the collective values of society, particularly in those areas where there may be limitations or shortcomings in societal values which the cultural personality is concerned with addressing. Second, there is the discrepancy between absolute and relative values, or values which are designed to manifest some sort of universal truth in contrast to values which are a function of a specific time or place. Here, the cultural personality is careful to avoid falling into the trap of thinking that values for one person must necessarily be values for all people. And finally, there is the realization that values must be constantly attended to if they are to be cultivated properly.

In the process of cultivating a viable set of personal values, the cultural personality becomes aware that values are not only the essential rudiments of a fully-developed personality, but also sources of integrity and inspiration. As a result they should be savoured and celebrated at every opportunity:

> There is a sense in which the whole of human culture is a struggle towards the higher values. Can there be any greater expression of culture than art? Art surely lifts us up, although it would not be likely to exist without us. . . . We were meant to actualize the higher values, and incidental to this task is the privilege of enjoying them.[6]

It is through the process of struggling to formulate, reformulate, and refine values that the cultural personality becomes aware of a deeper development that is starting to take place in the fertile soil of the self. It has to do with the formulation of a set of central organizing principles around which personal values are galvanized and coalesced.

These central organizing principles may be based on love, beauty, truth, integrity, creativity, caring, or any other worthwhile human attribute. Since they are finely honed over long periods of time, they have a

---

[6] James Feibleman, *The Theory of Human Culture* (New York: Humanities Press, 1968).

seasoned quality, stability, and solidarity about them. Nevertheless, no greater mistake could be made than to assume that they are fixed, immutable, and unchanging. On the contrary, they are constantly being broadened, deepened, and refined in order to remain in tune with the dynamic nature of society. For just as the world is constantly coughing up new problems, challenges, and possibilities, so the cultural personality is constantly redefining and reformulating its central organizing principles in order to bring them into line with the ever-evolving needs of humanity.

It is important to emphasize that these central organizing principles are what make it possible for the cultural personality to feel simultaneously rooted in the self, as well as flexible, adaptable, and responsive to the never-ending changes which are taking place in the world at large. By providing the fundamental focal points around which experiences and values are organized and arranged, these central organizing principles provide coherence, connectedness, and continuity in space and time. While they mature and ripen over time depending on individual needs and preferences, they nevertheless remain the benchmarks and touchstones which are imperative to the effective functioning of the cultural personality in the real world.

It is through the progressive refinement of these central organizing principles, or what some call the creation of a viable value system, that the cultural personality begins to fashion a very specific philosophy of life. In his book *Cosmic Understanding*, Milton Munitz explains why it is so essential to have such a philosophy:

> When acquired, such a philosophy provides a framework of basic principles that helps guide a person's reactions to the crises and opportunities of life, to the universal facts of human existence—being born and dying, being a member of society, being part of a wider universe. To have a set of basic guiding principles, whether accepted from some external source or worked out for oneself, is an inescapable requirement for a human being.[7]

What is significant about this philosophy for the cultural personality is how distinctive it is. Having taken the time and trouble to wrestle with all the diverse elements which go into making it, it can scarcely be otherwise:

[7] Milton K. Munitz, *Cosmic Understanding* (Princeton, N.J.: Princeton University Press, 1986).

A philosophy of one's own, grown tough and flexible amid the shocks of the world, is a far more important achievement than the ability to expound the precise differences between the great philosophic schools of thought. . . .

The art of self-culture begins with a deeper awareness, borne in upon us either by some sharp emotional shock or little by little like an insidious rarefied air, of the marvel of our being alive at all; alive in a world as startling and mysterious, as lovely and horrible, as the one we live in. Self culture without some kind of *integrated* habitual manner of thinking is apt to fail us just when it is wanted the most. *To be a cultured person is to be a person with some kind of original philosophy.*[8]

It is through hammering out this philosophy that the cultural personality begins to comprehend what it means to be centred in the self as well as rooted in the world. This is because there is growing awareness of the fact that a central rudder has been created which provides strength, durability, and a clear sense of direction to the life course. John Cowper Powys uses a botanical illustration to bring this point home with startling clarity:

Slowly, as life tightens the knot of our inner being, our outer leaves, like those of a floating water-plant, expand in the sunshine and in the rain of pure chance; but we still are aware of the single stalk under the surface, of the single root that gives meaning to all.[9]

It is doubtful whether the cultural personality can ever become fully conscious of the single root which provides centredness in life without becoming "authentic" or true to the self. It is this requirement that Thomas Carlyle had in mind when he penned his "great law of culture":

Let each become all that he was created capable of being; expand, if possible, to his full growth; resisting all impediments, casting off all foreign, especially all noxious adhesions; and show himself at length in his own shape and stature, be these what they may.[10]

---

[8] Powys, *The Meaning of Culture*, pp. 23, 8 (emphasis mine).
[9] *Ibid.*, p. 11.
[10] Thomas Carlyle, *Critical and Miscellaneous Essays, Volume I: Jean Paul Friedrich Richter* (London: Clay and Taylor, Printers, 1869), p. 16.

There are two aspects of this law which deserve our attention. First, there is the idea of the growth and development of the personality itself, not only in terms of the infinite expenditure of all those energies which are required to achieve maturity and full growth, but also in terms of the struggle that must be constantly waged to achieve real authenticity. It is cast in the form of a struggle because that is precisely what it is; it is a struggle that must be continuously waged within the self as well as with the world at large to "become what thou art." To do this is to resist the pressures of imitation and conformity and compel oneself to come to grips with one's real essence and fundamental purpose in life. Surely this is what John Calvin had in mind when he talked about fulfilling one's destiny or calling, as well as what Joseph Campbell had in mind when he talked about "following one's bliss," or never taking the easy way out but always striving to achieve one's full potential.

This struggle to realize one's full potential must surely be one of the most difficult challenges of all. It means plumbing the depths of one's being to confront the real self and achieve genuine identity, rather than giving in to what others might wish or succumbing to the dictates of society. Such a challenge is totally independent of one's station in life or geographical location in the world. It relates as much to the impoverished farmer in Africa and Asia and the landlord in Latin America as it does to the wealthy businessman in North America or the housewife in Europe.

There is another aspect to the "great law of culture" which also demands our attention. It has to do with the limits of authenticity, where one person's quest for authenticity ends and another person's begins. What happens, for example, when one person's quest for authenticity impinges on or interferes with the rights and freedoms of others? For the cultural personality, this always sets in motion the search for an alternative way—a way that preserves the right for authenticity without running roughshod over the needs, rights, and privileges of others. It is for this reason that the cultural personality deals with everything in context rather than in isolation. The quest for authenticity is never used as a licence for doing whatever one wants in life, or for achieving things at the expense of other people.

It is difficult to see how the cultural personality can achieve authenticity without becoming unique or one of a kind.

While it is often said that every individual has, in a purely physical sense, a double living somewhere else in the world, this is certainly never true in a cultural sense. In a cultural sense, all individuals are totally different and truly unique. From the moment they enter the world, their lives are filled with a continuous flow of situations, challenges, ordeals, and opportunities that are totally different from those of other people. Not only are there enormous variations in the way in which people interact with friends, family, relatives, strangers, and the natural environment, but also there are significant differences in the myriads upon myriads of special features and particular circumstances which govern their lives.

In the process of weaving together life's infinite elements to form an ordered whole, the cultural personality slowly but surely creates a life that is without duplication elsewhere in the world. This fact is worthy of reflection. It should be celebrated in good times as well as bad, in moments of pleasure as well as times of adversity. Not only does it speak volumes about the need that exists in every individual to be distinctive and different in his or her own right—to have a personal identity and life that is readily differentiated from that of any other—but also it supplies much of the fuel that is required to propel people to higher and loftier heights.

It is the ability of the cultural personality to meld together life's innumerable fragments and elements to form a life that is distinctly different from that of any other individual which makes the cultural personality not only unique, but creative.

As profuse and unpredictable as life's events and experiences may be, it is not the events and experiences themselves which make life a creative act. Rather, it is the way in which they are spun together to form a coherent unity. For in the process of weaving together the infinite strands of life's untold profundities and mysteries, the cultural personality is compelled to exercise an incredible amount of creativity. It is creativity which derives from the inalienable right of all individuals to fashion life in accordance with the demands and dictates of their own experiences. Every individual, regardless of educational background, professional circumstances, social situation, religious persuasion, or spiritual necessities has the right to fashion life in such a way that it is highly creative in its design, development, and execution.

While the type of creativity we are talking about here may not be the kind of creativity that is often associated with artists, intellectuals, or scientists, it is creativity nonetheless. It probably will never manifest itself in the production of rare paintings, unusual compositions, fine books, or famous inventions, that is to say, in creation of great works of art, science, or scholarship capable of withstanding the test of time. It is creativity nonetheless, since it involves taking the infinite building blocks of life and arranging them in such a way that the result is a life that is without parallel elsewhere in the world.

It follows from this that life is dynamic rather than static. It is in a constant state of evolutionary flux, not only in the way in which experiences and values are constantly being arranged and rearranged, but also in the way in which the central organizing principles and underlying philosophy of life are perpetually being enlarged, reformulated, and recreated. Ralph Linton, writing about the relationship between culture and personality, refers to this dynamic property this way:

> Personalities are dynamic continuums, and although it is important to discover their content, organization and performance at a given point in time, it is still more important to discover the processes by which they develop, grow, and change....[11]
>
> Each individual is born with a unique configuration of physical and psychological potentialities, and from the moment of birth finds himself in interaction with his environment. *The process of personality development is one of continual assimilation and organization of the experiences which he derives from this interaction.* As each new item of experience is integrated it becomes a factor in later interactions with the environment, and consequently in the production of new experience.[12]

It is this dynamic property which renders to the cultural personality an ability to continuously adjust to a world that is in perpetual motion. While it is important to develop this ability in the short run, it is even more essential to develop it in the long run. For every individual must confront the realization that a kind of "psychological death" or "static malaise" can set in at any age of life if the appropriate precautions are not taken to prevent it. Regardless of whether the individual is in the prime of life, mid-career, early retirement, or the final stages of life's ever-unfolding mystery, there is the perpetual risk of becoming so mired in the muck of reality that it is impossible to extricate oneself and get back on course. If

[11] Ralph Linton, *The Cultural Background of Personality* (New York: Appleton-Century Crofts, 1945), p. 3.
[12] Francis L. K. Hsu, ed., *Aspects of Culture and Personality: A Symposium* (New York: Abelard-Schuman, 1954), p. 202 (emphasis mine).

the creative and dynamic capabilities of the personality are not swung fully into action here, what results is a deadening process which slowly but surely sucks every ounce of energy and vitality out of the life process.

The cultural personality is not only fully aware of this but is constantly and methodically taking steps to overcome it. It does so by drawing on its own inner reserves and innovative abilities to ceaselessly create new challenges and opportunities. No sooner is one challenge met or opportunity realized than others are put in their place.

It is unlikely that the cultural personality will achieve this without acquiring one of the noblest human characteristics of all. We are referring of course to altruism, or the ability to give to others and make commitments to causes which are greater than the self.

Throughout history, there have been numerous examples of individuals who have set aside their own personal ambitions and interests in order to devote themselves to the service of others. As indicated earlier, the examples of Mahatma Gandhi, Albert Schweitzer, and Mother Teresa come quickly to mind. Each in his or her own way gave up promising careers and personal aspirations in order to dedicate themselves to serving society on a global scale. As impressive as these examples are, they should never be allowed to obscure the fact that there are people working at every level of society, and in every conceivable part of the world, to promote the interests of humanity as a whole.

For the cultural personality altruism is not seen as an alternative to egoism. Rather, both characteristics are seen as dual aspects of the same reality. While the cultural personality is very much interested in the development of the self, this is not seen as an end in itself, but rather as a means to serving broader interests and the needs of humankind as a whole. Why is this so essential? It is essential because, as Samuel Butler so wisely observed, the works of all individuals, whether they are in literature, music, pictures, architecture, or anything else, are always portraits of the self. And the more people try to conceal this, the more clearly their characters will appear in spite of it.

While altruism is a fundamental characteristic worthy of much thought and reflection, it is not sufficient in and of itself to ensure that the cultural personality is humane.

It is far from easy to determine how to address this final and most important characteristic. Perhaps the best place to start is to return to the idea of the harmonious unification of all the characteristics and attributes which in totality comprise the cultural personality.

In the process of uniting all of these characteristics and attributes, the cultural personality is forced to develop many of the sensitivities and sensibilities which are needed to become fully human and truly humane. It is here that the heart, the soul, and the senses are fused with the mind, the spirit, and the intellect; egoism is tempered with altruism; beauty, truth, and creativity are brought into line with equality, justice, and integrity. The result is an individual who is not only more settled in the self, but also more compassionate and respectful of the needs and rights of others.

It is difficult to see how the cultural personality can become humane without plunging deeply into questions of morality. Viewed from this perspective, the current moral malaise that is sweeping the globe must be viewed as a cause for concern. For in the act of attempting to assert human dominance over nature and making gods of technology and economic growth, are human beings not in danger of losing those moral convictions and ideals which lie at the very heart of the human personality?

Perhaps what we need most is the development of a secular moral code capable of assigning to human beings all those fundamental responsibilities which have been traditionally assigned to God. Of what would these responsibilities consist? Surely they would consist of showing compassion and concern for the sick, the poor, the disadvantaged, and the elderly; lakes, rivers, oceans, and streams; flora and fauna; other species; and other planets and galaxies. Such commitments, particularly if they were taken seriously and addressed fully, would quickly compel the cultural personality to develop the sensitivities, sensibilities, and capabilities which are needed to become compassionate in the fullest and most complete sense of the term. For in the process of accepting these responsibilities, the cultural personality would be compelled to develop those deeper and more lasting moral values, principles, and practices which are needed to become fully committed to the wider cosmic reality and all that is contained in it. This would help to ensure that the cultural personality is not only holistic, centred, authentic, unique, creative, and altruistic, but also humane.

There is no more fitting way to end this section than to quote from Prem Kirpal, one of India's most talented and creative individuals. Not only does the following poem embody many of the qualities and characteristics which combine to form the cultural personality, but also it strikes at the heart of what the cultural personality is really all about:

The abiding quality of life-time
Conferred by God on each alive
Is comprised of care of each other,
Quest of love and peace of mind,
Quietness of spirit, and sheer delight
Of being oneself and belonging to all,
Loving and loved in life-time,
Experiencing bliss and ecstasy
With Serenity and Creativity!
May such Quality of Life
Embellish all in time to come
For a great new world of Humanity![13]

The Cultivation of the Cultural Personality

Of all the possible points of penetration into the problem of cultivating the cultural personality in fact, none may offer more promise as a point of departure than cultivation of "the art of seeing."

Cultivation of this particular ability requires constant attention and careful nurturing, since it requires the development of a number of interrelated capabilities: the ability to see things and see them whole; the ability to detect patterns, themes, and interrelationships among the component parts of the whole; the ability to broaden and deepen vision in all directions in order to come into closer and closer contact with the cosmos and the self; and finally, the ability to make intelligent choices and enlightened decisions about the future life course.

Why is it so essential for the cultural personality to develop this particular capability? It is essential because if we have lost one thing in the modern world, surely it is the ability to see things clearly and in proper perspective. Our existing perceptions seem so fragmented, distorted, specialized, and short-sighted that they lack wisdom, understanding, and common sense. When Fritjof Capra observed that all the difficult economic, environmental, social, political, and human problems of our times are really "different facets of one and the same crisis, and that crisis is essentially a crisis of perception,"[14] he surely underlined the quintessential

---

[13] On a personal card sent to the author and printed in India by Kamal Sales Publishers Pvt. Ltd.

[14] Fritjof Capra, *Uncommon Wisdom: Conversations with Remarkable People* (New York: Simon & Schuster, 1988), p. 232.

importance of "the art of seeing" as a basic prerequisite to effective problem solving.

Ken Wilber was preoccupied with this same problem in his book *Eye to Eye*. There, he talks about developing the three eyes of perception as the key to knowledge and understanding. First, there is the "eye of the flesh" which discloses "the material concrete world of our senses" and therefore the way we "perceive the empirical world of objects in time and space." Second, there is "the eye of reason" which discloses "symbols and images" and thus the "foundations of the psyche." And third, there is "the eye of contemplation" which discloses "direct knowledge of spiritual or trans-logical realities."[15]

Cultivation of the art of seeing was also uppermost in Goethe's mind when he said "it was with the eye more than with all the other organs that I learned to comprehend the world."[16] He was obviously focusing attention on the critical importance of sight as a fundamental prerequisite for coming to grips with the nature of reality as well as with the self. For how we perceive the world and all that is contained in it is of singular importance in determining how we assess and evaluate problems as well as how we choose to live our lives. It is to the development of the art of seeing, therefore, that we must direct our initial attention if we are to piece together a portrait of how the cultural personality is cultivated in fact.

There is much to be learned about the art of seeing from the artist. Since every work of art is an organic whole, perspective is of crucial importance to the artistic process. And the artist, always conscious of this, is constantly moving around a work of art and back and forth from it in order to see it from the best possible perspective. It is through this process that the artist begins to comprehend the holistic and multi-faceted nature of reality, and with it, the need to examine reality from a variety of perspectives rather than from a single perspective. This multi-dimensional capability is of paramount importance to the cultivation of the art of seeing. For it means that many diverse viewpoints are needed if the true nature of reality is to be revealed.

In the process of constantly moving around a work of art and back and forth from it, the artist reveals something else about the nature of reality which is of fundamental importance to the art of seeing. It is the inter-

[15] Ken Wilber, *Eye to Eye*, as referred to in R. Ralston, *Teaching the Stones to Speak* (Kelowna, B.C.: Vision Action Conference, Assembly of the B.C. Arts Councils, 1990).
[16] R. King, ed., *Goethe on Human Creativeness and Other Goethe Essays* (Athens, Ga.: University of Georgia Press, 1950), p. 236.

connected nature of reality, and with it, the fact that solutions to problems are not always where they are expected. For example, the solution to a problem of too much fullness in the face may lie not with altering the shape of the face, but rather with changing the colour of the hair. This is yet another valuable lesson in perspective, for it means that the inter-connectedness of problems must always be taken into account if effective solutions to these problems are to be forthcoming.

There is one final lesson to be learned from the artist. It has to do with where the viewer positions himself or herself in relation to the problems being viewed. Look at a problem from one point of view and it looks like a mountain. Look at it from another, and it looks like a hill. Look at it from yet another, and it disappears entirely. And what is true with respect to the spatial position from which problems are viewed is equally true with respect to the temporal context within which they are analyzed. A change in the time horizon within which problems are analyzed can radically alter their relevance or significance. This is yet another valuable lesson in perspective. For it means that where the individual chooses to situate himself or herself is of crucial importance in determining the ultimate nature of reality.

These lessons are extremely pertinent to the art of seeing. Regardless of whether it is a painting, a play, a composition, or a manuscript, it is not the individual objects, notes, scenes, melodies, or chapters which are of greatest relevance. Rather, it is the work of art *as a whole*. In effect, every work of art is a holistic entity in which the whole takes precedence over the parts. Excesses and imbalances among the parts are permitted, yes, but only in relation to the whole and never for their own sake. And what is true for works of art is equally true for people. Every individual is an organic whole in which the whole takes precedence over the parts.

If artists have a great deal to contribute to the cultivation of the art of seeing, so do scientists. Through their intensive investigation into all manner of things, from the smallest inanimate objects to the largest planetary and galactic systems, scientists also have a great deal to contribute to the evolution of this essential perceptual capability. By pro-gressively expanding and intensifying the dimensions of seeing, they make it possible to view reality in a systematic and disciplined way rather than in a spontaneous and random way. The result is a fuller and richer under-standing of reality, as well as a deeper and more profound comprehension of the cosmos.

If there is much to be learned from scientists about the art of seeing, there is also much to be learned from psychologists and psychiatrists. Whereas scientists stretch the dimensions of sight outward from the smallest and most minute objects to the farthest reaches of the universe, psychologists and psychiatrists push the dimensions of sight inward into the self. The one is as indispensable as the other. If it is essential to learn more about the nature of reality and the universe in an objective sense, it is equally essential to learn more about the self in a subjective sense. Just as the aim of science is to uncover the nature of external truth, so the aim of psychology and psychiatry is to uncover the nature of internal truth.

If it is the aim of psychologists and psychiatrists to stretch the dimensions of sight inward into the self, it is the job of historians and futurists to stretch the dimensions of sight backwards and forwards in time.

Why is it so essential to cultivate a capacity for looking backward into the past and forward into the future? It is essential in order to broaden and deepen our understanding of reality, and with it, the way in which the past impacts on the present and the future.

In an historical sense, there is a rich mine to be tapped here. It is essential to plumb the depths of this inexhaustible reservoir of accumulated knowledge, wisdom, insight, and understanding, or what Jung called "the collective unconscious." For not only is there a colossal amount to be learned from the past, but also it is necessary to avoid the pitfalls of the past and learn from our mistakes.

If the ability to travel back in historical time is essential in a collective sense, it is equally essential in an individual sense. Every individual possesses a personal history which includes an infinite variety of encounters and events, trials and tribulations, challenges and accomplishments, successes and failures. This vast reservoir of experience is a treasure-trove to be savoured in good times, but perhaps more importantly, to be learned from in times of adversity. For it is through this process of assessing and reassessing their past that individuals learn to confront the realities of their own experience and take control of their lives.

Just as it is necessary to train the eye to travel back along the continuum of time, so it is necessary to train the eye to travel forward along the continuum of time. Whereas the former requires an ability to see and learn from the past, the latter requires an ability to anticipate and prepare properly for the future.

The one is as difficult as the other. While it is exceedingly difficult to understand the past, particularly in a way that is meaningful, honest, and true, it is equally difficult to anticipate and prepare properly for the future. Predictions are precarious at the best of times, and much more so when the world is in a state of revolutionary change and dynamic flux. Nevertheless, it is crucial for people to be as concerned with the future as the past, with the work of futurists as well as the work of historians. As John McHale so astutely observed, "people survive, uniquely, by their capacity to act in the present on the basis of past experience considered in terms of future consequences."[17]

It is clear from all this that the art of seeing should be cultivated to the point where it acts as a window on the universe as well as on the self. In order to do this effectively, it should be extended as far as possible in all directions: past, present, and future; external and internal; spatial and temporal. Not only must it be finely tuned to the infinite mysteries of the cosmos, but also it must be clearly focused on the most mundane details of everyday life. In other words, it must be concerned with the perpetual enlargement of vision, as well as the progressive refinement of vision.

The cultural personality seeks to develop and refine the art of seeing not as an end in itself, but rather as the first step towards cultivation and refinement of all the sensory capabilities. For what is true with respect to the art of seeing is equally true with respect to the art of hearing, touching, smelling, tasting, and sensing. Cultivation and refinement of each of these sensorial qualities requires the same kind of constant care and attention that cultivation of the art of seeing requires. For aural acuity, tactile sensitivity, olfactory capability, taste discrimination, and intuitive understanding are equally essential if the object is to expand knowledge and understanding of the external world as well as the self. John Cowper Powys expressed this thought admirably when he said, "The very essence of culture is the conscious development of our awareness of existence."[18]

It is difficult to see how the conscious development of our awareness of existence can be attended to effectively without a comprehensive training in the arts. For education in the arts is quintessential to the opening up of our creative faculties as well as the development of our sensory capabilities. Through music, as noted earlier, there is exposure to sounds, rhythm, harmony, counterpoint, and composition. Through dance, there is exposure to touch, balance, movement, muscle control, and physical coordination. Through the visual arts, there is exposure to texture, mass,

[17] John McHale, *The Future of the Future* (New York: George Braziller, 1969), p. 3.
[18] John Cowper Powys, *The Meaning of Culture*, p. 18.

structure, shape, form, and proportion. And through drama, there is exposure to tragedy, comedy, satire, humour, and pathos. Not only do individuals learn more about the self and the world through intensive education in the arts, but also they learn to deal creatively and constructively with the problems and possibilities encountered in everyday life.

What education in the arts does for the development of the senses and creative abilities, education in health and physical fitness does for the development of the body. Without adequate training in terms of diet, nutrition, disease prevention, and proper exercise of the various components of the body, the body will not function properly. Regardless of whether it is through callisthenics, tai chi, yoga, a vigorous walking program, swimming, or any other physical activity designed to loosen muscles and lubricate the limbs, care should be taken to ensure that the body is kept in sound physical condition and prime working order.

The cultural personality is careful to attend to the cultivation of its mental capabilities every bit as much as its physical capabilities. Clearly, development of these capabilities requires the ability to cut through the shell of illusion in order to get to the basic principles, premises, and assumptions which underlie all things. Far too often, too much attention is directed to outward appearances, thereby leaving too little time to get to the real essence of things. As a result, we usually end up dealing with secondary symptoms rather than generic causes.

It is through cultivation of the senses, the body, and the intellect that the cultural personality begins its ascent into some of the more profound and hidden dimensions of the self. In much the same way as the art of seeing opens a window on all of the other senses, so the senses, the mind, and the body open a window on the heart, the soul, the emotions, and the spirit.

The development of each of these human faculties is attacked with the same vim, vigour, vitality, and determination as the development of the senses, the body, and the intellect. The goal is always self-improvement or self-actualization, to use Maslow's evocative phrase.

Considerable care must be taken to ensure that the idea of self-improvement is not confused with the idea of perfectibility. For the cultural personality, perfectibility is something worth striving for, but is ultimately unattainable. In the first place, it demands perfect knowledge and understanding, which, as we have been at pains to point out, stands well beyond the capabilities and potentialities of the cultural personality.

For regardless of how much the cultural personality sees, senses, feels, or knows, it is always possible to see, sense, feel, and know much more. This is why "the whole" is always defined in dynamic rather than static terms, as an open agenda rather than a closed system. Moreover, the cultural personality is always aware of its own imperfectibility. Thus, while perfectibility is a goal worthy of pursuit, the cultural personality is always conscious of the inherent limitations and shortcomings which stand in the way of ever actually achieving this.

It is through recognition of the necessity and inevitability of imperfectibility that the cultural personality slowly but surely develops the sense of humility, awe, and appreciation which forms the basis of cosmic consciousness. Clearly, this cosmic capability lies at the very heart of the cultural personality. It is external in the sense that it radiates outward in order to embrace ever-expanding dimensions of the universe. It is internal in the sense that it penetrates deeply into the psyche in order to embrace all that it is possible to know and understand about the self. As a result, it stretches as far as possible in all directions, even though it is never possible to know what exists at the outer edges of the universe or the inner edges of the self.

Some contend that cosmic consciousness is such a rarefied affair that it can only be experienced by very select individuals. In his book *Cosmic Consciousness: A Study in the Evolution of the Human Mind*, the Canadian medical doctor, Richard Maurice Bucke, distinguishes three types of consciousness: *simple consciousness*, or awareness of one's bodily organs as well as the things that go on around one; *self-consciousness*, or awareness not only of one's bodily organs and the immediate external environment but also awareness of oneself as a distinct entity apart from all the rest of the universe; and *cosmic consciousness*, or awareness of the cosmos as a whole.[19] Having set out these three different types of consciousness, Bucke goes on to describe cosmic consciousness in more detail:

> Along with the consciousness of the cosmos there occurs an intellectual enlightenment of *illumination* which alone would place the individual on a new plane of existence—would make him almost a member of a new species. To this is added a state of moral exaltation, an indescribable feeling of elevation,

---

[19] Richard Maurice Bucke, *Cosmic Consciousness: A Study in the Evolution of the Human Mind* (New York: E.P. Dutton, 1969), pp. 1–2.

elation, and joyousness, and a quickening of the moral sense, which is fully as striking and more important both to the individual and to the race than is the enhanced intellectual power. With these come, what may be called a sense of immortality, a consciousness of eternal life, not a conviction that he shall have this, but the consciousness that he has it already.[20]

Using the impersonal rather than personal pronoun to describe his own particular encounter with cosmic consciousness, Bucke goes on to describe the intensity of his own experience with this fascinating phenomenon:

His mind . . . was calm and peaceful. He was in a state of quiet, almost passive enjoyment. All at once, without warning of any kind, he found himself wrapped around as it were by a flame-coloured cloud. For an instant he thought of fire, some sudden conflagration in the great city; the next, he knew that the light was within himself. Directly afterwards came upon him a sense of exultation, of immense joyousness accompanied or immediately followed by an intellectual illumination quite impossible to describe. Into his brain streamed one momentary lightning-flash of the Brahmic Splendor which has ever since lightened his life; upon his heart fell one drop of Brahmic Bliss, leaving thenceforward for always an aftertaste of heaven. Among other things he did not come to believe, he saw and knew that the Cosmos is not dead matter but a living Presence, that the soul of man is immortal, that the universe is so built and ordered that without any peradventure all things work together for the good of each and all, that the foundation principle of the world is what we call love and that the happiness of every one is in the long run absolutely certain. He claims that he learned more within the few seconds during which the illumination lasted than in previous months or even years of study, and that he learned much that no study could ever have taught.[21]

According to Bucke, eventually the human species as a species may be able to achieve this Utopian state of affairs, even though it is limited to a very few select individuals at present. Whether or not this ethereal state of

[20] *Ibid.*, p. 3.
[21] *Ibid.*, pp. 9–10.

affairs may ever actually be attainable, are there not grounds for asking if the experience of cosmic consciousness is not far more common than is generally realized? While cosmic consciousness may be a highly personal affair which defies scientific quantification or interpersonal comparison, who has not at one time or another experienced the feeling of Brahmic splendour or bliss which Bucke describes, where the sense of ecstasy and serenity which comes from some unique encounter with other people or the natural environment is so profound and intense that for the flash of a second there is a feeling of immortality and the entire universe and all of humanity seem united as an ordered whole? Surely cosmic consciousness is more commonplace than some people are willing to admit.

Was it cosmic consciousness that Herman Hesse had in mind when he wrote the following passage in *The Glass Bead Game*?

> World history is a race with time, a scramble for profit, for power, for treasures. What counts is who has the strength, luck, or vulgarity not to miss the opportunity. The achievements of thought, of culture, of the arts are just the opposite. They are always an escape from the serfdom of time, man crawling out of the muck of his instinct and out of his sluggishness and climbing to a higher plane, to timelessness, liberation from time, divinity.[22]

In the process of striving to achieve this desirable state of affairs, the cultural personality comes face to face with the holistic nature of life in particular and the cosmos in general. When Goethe said, "He who wills the highest, must will the whole," he put his finger on the crux of the matter. For in the process of willing the highest, the cultural personality not only comes face to face with the holistic nature of life and the universe, but also with the means of uniting all the various human faculties and capabilities in a symbiotic and unitary relationship. The senses, the body, the intellect, the mind, the heart, the soul, and the spirit become one, so to speak, indispensable ingredients in the total make-up of the individual. Surely this is what Jan Christiaan Smuts had in mind when he made the following observation:

> The great practical problem before the Personality is thus to effectuate and preserve its wholeness through the harmonizing

[22] Herman Hesse, *The Glass Bead Game* (New York: Bantam Books, 1977), p. 55.

of its several activities, and the prevention among them of any random discord or sedition, whereby one or other might be enabled to assume ascendency over the rest and so prepare the way for the disintegration and destruction of the whole. . . .

In proportion as a personality really becomes such, it acquires more of the character of wholeness; body and mind, intellect and heart, will and emotions, while not separately repressed but on the contrary fostered and developed, are yet all collectively harmonized and blended into one integral whole; the character becomes more massive, the entire man becomes more of a piece; and the will or conscious rational direction, which is not a separate agency hostile to these individual factors, but the very root and expression of their joint and harmonious action, becomes more silently and smoothly powerful; the wear and tear of internal struggle disappears; the friction and waste which accompany the warfare in the soul are replaced by peace and unity and strength; till at last Personality stands forth in its ideal purity, integrity and wholeness.[23]

It is difficult to see how the cultural personality can stand forth in all its ideal purity, integrity, and wholeness without evolving a comprehensive, compassionate, and enlightened worldview. In the process of developing this worldview, the cultural personality learns to take a passionate and consuming interest in everything. To do this effectively requires detailed exploration of all things, large and small, esoteric and commonplace, popular and serious. Nothing is rejected, ignored, or taken for granted, since everything that is germane to the human condition and the cosmos is examined in great interest and great depth. Whether it is the arts, the sciences, religion, politics, philosophy, economics, or the environment, all fields of knowledge and all disciplines are openly and actively cultivated because they contain valuable clues to the effective formulation and implementation of this highly personal way of looking at life, other people, other species, the universe, and the cosmos as a whole.

Cultivation of this highly personal worldview will require the development of educational and learning processes which are at variance with those that are in vogue today. Whereas most contemporary educational and learning processes are focused on the mastery of a single discipline and acquisition of a narrow set of specialized skills, the educational and

[23] Jan Christiaan Smuts, *Holism and Evolution*, pp. 296 and 298.

learning processes advocated here are predicated on exploration and discovery of all disciplines, as well as acquisition of a very diverse set of skills and abilities. Not only is this more in keeping with the true nature of the cultural personality, but also it is more in tune with the newly-emerging global reality.

Development of this significantly broader approach to education and learning will be no easy matter. All people are products of their culture to the point where they take many aspects of their culture for granted and accept them without reservation or qualification. To develop an educational and learning system which is finely tuned to the realities of the present and demands of the future does not necessarily mean rejecting those aspects of one's own culture which are taken for granted. Rather, it means critically examining every aspect of one's own culture to determine what is relevant and what is not. One of the very best ways of achieving this is to juxtapose and compare one's own culture with the cultures of other countries. For intercultural comparison is one of the best means of exposing the strengths and shortcomings of one's own culture, as well as those aspects of one's culture which are most germane to the human condition.

However difficult it is to stand outside one's culture in order to evaluate it with an objective and critical eye, it is even more difficult to stand outside the self in order to view oneself in a detached and truthful manner.

If only we could see ourselves as others see us! If we could, we would be able to deal with our problems and our lives far more effectively. Things which are so patently obvious to others are often so clouded and obscured to the self. To see ourselves as others see us—our strengths and shortcomings, our insecurities and instabilities, our problems and possibilities—would be to take a giant leap forward in developing a fuller and more complete understanding of the self. Perhaps this is why the cultural personality is always engaged in actively searching out the opinions of others, as well as using other people as a mirror for the self. For as difficult as this art of self-assessment is, it is quintessential to the effective cultivation of the cultural personality.

It is through the ability to see the self as others see it, and to evaluate the self with a discerning and critical eye, that the cultural personality comes face to face with its real essence. What is it in the final analysis that gives the cultural personality its real meaning and identity? In the end, it is the sense of fulfillment that comes from taking the time and trouble to develop a total worldview that is consistent with the nature of reality and the dictates of the cosmos. By its very nature, such a worldview is indigenous rather than imitative. Not only is it hammered out on the anvil of personal experience, but also it is highly original and authentic in every way. In effect, it is fashioned not by allowing others to dictate what is important or how to live one's life, but rather by deciding for oneself what is important in life as well as how to live one's life and accept full responsibility for it.

In the process of hammering out this highly personal worldview and accepting full responsibility for it, the cultural personality recognizes that it has mastered not only the art of seeing, but more importantly, the art of being. The reason for this is now crystal clear. In the act of dealing with all the trials and tribulations which manifest themselves in the external world of reality and the internal world of self, the cultural personality is compelled to cultivate those capabilities, sensitivities, and sensibilities which are most needed to live life as an integrated, ordered, and harmonious whole.

CHAPTER EIGHT

The Culturescape:
Self-Awareness of Communities

A community is like a shattered mirror. Each person possesses a piece that is large enough to see his or her own reflection. However, no one has a piece that is large enough to provide a reflection of the community as a whole.

A culturescape is a tool that enables people everywhere to participate in putting the shattered mirror of the community back together again.

C ommunities are fascinating places.[1] Ranging in size all the way from small towns to sprawling cities, they are filled with endless panoramas of sights, sounds, smells, textures, tastes, shapes, structures, mysteries, and intrigues. As such, they provide residents and visitors alike with infinite possibilities for experience and delight. Yet, communities everywhere are in deep trouble. Due to the rapid population expansion, the shift from rural to urban areas, uncontrolled pollution, traffic congestion, overcrowding, the nature of contemporary technology, and the excesses of economic systems, there is the mounting danger that many of the more pleasurable and rewarding aspects of community life

[1] This article is based on a highly exploratory study the author directed for Ontario's Ministry of Culture and Recreation. The study, which involved in-depth probes into four communities in Ontario, was published under the title *Explorations in Culturescapes: A Cultural Approach to Community Development*. The author wishes to thank the Ministry for permission to draw on this study in the preparation of this article. In addition, the author also wishes to thank the editor of *Cultures*, Dr. G. S. Métraux, for several valuable suggestions concerning the development of this article.

will disappear. In fact, if the proper precautions are not taken, and taken soon, community living could quickly and easily become a nightmare.

If local life is to prove pleasant rather than painful, two developments are imperative. First, we must begin to treat our communities as total rather than partial environments, since this is the only way we will be able to make effective calculations of the various costs and benefits involved in change. Second, we must create tools which allow citizens to articulate their needs and participate fully in shaping all aspects of local life. We must adopt a cultural approach to community development. Fortunately, the culturescape process satisfies these two imperatives for future living most admirably.

Communities as Total Environments

In historical terms, the approach to community development has almost always been partial rather than total. As such, community life has usually been dominated by a single, specialized activity, thereby limiting the perspective from which community development was viewed.

In the Middle Ages, the approach was primarily religious. As a result, the church became the focal point and dominant institution in the community. Not only did all roads lead to and from the church, but also, in sheer physical terms, the church towered over the community, thereby creating a sense of psychic dependence among the resident population. Even the sonorous ring of the church bells played its part. It defined the outer limits of the community. To live within reach of the sound of the bells was to live within the community; to live beyond its reach was to live outside the community.

During the Renaissance, the approach was predominantly social. In a purely physical sense, the square replaced the church at the core of community life. Whereas the church was sacred, the square was secular. Whereas the church was designed to serve religious functions, the square was meant to serve social functions. Not only was the square an important place to meet friends and pass away the time of day, but, like the church, it was designed to uplift and inspire people. Through its use as a place to enact rituals and celebrate communal occasions, it brought people into close contact, thereby strengthening the social bonds between them.

In our own time, communities have been designed to serve economic functions. Their primary object is to satisfy the needs of industry, trade, and commerce. Even the terms we use—terms such as *industrial zone, residential district, ghetto, worker's tenement, middle-class* or *bourgeois neighbourhood*—betray the economic shadow which hovers over contemporary perspectives of the community.

Unfortunately, the negative effects of this exclusive economic orientation are mounting daily and are threatening everywhere to run out of control. People are swarming to large and small communities looking for work, particularly as economic opportunities disappear from the hinterland due to the onslaught of technological change. The result is a great deal of overcrowding, and its attendant problems of sanitation and health. In order to reduce transportation costs and profit from locations in close proximity to expanding urban markets, more and more companies are locating in urban environments, thereby creating major zoning problems and tightening an industrial knot around the centre of most communities. More industries mean more traffic, since more trucks and vans are needed to haul produce. The result is an astronomical increase in traffic on city streets, causing maintenance costs to soar, traffic congestion and major transportation and communications problems to appear. Due to the tremendous expansion of all types of vehicular traffic and the urban location of industries, severe pollution problems arise. A layer of film is added to buildings and a solid band of smog settles over community skies, thereby permitting less and less sunlight. At the same time, pollution affects the aesthetic appearance of the community and causes it to deteriorate. Nor is this all. Increasingly, the community becomes segregated, as one economic class attempts to protect itself from the effects of industrialization or the steady encroachment of other economic classes whose fortunes have been less favourable. The effect? The community becomes compartmentalized and fragmented, which leads to a serious deterioration in its emotional make-up and moral fabric. Alienation reaches alarming proportions, as an increasing number of people lose touch with their environment and become faceless people in a lonely crowd. And what replaces the church or the square at the physical core of community life? In all probability, it is a factory, a smokestack, or the head office of a bank, an insurance company, or a multinational corporation, towering over the community and stretching halfway to the heavens.

Of course, the problem here is that there are numerous side-effects to economic growth which are seldom taken into account in planning community change. Too often, the calculations are exclusively economic in nature. If economic benefits are expected to outweigh economic costs, change takes place regardless of sensory, aesthetic, social, or human consequences. What is too often overlooked is the fact that the relationship between people and their environment is interactive and reciprocal. People's actions have a profound effect on the environment; at the same time, the environment affects people. In effect, actions invite retaliation. If people treat their environment with disrespect or fail to take the environmental effects of change into account, the environment will strike back by affecting people in some adverse way, as polluted environments do by destroying the mood and morale of people and the aesthetic quality of community life. Obviously, what is required here are cost-benefit calculations which stretch across all dimensions of community life. These are not the traditional calculations of cost-benefit analysis; on the contrary, they are new calculations which treat communities as total environments. Fortunately, the culturescape process provides a basis for such calculations since it treats communities as total entities constituent of many diverse social, political, economic, aesthetic, religious, and human components.

Interactive and Participatory Methods. If communities are to achieve desirable states of development, it is critical to evolve integrative and participatory methods which can be used by citizens and professionals for the collective betterment of society. However, those interested in the practical, methodological side of community development will be struck by two principal considerations: first, by the lack of effective methods which can be used by citizens at large for participatory purposes—to this extent, the average citizen is presently locked out of community development; and second, they will be struck by the comparative wealth of scientific methods which can be applied to community development compared with the paucity of methods available in the artistic domain which can be used for similar purposes.

The lack of effective methods which can be used by citizens at large to promote community development is understandable—community development is a comparatively new field of interest. In more established fields of activity, such as in economic, social, educational, or political development, methodological techniques tend to be in far greater supply as well as substantially more developed. Here, the challenge is often to apply existing techniques to specific situations in order to learn from the results. In contrast, the challenge in community development at the moment is to fashion a set of innovative methods capable of integrating the many diverse elements of local life as well as stimulating active citizen participation in the process.

The adverse imbalance that exists between the availability of scientific as opposed to artistic methods poses an equally serious problem.

In general, techniques which have been shaped in the scientific domain—such as observational analysis, experimentation, sampling, directive and non-directive interviewing, time-budget and expenditure studies, attitudinal surveys, and opinion polls—are already in a high state of sophistication. Unfortunately, however, they are largely descriptive in nature and are far better suited to describing problems than providing solutions. In consequence, they contribute little that is of sustained value in coming to grips with community needs. A huge gap still remains between knowing what the problem is and dealing with it. In addition, they are largely designed for professional use; they preclude all but a very limited number of researchers, experts, and specialists from participation in the process.

In broad comparison, techniques which have been shaped in the artistic domain are still in their infancy. In an historical sense, it is true that many artists have been highly sensitive to the aesthetic quality of communities and have devoted important segments of their works to depicting different aspects of this life in detail. In this connection, Brueghel with his scenes of lively Dutch social celebrations and peasant life, Canaletto and Guardi with their colourful presentations of Venice, Zola with his portrayal of the vivid colours and pungent aromas of Paris, Turgenev with his incredible descriptions of Russian life, and Renoir and Whistler with their captivating street scenes and cityscapes come quickly to mind. Why, the English composer Coates even used a musical composition to immortalize three English communities—Covent Garden, Westminster, and Knightsbridge! Nevertheless, while artists generally have been successful in capturing the aesthetic character of different communities for posterity, they have failed to fashion the artistic methods which are urgently needed to evaluate the aesthetic state of communities—methods which might also be used by citizens to improve the aesthetic quality of their surrounding environments. In short, artists have not extended the arts sufficiently into the environment so that they can begin to affect the attitudes of people and the decisions of politicians. The arts remain imprisoned behind the institutional walls of galleries, museums, theatres, concert halls, and cultural centres, thereby failing to become an integral ingredient in the planning process as they should be. As a result, the aesthetic state of most communities is nothing short of abysmal and the prospects for the future are not good. This tragedy is compounded by the artistic experiences of most citizens. Although many citizens have their artistic sensibilities destroyed in school, all citizens have artistic tastes and are constantly making aesthetic judgments throughout their lives. The problem here is that these tastes and judgments are bottled up and remain hidden from view. What is required is the development of methods which can provide an outlet for these tastes and judgments, especially for people who have little intention of becoming involved in the institutional side of the arts. Why is this so essential? Precisely because the aesthetic character of our communities will not change until it becomes every citizen's business, and this will not happen until ways and means are created which permit the large majority of people to participate in the aesthetic transformation of community life.

If new methodological techniques are to be created which can be used effectively by citizens, civic authorities, planners, and professionals to raise community consciousness to new and loftier heights, it is as essential to fuse the scientific and artistic components to form a methodological whole as it is to promote active citizen participation in the process. Here again we encounter the advantage of the culturescape. It acts as both a catalyst and synthesizer. As a catalyst, it prompts people everywhere to get involved in the design and development of their environmental habitats. As a synthesizer, it provides the common ground for science and art to unite for the cultural enrichment of community life. The reason for this is that the culturescape process possesses three properties—the properties of exploration, education, and discovery—which are fundamental to all artistic and scientific activity.

Culturescape Constructions

There is nothing mysterious about the idea of a landscape. In effect, a landscape is a visual exposition of the natural and man-made sights of an environment. It exposes the way in which the eye surveys an environment, sometimes stopping to focus on distinctive features, often roving rapidly over features it takes for granted, but always snapping mental pictures and making selections as it moves.

Nor is there anything mysterious about the idea of a soundscape. A soundscape is the ear's answer to the eye. It is an aural exposition of the different sounds of an environment. It reveals the way in which the human ear samples natural, mechanical, and human sounds, opening wide to sounds which are soothing and closing off sounds that are unsettling.

It follows from this that a culturescape is an exposition of all the different cultural features—natural, historical, sensorial, social, economic, political, aesthetic, and human—of an environment. It is an environment assaulted by all the human faculties—an explorer's curiosity set loose on the incredible panorama of sights, sounds, smells, tastes, textures, institutions, activities, and events encountered in daily life.

Landscapes and soundscapes cut down into environments. They are discrete notions, designed to look at environments through the vertical lenses of specialization. As such, they are structured to explore similar facets of life. In contrast, culturescapes cut across environments. They are integrative, horizontal notions, designed to reveal the infinite and inter-related nature of many diverse facets of life. They are structured to bring things together, not set things apart

One of the most fascinating characteristics of landscapes and sound-scapes is the way in which they can vary so much from individual to individual. What may be significant for one person may be quite in-significant for another. Two artists can paint the same landscape and the attention given to layout, detail, colour, shading, and overall composition can be so varied that an observer would swear that two different land-scapes have been portrayed. Two composers can listen to the same sequence of sounds and hear entirely different compositions. In much the same way, two people selected at random can be exposed to the same landscape and their eyes will settle on entirely different natural and architectural features. Or they can be exposed to exactly the same sound series—vehicular traffic, human voices, different languages, or orchestral music—and react very differently to these sounds.

Like landscapes and soundscapes, culturescapes can be highly personal affairs. They can be simple or complex, conscious or intuitive, depending on the amount of detail that people's sensory and intellectual faculties have chosen to record. Two people can spend three days exploring Paris, London, Mexico City, New York, Marrakech, Istanbul, Calcutta, or Beijing and their experiences will be totally different. Whereas one person will be highly sensitive to sights and sounds, the other will be highly responsive to smells and tastes. Whereas one may be extremely curious about the history of the city being explored but rather indifferent to its natural features, the other might be wildly enthusiastic about its parks, con-servation areas, and topographical features but completely bored by its historical accomplishments.

Such experiences reveal much about the different phases which com-prise the culturescape process. First, there is the absorptive phase in which people soak up many details about the surrounding environment. Next, there is the evaluative phase where people imprint their likes, dislikes, and habits on the environment. This is the highly subjective part of the process. Finally, there is the responsive phase where individuals respond to the mental blueprints they tuck away in their minds. These three phases usually happen so instinctively that they form a continuous process. But how does the process get started? How does it gather momentum? More importantly, how does it become an integral part of local life, a tool for community improvement?

Building a Sensory Profile of the Community. Respecting citizens for the important contributions they can make is the key to successful initiation of the culturescape process. Through respect for each citizen's contribution, more and more people will be anxious to participate in the process. When this happens, every community becomes a hidden treasure with all sorts of fascinating gems sunken just below the surface. But, as citizens, how often do we take the time to dig into our communities to become acquainted with their treasures? How often do we take our communities for granted, assuming that we know what services they provide as well as what programs are available to enrich local life? How much do we really care about the aesthetic state of our communities—their captivating or disturbing sights, sounds, smells, textures, and tastes? Perhaps we assume too much and explore too little.

Given the strong visual orientation of contemporary life, as soon as we commit ourselves to in-depth exploration of our communities, we will probably find that the visual aspects will predominate. Every community contains an endless array of visual images—flowers and trees, parks, homes, gardens, factories, stores, office buildings, billboards, halls, malls, and shopping centres. Our eyes may instantly fasten on many of the larger visual attractions—homes, buildings, and offices. However, this should not be allowed to overpower many of the smaller visual delights of the community—lights, benches, flower pots, kiosks, clocks, gables, and pieces of sculpture—or lack of them. At the same time, the eye would also be well advised to pay particular attention to the floor of the community—its pebbles, cobblestones, cut stones, bricks, asphalt, soils, grids, and drains—as well as to the roof of the community—the daytime or night-time silhouette it etches against the eternal sky.

Visual exploration of the floor, roof, and street furnishings of the community should help train the eye to focus on larger visual patterns:

simultaneous movement systems of people and vehicles, city blocks, communal squares, street furnishings, landscaping, and planning arrangements. At the same time, aesthetic faculties should be called into play. Not all of the sights will be pleasing. In fact, many will be disturbing: traffic congestion, obnoxious signboards, commercial strips, jungles of wires and poles, littered streets, run-down store fronts, shortages of people places, and the surfeit of splashy advertising enticements.

The strong visual overtones of the community should not be allowed to obscure other sensory characteristics—textures, smells, tastes, and sounds. The satisfaction derived from visual exploration and discovery should help to activate interest in the other sensory dimensions of the community.

At the same time that the community possesses a fascinating admixture of sights, so it also contains an incredible assortment of textures, each calling out to be caressed. For example, take the building materials of the community. What a vast array of different woods, metals, stones, and bricks abounds everywhere—some of these materials are smooth and fine; others are rough, granular, and full of interesting indentations; some are highly finished; others are left in their natural state. Each ready to reward the tactile explorer with their intimate secrets.

Are the community's smells and tastes any less important than its sights and textures? Yet, how indifferent we tend to be to the various smells of the natural and man-made environment, primarily because pollution has dulled our sensory faculties. However, it would not prove overly difficult to piece together an olfactory profile of the community. Such a profile might include the enchanting scents of favourite flowers in the local park, the intoxicating smells of various perfumes and colognes, the gaseous vapours of exhaust fumes, the distinctive scents of spring saplings or decomposing fall leaves, the pungent odours of local industries, or the beckoning aroma of the local pastry shop.

A visit to the local pastry shop to sample its oven-fresh pies, cakes, breads, or rolls should help to open up the world of taste. This may be followed up at home by experiments which expand gastronomic knowledge of different vegetables, meats, wines, sweets, spices, and herbs. Here, the emphasis may not be on what is habitually pleasing to the taste buds, but rather on what needs to be known about the incredible diversity of tastes. Families of spices and herbs—cinnamon, mace, nutmeg, and cloves, or basil, thyme, marjoram, oregano, and tarragon—will be sampled in succession to expand culinary awareness. New vegetables, such as chicory, escarole, endive, garbanzos, leeks, and parsnips, will be added to salads to enhance their taste. Questions will be asked in local supermarkets about the need for artificially produced tastes or prepackaged foods. More requests will be made in local restaurants for regional specialities and home-cooked delicacies. Slowly, prepackaged, plastic tastes may even yield to local, indigenous tastes as more and more residents express their demands for culinary reform.

The sensory side of the culturescape composition is not only scored for sights, smells, textures, and tastes. It is also scored for sounds. No less an authority than John Cage contends that music is sound, the sound we hear around us, whether inside or outside the concert hall. An increasing number of contemporary composers share this conviction.

A group of composers connected with the World Soundscape Project believes that there is a soundscape of natural, human, and mechanical sounds which corresponds to the landscape of physical and architectural sights. They contend that the soundscape of the world is in reality a vast musical composition which has been badly orchestrated in the present century. There has been an imperialistic spread of many of the most grotesque and taxing sounds imaginable. The hard-edge sounds of modern technology—from power tools, lawnmowers, factories, machines, cars, trucks, planes, motorcycles, and other mechanical devices—have masked out almost all human and natural sounds in many parts of the world. In pre-industrial and rural cultures, natural and human sounds account for up to 95 per cent of all sounds, with the sounds of tools and technology accounting for the remaining 5 per cent. In industrialized and urban cultures, the proportions are virtually reversed. The sounds of machine technology account for an alarming 70 per cent of all sounds—and at progressively higher and higher decibel levels. This has brought in its wake two concomitant developments. First, it has caused increased deafness and impaired hearing. Second, it has turned most communities in industrialized societies into sonic sewers. By promoting improvements in noise abatement legislation and aural acuity—through "ear-cleaning and ear-training" exercises, sounds museums, and sounds walks—the World Soundscape group hopes to inspire a universal movement for a better world soundscape—a soundscape which will prove vastly more satisfying to ear and mind.

Determined explorers will not allow the local soundscape to pass unnoticed. Rather, they will store sounds away in the bank of memorable acoustical experiences—wind rattling against metal, birds singing at dawn, rain drops on a tin roof, train whistles, fog horns, factory sirens, revving motors, church bells, and the clatter of horses' hooves on pavement. Like the composers of the World Soundscape Project, committed explorers will soon discover that many of the most beautiful sounds are disappearing, due to the rapid onslaught of technological sounds and the lack of effective noise abatement legislation. This too will be added to the expanding sensoryscape of the community.

A Constellation of Community Profiles. At the same time that some residents will be contributing to the building of the sensory profile of the community, others will be involved in the piecing together of other types of profiles—natural, historical, scientific, institutional, human, and aesthetic. Each profile will possess its own peculiar characteristics.

Some citizens may become interested in fashioning a natural profile of the community and its environs. Here, probes will be conducted into the topographical contours of the community: its hills, valleys, rivers, streams, embankments, and overall geographic setting. Parks and conservation areas will be studied in detail for their scenic appeal, flora and fauna, fragile botanical systems, and distinctive ecological features. Others may be interested in painting an historical portrait of the community which illustrates why it was originally settled, how it grew in response to different types of needs, and when it underwent periods of profound change. To do this effectively, it may prove necessary to draw on museum holdings, archival material, old photographs, library records, and news-paper clippings. Through this, an impression will be gleaned of the different layers of culture which combine to form the overall cultural composition of the community. Still others may be interested in preparing a scientific profile of the community. This will entail probes into trans-portation and communication systems, changes in climatic conditions, meteorological studies, and the activities of different research agencies.

Active interest in the institutional profile of the community may result from visits to different community resources, such as museums, libraries, social agencies, government offices, factories, banks, insurance com-panies, commercial enterprises, boutiques, community centres, concert halls, and sports arenas. Standing behind this complex network of in-stitutions are the myriad individuals and organizations responsible for the numerous programs and services which are offered in the community. How unaware we tend to be of the various programs and services which are available to us either as residents or visitors to communities. How little knowledge we have of the real functioning of our numerous institutions. Travelling down this path is essential to the crystallization of a comprehensive community culturescape. Not only is there exposure to the inner workings of the community as a dynamic and evolving entity, but also much more is learned about the way in which complex decisions are made—decisions which affect the planning, design, and development of all our communities.

People who are determined to probe to the very depths of the cultural experience will be anxious to learn as much as possible about the human profile of the community. Initially, a probe into this area may start when an individual becomes interested in his or her own cultural patterns. Eventually, it will probably fan out to encompass an interest in the cultural patterns that are traced by others.

It is often said that human beings are the products of habit. Plotted over time, these habits form cycles; some of which—eating, sleeping, and working—are necessary for survival; while others—watching television, enjoying hobbies, reading, or attending meetings or parties—are highly optional. One of the best ways of documenting these cycles is to keep a cultural diary. A cultural diary differs from a general diary in that it is intended to record in systematic fashion that amount of time or money spent on life's different activities, rather than to chronicle those special little events and experiences which highlight the day. As such, a cultural diary breaks a given period of time in two ways: first, into minutes, hours, and weeks; and second, into different types of activities. Records are then kept of the actual amounts of time or money spent on these different activities. When these separate recordings are aggregated and plotted graphically on maps of the community or on charts, cycles are revealed which expose the extent to which all individuals are the products of different types of cultural habits and trace different patterns on their environment.

Cycles of human activity often act to highlight fundamental problems in community development. Much of the concern of cultural development—for greater human fulfillment in life, a more responsive environment, better conservation of resources, more citizen participation in decision-making, and a higher level of awareness—can only be accomplished by reinforcing or breaking with these established patterns of human activity. Simultaneously, new cycles are created; cycles which bring people closer to real satisfaction in their daily lives. Creation of these new cycles may require higher occupational turnover, variations in working hours, reduced consumption of goods and services, more recreational and artistic amenities, more effective urban renewal or abatement legislation, better control of water or air pollution, greater regulation of business and industry, and more democratic forms of decision-making. Such can often be the effects of cultural change.

To achieve a full understanding of the human profile of the community, excursions into the land of individual habits should be complemented by probes into the habits of friends, relatives, neighbours, and more distant residents. Although people often betray signs of similarity in external terms, in internal terms, their lives are very diverse, reflecting their different ethnic backgrounds, religious beliefs, upbringing, education, and personal preferences. A little friendly curiosity usually brings its own rewards. Often probing in this area reveals significant differences in the way people choose to live their lives, approach jobs, practise hobbies, celebrate events, cook dishes, observe holidays, and utilize leisure time. A rich human mine exists in every community and is always ready for the tapping.

If the door starts to swing open the moment the human profile is probed, it is thrust open wide as soon as the aesthetic profile is exposed. Here is where preferences run strong and feelings cut deep. The aesthetic experience is an exceedingly personal affair. Whereas one person may detest the sound of motorcycles, planes, or trucks, another person may revel in such sounds. One person may find billboards offensive; another may find them satisfying. Some may feel that the city core needs a facelift; others may be content to leave it alone. Unfortunately, we know very little about the aesthetic preferences of people: far too often they remain hidden from view due to adverse educational or social experiences. However, since they represent one of life's realities, they should be brought out into the open and confronted for what they really are: illustrations of the infinite spectrum of likes and dislikes which comprise all communities. Herein lies one of the real strengths of the culturescape process. By allowing many sides of an issue to surface, it knits many aesthetic preferences into the cultural fabric of society.

Culturescape Choreography
As material related to the constellation of community profiles is collected, it can be choreographed in different ways to yield different results. For example, factual information about the various sensory, natural, historical, scientific, institutional, human, and aesthetic profiles can be

classified according to the cultural sector it represents, thereby making it possible to prepare cultural inventories. Information in this form can be used as a basis for time-budget and expenditure studies or to undertake public opinion polls or attitudinal surveys. Or it might be transformed into symbolic form and used to prepare maps, walks, tours, itineraries, and exchanges which can be extremely valuable for administrative, animation, planning, and policy purposes. In one form or another, all this information relates to the supply and demand for community services. Synchronizing supply and demand in such a way that it meets the real needs of citizens and communities still constitutes the supreme challenge of all development.

Cultural Inventories. During the absorptive phase, the culturescape process acts like a sponge. It soaks up as much information as possible about community life—information which leads to a keener and deeper appreciation of the intricate interrelationships as well as the strengths and shortcomings of all community life. For purposes of administration and planning, it is possible to classify this information according to different sectors of culture. Taken separately, each sector has an identity of its own which results from the many institutions, facilities, programs, and services which comprise it. Taken together, these sectors combine to form an extremely valuable profile of the community as a total environment.

Artistic culture:	music, opera, ballet, drama, art, sculpture, concert halls, theatres, art galleries, craft shops, etc.
Folk culture:	festivals, fairs, carnivals, circuses, ethnology museums, community celebrations, etc.
Media culture:	newspapers, publishing houses, printers, radio and television stations, archives, libraries, film centres, cinemas, etc.
Recreational culture:	football, gymnastics, polo, hockey, stadiums, rinks, gymnasiums, etc.
Environmental culture:	parks, conservation areas, historic sites, streets, shopping centres, malls, residential districts, etc.
Scientific culture:	research institutes, meteorological stations, laboratories, etc.
Educational culture:	elementary and secondary schools, technical schools, universities, educational associations, etc.
Religious culture:	churches, synagogues, mosques, temples, religious organizations, etc.

Political culture:	national, regional, and local governments, political associations, etc.
Social culture:	pubs, cafes, restaurants, clubs, veterans' associations, legions, Rotary, Kiwanis, and other service organizations, etc.
Economic culture:	commercial establishments, banks, insurance companies, factories, industries, service stations, multinational corporations, etc.

Given the highly personal nature of each individual's contribution to the culturescape, it is highly unlikely that in combination they will contain enough factual information to build a comprehensive cultural inventory or present a picture of the community as a total environment. As a result, more systematic measures may have to be introduced to insure that each sector is fully represented in breadth as well as in depth. This may necessitate the collection of comparable data for each sector on the number and nature of organizations, the size and composition of memberships, funding patterns, the character and use of facilities, and the availability of programs. Such data is a prerequisite to intelligent planning and decision-making, since it sheds light on the supply side of the equation.

Like inventory data, data on the amount of time and money residents spend on different types of activities will not be provided in sufficient detail to provide a composite picture of how the community as a whole makes its various allocations. Where individuals have chosen to keep cultural diaries in a systematic fashion, these diaries will form the basis of larger community time-budget and expenditure studies. When conducted on a sample basis which is large enough to be representative, these studies will reveal the relative allocations of time and money for the various sectors of culture, thereby providing invaluable information on time distributions and financial transactions. Information on the distribution of time between work and leisure as well as expenditure on such things as books, radio and television sets, cinema attendance, admissions to theatres, concerts, galleries, sporting events, food, clothing, and shelter will help to fill in the demand side of the equation.

Attitudinal surveys and opinion polls can also make extremely valuable additions to the culturescape process. In one form or another, both techniques get residents thinking about the character of their own lives as well as exchanging ideas about how the community might be improved from a cultural point of view. Every resident makes a fundamental decision by choosing a place to live and a line of work to pursue. The factors affecting these decisions vary considerably, depending on the nature and location of the community, employment opportunities, proximity to nature, and the availability of social and artistic amenities and shopping facilities. Often surveys and polls which involve discussion of these factors help to bring individuals to new levels of awareness about why a particular community was originally selected or how it might be improved or utilized to better advantage. These discussions can easily lead to conversations in adjacent areas: what residents think of their community; what they like or dislike about it; how they propose changing the undesirable aspects of local life; or how they feel political authorities can best serve them in meeting their real needs. This is what makes the non-directive interview so valuable for detecting actual and latent needs. Through unstructured discussion, citizens are often pressed into closer contact with their own deeper desires.

One of the real strengths of the culturescape process is its susceptibility to mapping. Depending on the problem at hand and the symbols used, it is possible to prepare culturescape maps for informational, administrative, planning, policy, exploratory, or animation purposes.

It does not prove difficult to picture the numerous possibilities. For general purposes, it is possible to prepare inventory maps which depict the different sectors of culture as well as the various resources that are available within each sector. Visualize a community map in which different colours are used to denote the different sectors of culture—say blue for the political culture, red for the artistic culture, and green for the recreational or environmental culture—and different symbols are used to designate different kinds of resources—an actor's mask for a theatre, books for a library or school, a musical instrument for a concert hall, a greenhouse for a botanical garden, and so on. When the community inventory is plotted on such a map, an interesting graphic profile of the location and character of community resources takes shape. This type of map can be extremely useful in helping to acquaint residents and visitors alike with the vast inventory of cultural resources which is available to enrich local life.

With slight alterations, this inventory map can be transformed into administrative, planning, and policy maps which can be extremely valuable in pinpointing certain problems or plotting future directions. For example, by overlaying demographic statistics, transportation grids, and capacity data on an inventory map of this kind, it is possible to identify inequalities in the physical distribution of resources, persistent deficiencies in programs, capacity limitations on facilities, and transportation and parking problems with respect to accessibility to resources.

Inventory, administrative, policy and planning maps all share one thing in common. They all use objective "data"—such as physical locations, organizational types, user information, time allocations, expenditure patterns, and recorded responses—as their point of departure. Much of this data will have been systematically collected and recorded to provide an external portrait of community life. But there is another equally valid approach to culturescape cartography—an approach which grows out of the subjective side of human nature. It takes as its point of departure people's personal reactions to their environment and uses the frequency with which people refer to different likes and dislikes to arrive at an "objective" portrait of community reactions which is in reality an aggregation of many "subjective" impressions.

Suppose residents were asked to list their major likes and dislikes of a community. Now, picture a map on which these likes and dislikes are overlaid one on top of another. What begins to emerge is a highly impressionistic map which reveals at a glance many of the collective likes and dislikes of community residents. By denoting likes which have been referred to with the greatest frequency by spoked circles and dislikes which have been referred to with the greatest frequency by rectangular bars, a portrait of collective likes and dislikes quickly emerges. These impressionistic maps—which may reveal such things as favorite restaurants, special haunts, well-travelled streets, noisy intersections, obnoxious odours, traffic irritations, grotesque buildings, disturbing sights, and satisfying sounds—can be extremely valuable for planning and policy purposes. In fact, they may be the most salient planning vehicles of all, since they do not represent the attitudes of a few highly specialized, professional planners but rather the collective reactions of residents at large. To this extent, they help to explain those strong and often unexpected reactions which come from citizens when planners decide to change some aspect of the environment which citizens cherish very highly. Getting information about these reactions out in the open in advance helps to avoid needless confrontations among citizens, planners, and politicians.

In a sense, inventory and impressionistic maps represent dialectical approaches to culturescape cartography. Between these extremes, different types of maps can be produced which help to illustrate the constellation of possible culturescape profiles. For example, it is possible to produce maps which depict the range of sensory characteristics of the community, such as its sights, sounds, smells, textures, and tastes. These maps can be extremely valuable in prompting people to explore their surrounding environments, as well as in identifying aggravating sensory irritants. In much the same way, it is possible to prepare maps which reveal the different natural, historical, institutional, human, and aesthetic dimensions of community life.

Like landscaping, culturescaping describes a process which involves selections as well as collections. It draws information together, sifts and sorts it, and selects the information which most satisfies the objectives involved. Suppose the objective is to prepare a community walking tour. Using the inventory approach, information from the inventory can be used to identify prominent cultural monuments. This information can then be written up in capsule form, symbolized, and plotted on a map of the community. The result is a highly interesting walk which directs people to specific resources and special landmarks. Most guide books are prepared in this way. Through the collection of a vast amount of inventory information, they rank or star selective sights and provide a descriptive itinerary which is broken down according to the varying amounts of time that residents or visitors have to devote to a particular community. Research undertaken in connection with the development of this culturescape methodology reveals that this approach tends to highlight the monuments and institutions of the community—its art galleries, museums, community centres, old buildings, historic sites, festivals, fairs, theatres, factories, and athletic facilities. What is particularly significant is the fact that a much different walking tour results when the impressionistic approach is used. Much more emphasis is placed on the "magnetic cultural forces" which residents cherish about their local life—an interesting gable, an old dilapidated building, a pub, a city block of contrasting sights and sounds, the aroma of a favorite restaurant, a special haunt from which to view human interactions, a curio shop, or perhaps a mural in a building. These items reveal the more intimate character as well as the collective preferences of community life. By identifying, describing, and linking these together, a very different kind of tour is produced.

Discrepancies between the two approaches show up most clearly by asking residents to compare their own preferences with things they would recommend to visitors or friends who express an interest in getting to know their community better. Most often, residents' own preferences are subjective and impressionistic, often tinged with a touch of nostalgia. What is recommended to friends and visitors is usually much more objective and systematic. A curious difference? How often do we find ourselves in the position where we are in a strange community longing to know it the way residents know it, only to find that we end up religiously following a guide book of systematically prepared cultural monuments? How often have we found ourselves in the position where we have recommended tours to visitors and friends that have not even been remotely connected with the cultural experiences which bring joy and happiness into our own lives?

As far as the culturescape process is concerned, what is required here is a synthesis of the inventory and impressionistic approaches—a subtle blending of the best features of both approaches to form a fascinating excursion which exposes the "monuments" and "magnets" as well as the macrocosmic and microcosmic dimensions of community life. Here is the point where science and aesthetics fuse to form the art of culturescape choreography. Great care should be exercised to insure that many audio, visual, and verbal technologies—tapes, photographs, slides, sketches, written commentaries, and miniature replicas of the community—are brought to bear on the realization of this necessary synthesis. Extreme caution should be exercised in planning the character and extensiveness of maps, walks, and tours so as not to overload or overdefine them.

Maps, walks, and tours of the community should really be designed to promote curiosity and exploration as well as education and discovery. Curiosity and exploration are needed to uncover the richness of resources; education is needed to expose the fullness of community life; and discovery is needed to raise the community to new levels of consciousness. How are these best accomplished? Perhaps by using a little creative imagination in the preparation of various maps, walks, and tours. For example, if a visitor is interested in taking a tour, rather than laying out a prescribed route, possibly the visitor should be given a series of photographs which expose some of the more unusual details of the community— an unusually shaped eavestrough, an ornate gable, an old verandah, a small piece of sculpture. This should prompt an active search for those special items and objects which enrich all communities. These photographs might even be arranged in degrees of difficulty such that the visitor progresses from photographs which depict macro details to photographs which depict micro details. Very often, more can be learned about a community through an active search for its hidden treasures and small details than through in-depth documentation of its major monuments and historic sites.

Itineraries and Exchanges. Just as every person has a different set of likes and dislikes with respect to the community in which they are resident, so each person imprints a different pattern on the environment. Spurred on by unquenchable curiosity, some people explore environments in great depth. They are not satisfied until they have overturned many stones, thereby tracing out intricate patterns of movements and probes into many facets of local life. Others trace out much simpler patterns; patterns which reflect needs that are more habitual in nature. Nevertheless, all are valid, since all expose the infinite variety of human needs— needs which vary markedly from person to person. Close inspection of these needs reveals in the minutest detail how each person lives a life that is without duplication elsewhere. It is often said that every person has a double living somewhere else in the world. While this may be true for people's physical appearance, it is certainly not true for the cultural patterns they create.

As a result of these differences, another fascinating possibility in the field of culturescape choreography is to ask people to record their likes and dislikes of the community. These may be recorded in the form of itineraries which range all the way from "all likes" to "all dislikes" to various combinations of the two. These itineraries can be designed to take a morning, a day, or several days to complete. The advantage of having itineraries prepared in this way is that they can be exchanged one for another, thereby providing people with an opportunity to experience their community from perspectives that are different from their own. The act of exchanging itineraries is not dissimilar to the act of trading secrets about unusual wines or unique restaurants except that it is organized on a much larger and more formal scale. An interesting possibility in this regard is to ask school children at different levels of the educational system to prepare "culturescape itineraries" of their community. What is particularly revealing is how their perceptions of the community differ from the perceptions of adults not only in terms of their likes and dislikes, but also in terms of their most cherished cultural attractions. This is not really surprising. Remember as a child how many secret hiding places you had in the community where you could let your private thoughts take hold and your imagination roam. Another possibility along the same lines is to ask a group of adults to prepare similar itineraries. These itineraries are then exchanged and experienced by others. Following this, the group is reconvened in order to discuss the results. Here again, it is amazing what is learned about the values and perceptions of others as well as about the reactions of people to their environment and the richness of community life. What emerges is a dimension of the human personality which is seldom revealed in group therapies and encounter sessions, since it is based largely on reactions to the external rather than the internal environment. At the same time, this approach has the distinct advantage of sensitizing people to the quality of their environment and arousing their interest in community improvements.

Housing the Culturescape

Every individual possesses something unique to contribute to the community culturescape. In all probability, these contributions will take different forms. For some, they will be itemized itineraries of daily or weekly events. For others, they will be recordings of likes and dislikes. For still others, they may be actual objects, such as old photographs, artefacts, tapes of oral histories, antiques, maps, records, or other memorabilia of community significance. In any event, as the culturescape process takes hold and these contributions grow, facilities will be required to house all this burgeoning activity.

There is no prescribed home for culturescape activity. It will vary from community to community depending on a variety of factors: the extent of participation, the nature of citizen contributions, the availability of suitable space, the level of public commitment, the existence of special skills and audio-visual equipment, and the unique character of the community itself.

In some communities, activities which form part of the culturescape process are being carried out by various institutions under different names. Museums collecting and classifying local artefacts are engaged in one aspect of the process. Universities or colleges involved in taping oral histories of long-time residents are engaged in another aspect of the process. Likewise, centres dispensing information about basic services are also engaged in a prominent part of the process. By undertaking these functions, each of these institutions is making a valuable contribution. As such, each of these institutions would make a suitable home for the community culturescape.

Nevertheless, when all this activity is added up, it will be discovered that the most important part of all is missing. At the present time, there is virtually no community in the world that has a central source to which residents can bring their different contributions; through which they can become actively involved in planning the development of their community as a dynamic entity; and from which they can acquire information that has been choreographed in different ways to expose the diverse dimensions of community life. What is urgently needed is the establishment of Culturescape Centres in every community which are devoted to the collection and presentation of interesting community memorabilia; the orchestration of many different types of maps, walks, tours, itineraries, and exchanges for in-depth use by citizens and visitors; and the utilization of miniature replicas and planning models which illustrate how proposed and actual changes affect the sensory, economic, social, political, aesthetic, and human character of communities. When this happens, citizens everywhere will have an opportunity to weigh for themselves the relative costs and benefits of different changes on community life. Moreover, they will also have the necessary vehicles to express their discontent with certain types of proposed changes, as well as the tools to actively participate in future community improvements. In this way, community development will be shaped less and less by the desires of a few politicians and specialized planners and will be channelled more and more in directions which reflect the real needs of the citizenry at large.

What facilities, equipment, and skills are needed in these Culturescape Centres to accommodate the multifarious activities? These will vary according to local circumstances. A large, free, comfortable space, capable of hanging billboards and maps, displaying models, recording feedback, storing memorabilia and artefacts, and dispensing recommended walks and tours would be perfect for such purposes. This space should be complemented by people who possess special skills, such as photography, mapping, documentation, classification, exhibiting, and tour preparation. Local artists, craftsmen, librarians, historians, photographers, audio-visual experts, municipal mappers, and museum curators would be particularly useful in this connection. Where it is not possible to have a Culturescape Centre in its own right, suitable space should be provided in a museum, a library, an arts centre, a sports complex, or a community hall. However, given the enormous importance of this activity, an independent home in or near the centre of the community would be preferable, even if this home is not constructed specifically for these purposes. In fact, a deserted factory, an old warehouse, an abandoned building, a boarded-up shed, or a dilapidated railway station would all make ideal homes for piecing together the community's mirror image of itself.

Patterns of Development

As microcosms, all communities are unique—they make collective state-ments which reflect the myriad events and activities which comprise them. In terms of minute details—in the naming of streets, the location of shops, the design of parks, the laying out of transportation systems and sub-divisions as well as the celebrating of special events—no two communities are alike. Yet, as macrocosms, many communities exude similar patterns of development and betray routine ways of ordering the different aspects of daily life. By far the most prominent of these patterns of development are the imposed, the imitative, and the indigenous. In one way or another, most communities settle for one of these three patterns of development.

The imposed pattern traces out the most familiar design. On an inter-national scale, it is most easily identified as the product of imperialism, the process whereby some communities, due to their superior economic, political, or military power, are able to subject other communities to their will. In such cases, values, institutions, and technological practices which originate in the dominant community are imposed, either through physical force or subtle suasion, on subservient communities. This pattern may result from forces that are external or internal to the community. It may result from the actions of governments or large corporations which, through the use of enticements or sanctions of various kinds, manage to impose their desires on communities with strategic locations or favourable resources. Or it may result from outside experts who are imported into a community with the express purpose of implementing pervasive programs. Or it may be the product of actions by a mayor or the local authorities who are determined to see the community benefit from a particular project.

Regardless of whether it emanates from forces without or within, the imposed pattern usually is the result of a vision that is shared by only a few people who have powerful positions inside or outside the community. This is not to say that it is necessarily subversive or counterproductive. Due to the lack of techniques to detect real community needs, local leaders often find themselves in the invidious position where they are compelled to make assumptions about needs as best they can or to proceed with programs that are highly uncertain in their ultimate outcome. Often, their decisions are made with the very best of intentions. Nor are the results always undesirable. An examination of many of the world's greatest accomplishments reveals that many contributions have been made by leaders who imposed their visions on an unwilling citizenry—visions which were once extremely unpopular but which now enjoy great popular support. A survey of the development of many great cities confirms this. No, the real problem with the imposed pattern of development is not that it is subversive or counterproductive. Rather, it is almost always non-participatory; it excludes most people from active participation in the process.

Whereas the imposed pattern is tinged with exclusion, the imitative pattern is tinted with conformity. In effect, the imitative pattern involves copying what already exists elsewhere, often a place in close geographical proximity. Like the imposed pattern, the imitative pattern also has its strengths and shortcomings. It would be a mistake to assume that what happens in some other community does not have value or relevance, or that a community will necessarily suffer from duplicating what has proven successful elsewhere. A good part of the developmental process involves learning from the successes and failures of others. Moreover, the imitative pattern can also produce unexpected results. What starts out as inferior imitation can also end up as superior innovation, as any cursory examination of Japanese technological progress since the end of World War II will verify. Nevertheless, such experiences are rare. More often than not, communities that follow the imitative pattern fall into a trap. One of two things happens. Either duplication yields foreign matter—matter which never quite fits the new environment as well as the original environment which gave it birth. Or it proves to be too simple, thereby usurping the more creative urge that might better have come from within. In either case, the effect is often surface, rather than substantive, development.

Whereas imposed and imitative development often seem artificial, there can be little doubt about the stamp of authenticity which marks indigenous development. However, indigenous development can take its toll. By digging deep into the soil of the community, as well as by opening up all the nooks and crannies of local life, indigenous development can turn a town topsy-turvy. It can cause strife among various groups and hostility among different factions. In consequence, of the three patterns of community development, the indigenous pattern produces the greatest amount of change, change which can be exceedingly painful at times. This is what makes this pattern by far the most infrequent as well as the hardest to achieve. Nevertheless, once achieved, it can also be by far the most rewarding. Not only does it come closest to meeting the real cultural needs of citizens and communities, but also it necessitates maximum public participation in the process of development. To this extent, it does not really represent an alternative to imposed or imitative development. By leaving no stone unturned in its search for genuine answers to pressing problems, it merely digs deeper than the other approaches to development. It involves greater risks but promises more substantial rewards.

In addition to responding to the real needs of communities and encouraging maximum citizen participation in the process, indigenous development solves several other pressing problems as well. In the first place, it satisfies the need for self-identity which underlies much of the current demand for cultural development. It is far from coincidental that much of the contemporary literature on cultural development is filled with demands for greater decentralization and more self-assertion. In one way or another, both these demands relate to the need for indigenous development: the demand for decentralization in terms of the need to create decision-making structures which respond to forces from within rather than without; and the demand for self-assertion in terms of the need for more authentic expression. Concurrently, indigenous development also satisfies the quest for diversity rather than conformity which forms an integral part of the contemporary literature on cultural development. Due to the accumulating power of modern technology and the pervasive influence of the mass media, the world is in danger of becoming a uniculture—an homogeneous culture in which consumer products, food-stuffs, clothing styles, architectural designs, and lifestyles look more and more the same. The uniform, plastic world of this uniculture looms more and more frightening in the human imagination as time goes on. In contrast, by placing emphasis on the unique, the authentic, and the creative, indigenous development promises to provide a world that is richer as a result of its differences and more humane as a result of its integrity.

Towards a World Culturescape

Over the last few decades, it has become obvious that communities are destined to play a prominent role in determining the future quality of life for the large majority of the inhabitants of the globe. Already, well over half of the population of the world is living in communities of varying shapes and sizes. Moreover, as population increases, and as technologies are invented and applied which release more and more people from rural areas, communities, from towns and hamlets to major urban centres, are destined to grow steadily in importance as they have done virtually without interruption from the dawn of recorded time.

It is a cliché to say that people get the governments and political systems they deserve. However, what holds true for governments and political systems also holds true for communities. People will get the communities they deserve and whether these communities prove to be sources of joy and inspiration or deprivation and misery will depend fundamentally on the collective ability of people to make intelligent use of spaces and effective decisions about changes in their communities.

It is often said that people's homes are their castles. In what sense is this true? Surely it is true in the sense that regardless of wealth or their station in life, most people get highly involved with their homes. This involvement takes many forms. For the wealthy, it means working with architects on the physical layout and design of the home, supervising builders on the actual construction of the home, and sharing with interior decorators the task of selecting home furnishings. For the less fortunate, it means anything from rearranging furniture, planting a small garden, hanging a picture, using a craft object to enhance a special space, or employing a carpet to warm a room, to sweeping floors and scouring walls to keep the home free of dirt and troublesome insects. In most cases, however, people take pride in their homes. By arranging and rearranging the objects in their domestic environment, they find an outlet for their creative energies. Their environment responds to care and attention by becoming a place where it is possible to find tranquillity, comfort, security, and most of all happiness.

What has been true for the home in the past and at present must be true for communities in the future. In effect, communities must become people's castles; they must be known with the same intimacy and cared for with the same affection and attention to detail. For it is only in this way that it will be possible to create decent and agreeable living arrangements for the world's rapidly expanding population. This is why the culturescape process is so essential. It strikes at the very heart of community problems. At the survival level, it examines and reports on the basic conditions of human habitation, ranging all the way from sanitation, sewage, and the adequacy or inadequacy of accommodations to basic transportation and communications requirements. At the sensory level, it documents the dangers arising from excessive amounts of visual, aural, olfactory, and tactile pollution. At the aesthetic and human levels, it exposes major shortcomings in the quantity of services and the quality of life. But the critical eye of the culturescape not only pinpoints problems. It also signals the way to solutions. By getting people involved and committed to their surrounding environment, it creates the necessary groundswell for a collective assault on troublesome problems. By paving the way for more realistic cost-benefit calculations, it helps to prompt action—action which can cancel out many of the irritants and reinforce many of the pleasurable aspects of local life.

Commitment to the culturescape process carries with it one other significant advantage. It can help to promote greater international understanding and respect for different cultural traditions. It is obvious that if the culturescape process was applied to four or five communities in various parts of the world, the results would be totally different. This is due to the fact that the emphasis placed on different sensory capabilities and cultural values varies markedly around the globe. In some cultures, such as the Western cultures, sight predominates. In other cultures, in Africa and Asia, sound plays a more important role. Hence the significance of the oral tradition and the escalating desire to preserve it. In still other cultures, in the Middle East, for example, smell may play a stronger role. Like the great oral tradition, the olfactory tradition, which is perhaps best epitomized by the pungent aromas of a Middle Eastern market, betrays a different sensorial dependency. What is true for sensorial dependencies is equally true for all the other cultural ingredients—natural, scientific, historical, social, economic, political, and aesthetic—which together comprise the culturescape process.

On an international scale, surely all these cultural and sensorial variations are worth preserving and extending. What we must move away from is the belief that there are inferior and superior cultures. What we must move towards is the realization that cultures are not better or worse, but merely different, and it is precisely because they are different that they are worth respecting and preserving. By highlighting these differences, the world culturescape gives stature to all communities and all cultures, regardless of their size, status, or geographical location in the world.

CHAPTER NINE

Culture and Spirituality: Key to Life and Living in the Twenty-First Century

... who wills the highest must will the whole.

—Johann Wolfgang von Goethe[1]

I have had the good fortune to become deeply immersed in culture over the course of my life.

This has enriched my life in many ways. It has made it possible for me to experience a great deal of joy and happiness in life, learn an enormous amount about the different cultures of the world, and achieve my basic goals and objectives. It has also enhanced my understanding of what is most valuable in life, as well as why I believe a cultural age is so essential for the future. However, the most interesting thing of all is the fact that the more I have become immersed in culture, the more my life has become spiritual in nature.

Of course, there is no single path to spirituality. There are many paths to spirituality, just as there are many paths to happiness, contentment, and fulfillment in life.

For many people, spirituality is achieved through religion and involvement in a specific religion and religious group. Not only is this the key to living a full, upright, and moral life, but also it is the key to experiencing higher and higher levels of spirituality and possibly even encounters with the divine. Virtually all the diverse religions of the world—Buddhism, Hinduism, Islam, Christianity, Judaism, and so forth—believe that spirituality is achieved by making a strong commitment to the

---

[1] R. King, ed., *Goethe on Human Creativeness and Other Goethe Essays* (Athens, Georgia: University of Georgia Press, 1950), p. xiii.

values, teachings, and beliefs of the faith and adhering to these values, teachings, and beliefs as fully as possible.

Others have a different view of this subject. They believe spirituality is best achieved through meditation, yoga, the teachings of individuals like Eckhart Tolle, Deepak Chopra, and Wayne Dyer, or the preaching of countless mystics, evangelists, and others who possess strong convictions about spirituality and how it can be realized. This is also possible through involvement in other activities, such as the arts, sciences, humanities, education, recreation, and appreciation of the natural environment.

To date, little consideration has been given to the role that culture is capable of playing in opening the doors to spirituality. This is probably because culture can be perceived in many different ways—such as the arts, the finer things in life, the legacy from the past, a complex whole, a total way of life, the relationship between human beings and the natural environment, and the organizational forms and structures of different species[2]—and this causes confusion and misunderstanding for many people.

While many people see the different ways culture can be perceived as a distinct liability, I see it as a powerful asset. This is because each of the "perceptions of culture" referred to above possesses the potential to open the doors to spirituality in one form or another, as will become apparent from the personal experiences I have had with each of these perceptions over the years and what many cultural scholars have had to say about this subject. This makes culture an ideal vehicle for achieving spirituality in my view.

My first real encounter with spirituality was in the arts. This is not surprising in view of the fact that many people treat "the arts" and "culture" as synonymous and it is a well-known fact that the arts possess a remarkable potential to lift people to lofty heights and transport them to ethereal places and spaces. As George Bernard Shaw said in *Back to Methuselah*, "You use a glass mirror to see your face; you use works of art to see your soul."

When I was young, my parents enrolled me in art classes at the Art Gallery of Toronto, now the Art Gallery of Ontario, arranged piano lessons for me, and put me in a choir at Grace Church on-the-Hill. It wasn't long

---

[2] These are usually referred to as the artistic, humanistic, historical, anthropological, ecological, and biological perceptions of culture. Detailed information on this is contained in the first four chapters of *Culture: Beacon of the Future*, which was published by Adamantine Press in England and Praeger/Greenwood in the United States in their Twenty-first Century Series in 1998.

before I was aware of the intimate connection between the arts, culture, and spirituality, since many of these activities lifted me out of the commonplace and propelled me to very high heights.

Whether it was painting pictures, playing pieces on the piano, or singing hymns and anthems in the choir, I felt a certain awe come over me whenever I was engaged in any of these activities. This was especially true for singing in the choir, since a great deal of beautiful music was combined with exquisite architecture and an enormous amount of sacred liturgy and pageantry. I soon realized that spirituality is not confined to adults or people in their twilight years. It can be experienced at any age and in any walk of life, and often in profound, moving, and very powerful ways.

Awareness of the intimate bond between the arts, culture, and spirituality has broadened and deepened substantially in me over the years. Many musical compositions, plays, paintings, poems, architectural masterpieces, and the like produce spiritual feelings in me that border on the sublime and occasionally on the divine. While there are too many to list here, I can't resist the temptation of providing a few examples of this in order to give you an idea of what moves me the most and produces strong spiritual sensations in me.

Undoubtedly, music heads the list. There is something about music—all music but especially certain pieces of music—that puts me in a spiritual state. While music affects people in different ways and every person has his or her favourites and personal preferences, I am transported into a spiritual state whenever I hear Handel's *Ombra mai fu*, *Lascia ch'io pianga*, *Zadok the Priest*, or the *Minuet* from *Berenice*, Striggio's *Mass in Forty Parts*, Tallis's *Spem In Alium*, Rachmaninoff's *Second Piano Concerto*, Mahler's *Resurrection Symphony*, and Brahms', Beethoven's, and Tchaikovsky's violin concertos. I am also in a spiritual state whenever I hear Strauss's *Four Last Songs*, Mendelssohn's *Song Without Words*, Opus 38, No. 6 (Duet), Chopin's *Étude Opus 25, No. 13* (Aeolian Harp), Schubert's *Impromptu Opus 90, No. 3*, Liszt's transcription of Schumann's *Widmung (Dedication)*, Mascagni's *Intermezzo* from *Cavelleria Rusticana*, Fauré's *Cantique de Jean Racine*, and the second movement of Albinoni's *Concerto Opus 9, No. 2 in D Minor*. Speaking candidly, I am "halfway to heaven" whenever I hear the first few bars of any of these pieces.

One night, I even went all the way to heaven, or at least so it seemed at the time. Here is how it came about.

For many years, I have been in the habit of turning my radio to a particular radio station before falling asleep. The station plays soft and soothing music—a rare commodity these days—to help people end their day on a pleasant and peaceful note.

One evening in the fall, I turned my radio to the usual station and fell fast asleep. I don't know how long I was sleeping, but I slowly became aware of the fact that I was hearing one of the most exquisite pieces of music I have ever heard in my life. As I lay there in a semi-conscious state, I remember thinking I had died and gone to heaven. *The music was just that beautiful!* Then I heard the announcer say, "You have been listening to Mendelssohn's *Grant Us Peace*. It was sung by the Corydon Singers."

Talk about a spiritual experience! As soon as I heard the announcer say the music was written by Mendelssohn, I knew that I had not actually died and gone to heaven although it certainly seemed like it that night. This piece of music has a wonderful melody, which is sung first by one section of the choir, then another, and finally by the full choir. I have often thought this piece should be adopted as humanity's "universal anthem." Not only is it exceedingly beautiful, but also it would serve a useful purpose at this time, much as Beethoven's *Ninth Symphony* does as the official anthem of the European Union and Council of Europe.

I hope you don't get the impression that it is only classical music that puts me in a spiritual state because this is not the case. Musicals do this too, especially specific songs in musicals. Most prominent in this regard are "If I Loved You" and "You'll Never Walk Alone" from *Carousel*, "Climb Ev'ry Mountain" from *The Sound of Music*, and "I Dreamed a Dream," "On My Own," and "Take My Hand" from *Les Misérables*.

What I find spiritually uplifting about these songs is not only the music, but also the lyrics. A good example of this is found when Richard Rodgers' captivating music is combined with Oscar Hammerstein II's inspirational lyrics. Who can forget "You'll Never Walk Alone" from *Carousel*, with its compelling promise of hope and deliverance when the storm is done? And words mesh perfectly with music in the even better known "Climb Ev'ry Mountain" from *The Sound of Music*, with its admonition to never give up till one achieves one's dreams. Similar feelings well up in me when I listen to certain pieces of film music—such as Ennio Morricone's "Gabriel's Oboe" from *The Mission* and "Dinner" from his *Lady Caliph Suite*—as well as popular songs like "Moon River," "Unchained Melody," "I Believe," "Stranger in Paradise," and many others.

This is equally true for certain paintings, poems, architectural edifices, and the like. Paintings like Monet's *Water Lilies* and van Gogh's *Starry*

Night, poems like Keats's *On First Looking into Chapman's Homer*, Byron's *She Walks in Beauty*, and Rumi's *Divan-e Shams*—as well as numerous mosques, pagodas, gothic cathedrals, and architectural wonders like the Taj Mahal—lift me to incredible heights because they are sublime and perhaps even border on the divine. As John Keats said, "A thing of beauty is a joy forever."

What is it about the arts in general—and certain artistic works in particular—that makes the artistic perception of culture one of the most effective vehicles for opening the doors to spirituality of all? Surely this. Not only are the arts capable of lifting people out of the doldrums and propelling them to incredible heights—largely through the sounds and images they exude and the feelings and emotions they convey—but also they enhance our awareness of virtually everything that exists in the world and in nature. In the case of nature, this is perhaps best realized by much of the piano music of Schumann and particularly his song *Der Nussbaum* (*The Nut Tree*). I can smell the sweet fragrance of this tree and picture its leaves gently rustling in the breeze whenever I hear this song. Perhaps this is why Beethoven was always so anxious to escape the hustle and bustle of the city and get out in nature to enjoy its babbling brooks and serene calm after the summer storm, as expressed so movingly in his *Pastoral Symphony* (*Symphony No. 6*).

If the arts provide one example of the rich potential culture possesses to open the doors to spirituality, the finer things in life provide another. Many of these things are inherent in the humanities—ethics, education, philosophy, and the like—and include the quest for peace, order, equality, and justice; the pursuit of knowledge, wisdom, beauty, and truth; and the importance of caring, sharing, cooperation, and compassion.

I often think of Albert Schweitzer when I reflect on these matters. Not only did Schweitzer give up a highly successful career in Europe as a medical doctor and outstanding musician to go to Africa to work and live with lepers—risking his life and his health in the process—but also he was a great proponent of reverential thinking and reverential action as one of the principal keys to spirituality. For Schweitzer, all living things were precious, and therefore deserved to be treated with dignity and respect.

I also think of Mahatma Gandhi, Nelson Mandela, Mother Teresa, and Dr. Martin Luther King, Jr., when I reflect on such matters, largely because they led exemplary lives in numerous respects. Whenever I think of all the painful experiences they were forced to endure—and how the lives of Gandhi and Dr. King were snuffed out instantly and so brutally—I recall Dr. King's comment towards the end of his life that he wanted nothing more than to leave behind him a life totally devoted to a cause, or words to this effect.

If the arts and finer things in life have a great deal to do with spirituality, so does the legacy from the past. This is probably why many people think the legacy from the past is one of culture's greatest gifts of all.

If I were able to travel backward or forward in time, I would definitely choose travelling backward in time. This is partly because I am not too excited about certain present and prospective developments—a gothic cathedral does much more for me than a colossal office tower—but it is largely because I am fascinated with the past and the magnificent legacy we have inherited from the past.

Little wonder, as noted earlier, that Jacob Burckhardt—the great Swiss cultural scholar who did so much to shed light on the Italian Renaissance and Greek and Roman culture in classical times—called this precious gift "the silent promise" that possesses the potential to transform the entire past into a "spiritual possession."[3]

The great English cultural scholar Matthew Arnold had similar thoughts on this matter, although he confined them more to knowledge, ideas, and education. Here is what he said about this in his popular book *Culture and Anarchy*:

> The great men [and women] of culture are those who have had a passion for diffusing, for making prevail, for carrying from one end of society to the other, the best knowledge, the best ideas of their time; who have laboured to divest knowledge of all that was harsh, uncouth, difficult, abstract, professional, exclusive; to humanize it, to make it efficient outside the clique of the cultivated and learned, yet still remaining the *best* knowledge and thought of the time, and a true source, therefore, of sweetness and light.[4]

One institution that has taken Arnold's and especially Burckhardt's beliefs in this area to heart is UNESCO. This remarkable organization has been steadily and systematically translating lofty ideals like this into concrete realities for more than half a century. Not only does it place an

[3] Karl J. Weintraub, *Visions of Culture: Voltaire, Guizot, Burckhardt, Lamprecht, Huizinga, Ortega y Gasset* (Chicago: University of Chicago Press, 1966), pp. 117–118.
[4] Matthew Arnold, *Culture and Anarchy* (Cambridge: Cambridge University Press, 1960), p. 70 (italics Arnold's; gender insert mine).

extremely high priority on the tangible and intangible cultural heritage of humankind and all the world heritage sites located throughout the globe, but also it places an exceedingly high priority on preserving and protecting this priceless legacy and making it accessible to present and future generations.

We are the beneficiaries of this profuse legacy of artefacts and accomplishments. This is becoming increasingly apparent through developments in contemporary communications that make it possible for people and countries in all parts of the world to enjoy all the incredible cultural achievements from the past. I get elated whenever I think that virtually every individual, institution, country, and culture in the world today possesses the means—or has access to them through new technologies and devices—to tap into these achievements regardless of where they are situated in the world.

In many ways, this is where things stood for me with respect to culture and spirituality until I was in my late forties. My experiences in this area were limited largely to "specific moments of spirituality" that tended to occur when I was exposed to certain works related to the arts, finer things in life, and legacy from the past. What I was not experiencing, however, was anything that might be called a "permanent state of spirituality."

Things started to change in this regard when I had a fortuitous experience one day in Bladen Library at the University of Toronto. I was in the library doing some research on culture—which had become my main passion and principal preoccupation in life by this time—when I happened to come across a book by Sir Edward Burnett Tylor—one of the world's first anthropologists if not *the* first—called *The Origins of Culture*. No sooner had I opened the book to the first page than the following definition of culture was staring me in the face:

> Culture . . . taken in its wide ethnographic sense, is that *complex whole* which includes knowledge, belief, art, morals, law, custom, and any other capabilities and habits acquired by man as a member of society.[5]

This definition struck me like a thunderbolt. I had long believed that there was far more to culture than the arts, finer things in life, and the legacy from the past—essential and fundamental as these are—because I had

[5] Edward Burnett Tylor, *The Origins of Culture* (New York: Harper and Row, 1958), p. 1 (italics mine).

come across numerous references to many other activities that cultural scholars thought should be included in culture. Here, at long last, was official confirmation of this.

What stood out with respect to Tylor's definition was the fact that culture was defined in terms of "the whole," and not just a part or parts of the whole. This elevated culture to a much higher plane in my view because it is a well-known fact that the whole is greater than the parts and the sum of the parts because new properties are brought into existence when the whole is created that are not in the parts taken separately.

The origins of this "holistic definition of culture" can be traced back to the late nineteenth century when Tylor and other anthropologists began to study culture and cultures in depth and in the field in many different parts of the world. What they discovered was that people had all sorts of words for the specific activities in which they were engaged as they went about the process of meeting their individual and collective needs. What they did not have was a word that described how all these activities were woven together to form a whole.

Culture, as we have already seen, was the word they used to designate this phenomenon. It resulted from the fact that all the various activities in which people were engaged—economics, education, religion, politics, technology, the arts, the sciences, recreation, and so forth—were tied together in specific combinations and arrangements to create a whole that was greater than the parts. While culture is not the only field to be concerned with "the whole"—it is also of concern to philosophy, religion, science, medicine, and other fields—Tylor's definition of culture struck a responsive chord with me because it confirmed my belief that culture is concerned with the whole and not just a part or the parts of the whole. It also struck a responsive chord with me because I felt the world—and virtually everything in the world including people, communities, countries, cultures, civilizations, plants, animals, and so forth—are wholes made up of many parts, not parts taken in isolation or by themselves.

Ever since that fortuitous day in the Bladen Library, I have been strongly committed to—and extremely interested in—the whole in all its diverse aspects and manifestations. Most prominent in this regard are holism in general and the holistic understanding of culture and cultures in particular. Indeed, it would not be far off the mark to say that the whole, holism, and the holistic perception of culture and cultures have been the guiding features and principal preoccupations of my life ever since.

Some may call what occurred in the Bladen Library that day an "epiphany," since it caused me to see the world in a new and different way. However, I would call it a "cultural transformation," since it helped me to see the world—and the vast majority of things that exist in the world—as they really are, rather than how they are presented to us as a result of specialization and our penchant for dividing the whole up into parts in order to study the parts in detail.

The implications of this for spirituality were clear and unequivocal. Focusing attention on the whole, holism, and the holistic understanding of culture and cultures provided me with a far more all-encompassing and inclusive way of seeing and understanding reality and the world around me. It also provided a gateway to living life on a higher plane of existence.

From that point on, I began to focus on the whole in everything I did and thought. When I walked in the neighbourhood, I walked in it as a whole, soaked it up as a whole, cherished it as a whole, and experienced it as a whole. When I thought about my community—Markham—or my country and its culture—Canada and Canadian culture—I thought about them as wholes made up of countless parts. When I thought about other countries, other cultures, and the world at large, I thought about them as wholes and not merely smorgasbords of disconnected and unrelated pieces. My focus was always on the whole, and with it, what brought things together rather than split them apart.

This was especially true for people. I was fascinated with this because years earlier I had come across several cultural scholars who had written about "the whole person." While I tucked this information away in my mind at the time, it took on far greater significance and meaning when I became aware of the whole and holism as it relates to people and made a strong commitment to this.

One of the scholars who wrote about the whole person was Matthew Arnold, who was referred to earlier. He believed that the central challenge in the evolution and education of the whole person is to attend to the harmonious development of all the faculties and factors that constitute human nature. John Cowper Powys had similar thoughts in mind, although he expressed them even more eloquently when he said:

> The whole purpose and end of culture is a thrilling happiness of a particular sort—of the sort, in fact, that is caused by a response to life made by a harmony of the intellect, the imagination, and the senses.[6]

---

[6] John Cowper Powys, *The Meaning of Culture* (New York: W. W. Norton and Company, 1929), p. 77.

These insights were very helpful to me because I was struggling to become a whole person and they emphasized how essential it is to achieve balance and harmony among all the diverse faculties and factors that constitute human beings and human nature: material and non-material; mind and body; work and leisure; egoism and altruism; the self and the other; and all the other dichotomous divisions that are often associated with people and used to describe them.

It was about this time that I had another fortuitous experience that had a profound effect on me. It happened when I accidentally came across a quotation by Johann Wolfgang von Goethe, the great German playwright and cultural scholar. The quotation was "Live in the whole, in the good, in the beautiful."[7]

This quotation had a profound effect on me for several reasons. In the first place, it summed up better than anything I had ever seen what the four perceptions of culture we have considered thus far—the arts, the finer things in life, the legacy from the past, and a complex whole—are really all about. In the second place, it stated in a few, simple words what I was desperately struggling to achieve in my own life. In the third place, and perhaps most importantly, it gave me an ideal that I could work towards in the years and decades ahead. In so doing, it produced not only another cultural transformation in my life, but also a transcendental experience in my life. Quite frankly, my life has never been the same since.

It was also very helpful in enabling me to understand that culture, like life, is not just a whole made up of many parts, but also a "total way of life." Here was yet another perception of culture that had strong implications for spirituality. Interestingly, it seemed to apply not just to me and my life, but to many of my friends, colleagues, and people I have known over the years and their lives. They all seemed to be struggling to achieve what Goethe had advised in his short, sage, and insightful statement.

I began to refer to this as "the cultural way of life" because it was concerned not only with the need to live in the whole, in the good, and in the beautiful, but also to achieve balance and harmony among all facets and components of life. I started to realize that my own life was filled with much more creative exuberance and exhilaration—and over substantially longer periods of time—when I made a commitment to the cultural way of

---

[7] *Ibid.*, p. 251.

life. Not only did it make it possible for me to live life on a higher plane of existence—what some spiritual leaders call elevated forms of consciousness—but also it helped me to soar to greater heights, much as eagles do in many popular songs. With this came the hope that the cultural way of life would be transformed into a spiritual way of life that was not confined to specific moments of spirituality but became a permanent state of spirituality.

This hope was reinforced when I came across another quotation that had a profound effect on me. It was Joseph Campbell's advice to "Follow your bliss." While Campbell is best known for his prolific writings on the great cultures and religions of the world and especially on myths, myth-making, and mythology, he had many valuable things to say about life, living, spirituality, and how they can be achieved most effectively.

Many people think Campbell was talking about happiness when he said "Follow your bliss." However, what he actually meant was that people should do the thing that is right for them and what they were intended to do with their lives, something which can produce a great deal of happiness but be very painful at times. To struggle to achieve this in Campbell's opinion was to find real meaning, purpose, and fulfillment in life. This had a great deal of relevance to my own life because I felt I was following my bliss when I was engaged in the quest to broaden and deepen knowledge and understanding of culture and cultures and the central role they are capable of playing in the world.

Thus far, I have said little about the overall relationship between human beings and the natural environment, yet another perception of culture with profound implications for spirituality. The time has come to address this requirement, since there is an intimate connection between human beings, the natural environment, culture, and spirituality that must likewise be taken into account.

Interestingly, culture's association with these matters can be traced back to classical times. As indicated earlier, this is because culture as a word and as an idea derives originally from the Latin verb *colere*, meaning "to grow," "to till," or "to cultivate." At least this is the way Cicero, the great Roman orator and statesman, used the word and the idea for the first time in history when he said "*Cultura animi philosophia est,*" which is usually translated as "Culture is the philosophy or cultivation of the soul." Interestingly, Herder expressed something similar many centuries later when he said, "The cultivation of a people is the flower of its existence."[8] The connection to the natural environment and spirituality is clear and unequivocal here. Despite the fact that this connection has been largely ignored in the modern era, it explains why (as mentioned earlier) we have terms in our vocabulary like agriculture, horticulture, silviculture, viticulture, and wolf culture that confirm the fact that there has been an intimate relationship between human beings and the natural environment dating back more than two thousand years.

Many cultural and ecological scholars have written at length and very passionately about this relationship in recent years, including Arne Naess, Fritjof Capra, David Suzuki, George Sessions, James Lovelock, and many others. However, no scholars have written more compellingly about this relationship—and the dire need to transform it—than Brian Swimme and Thomas Berry. In books like *The Universe Story*, *Dream of the Earth*, and others, Swimme and Berry have made a convincing case for "deep ecology," as well as treating the natural environment as a "spiritual gift" in much that same way that Jacob Burckhardt made a powerful case for treating the legacy from the past as a "spiritual possession."

The arts have a great deal to contribute here in terms of enhancing our respect and reverence for the natural environment in all its diverse forms, manifestations, elements, and seasons. Think, for example, of van Gogh's many landscape paintings, Claude Monet's splendid depictions of his gardens at Giverny, France, Respighi's *The Birds* (*Gli Ucceli*), Schubert's *Trout Quintet*, Alan Hovhaness's *Mysterious Mountain* (*Second Symphony*), Vivaldi's *The Four Seasons*, Saint Saëns's *Carnival of the Animals*, Smetana's *Moldau*, John Williams' *Five Sacred Trees*, and Toru Takemitsu's *Tree Line*. These works, and countless others, are designed to enhance our awareness and appreciation of the natural environment and the need to preserve, protect, and revere it. In a spiritual sense, this is perhaps best epitomized in the last movement of Sibelius's superb *Symphony No. 5*, where he expresses the awe, rapture, and sense of communion he experienced with nature and the sublime when he witnessed a flock of swans flying high over his farm in Finland late one afternoon. He is reputed to have exclaimed, "God, how incredibly beautiful!" after experiencing this memorable event.

My own experience with the natural environment dates back several decades to a time when I was experiencing some difficult health problems. I first went to doctors to get some help with these problems, much as most

---

[8] Patrick Gardiner, *Theories of History* (Glencoe, Ill.: The Free Press, 1959), p. 40.

people do. When this didn't work, I sought the advice of family and friends and read many books and articles on the specific health problems I was experiencing. While this helped a little, it didn't provide the lasting solution I was looking for. Finally, in a fit of desperation, I turned to nature. I started taking long walks in the countryside near our home. There seemed to be nothing quite like "getting out in nature" and experiencing everything nature had to offer—much like Beethoven!—that slowly but surely provided a lasting solution to these problems. The process of enjoying the flowers, trees, birds, streams, sunsets, and especially the leaves turning many shades of green in the spring and gold, orange, yellow, and red in the fall provided the tonic that was required to restore my health to normal.

Since that time, I have been actively engaged in nature and the natural environment in many ways. I take long walks in the forest near our home as often as possible, especially the Durham forest that is divided into an oak trail, a maple trail, a birch trail, and a hemlock trail. I also walk regularly in the many parks and conservation areas that exist in Markham and York Region, as well as enjoy many of the paintings of Canada's Group of Seven artists that are concerned with the country's magnificent landscapes and wilderness areas. And perhaps most importantly, I do exercises five mornings a week with a group that does what are called *Yuanji Dances*. Most of these exercises—which involve a combination of tai chi and qi gong set to the most beautiful music imaginable—are based on nature's flows, rhythms, and elements. This is not surprising in view of the fact that nature figures prominently in Chinese, Indian, and most other eastern cultures.

All this activity has helped me to sustain a good state of health and bring me one step closer to experiencing a permanent state of spirituality rather than just specific moments of spirituality. It has also helped to open the doors to the final perception of culture we are considering here, namely the organizational forms and structures of different species, both human and non-human.

I have long been interested in the organizational forms and structures of human beings and all the various cultures they create because they are so diverse, complex, and sophisticated. This is largely because they are based on different worldviews, values, customs, beliefs, traditions, and ways of life. In consequence, some cultures are best known for their architectural achievements and culinary accomplishments—Chinese, Indian, French, Thai, and Turkish cultures for example—whereas others are best known for their religious, political, and athletic capabilities, such as Buddhist, British, and American cultures. There is no single pattern or characteristic that fits all the diverse cultures of the world. They are all different and unique in one way or another.

Lately, I have become fascinated with the organizational forms and structures of other species and the cultures they create. This is because their cultures are also wholes made up of many parts. The cultures of bees, ants, trees, and other species in the natural realm confirm the fact that animals and plants have cultures just as people do, and create them in much the same way that human beings create their cultures.

An excellent example of this—one that was noted earlier but bears repeating because it is so relevant to human beings and human cultures—is the culture and cultural creations of elephants. It is a well-known fact that elephants have phenomenal memories—memories that may even be better than the memories of human beings. However, what is becoming increasingly apparent as a result of contemporary research is the fact that elephants have highly complex and very sophisticated cultures—cultures that are predicated on a great deal of caring, sharing, intimacy, and compassion. Not only do elephants bond with each other in much the same way that human beings bond, but also they are each other's keepers in the sense that they look after each other very attentively when they are sick, elderly, in distress, or threatened in some way. Moreover, they look after their young in much the same way that human beings do, doting over them in countless ways and actively participating in their evolution, upbringing, and development.

What is true for elephants is true for all other animal and plant species, even if less intensely and not to the same degree as human beings. Every species has its own cultures and forms of cultural creation, including its distinctive methods of procreation, habitat, social bonding, community organization, networking, and consumption and production activity. This is not surprising in view of the fact that animals and plants, like human beings, are living organisms, and, as such, obey the laws governing all living things.

What does all this have to do to spirituality? Surely this. Culture and cultures are without doubt the highest forms of creation when they are looked at in holistic terms, regardless of whether they are created by human beings or other species. This is because they are highly complex wholes made up of many parts and there is little else in the world that can compare with this. As Jin Li points out in her book *Cultural Foundations of Learning: East and West* when talking about the quintessential importance of culture for human beings: "Culture, as the largest human created system (as opposed to our biology), penetrates so profoundly into all spheres of human life that it alters human cognition, emotion, and behaviour. . . . Culture is like the air we breathe; we are completely dependent on it."[9] And what is true for human beings is equally true for other species.

Like the incredible breakthroughs that are now being realized in science—which are also part of culture and are designed to broaden knowledge of the smallest molecules and particles and deepen understanding of the universe and the cosmos—this most expansive perception of culture of all possesses the potential to produce higher and higher levels of awareness and states of consciousness with respect to virtually everything that exists in the human and natural domains. Whether these levels and states have to do with the divine may only be revealed in the fullness of time, if at all. However, this does not alter the fact that the organizational forms and structures of all the various species in the world have a great deal to do with spirituality and the sublime in countless ways.

And this brings us to the remarkable potential culture possesses to open the doors to spirituality when it is considered in comprehensive terms. It possesses this potential because culture can be perceived in many different ways and each of these ways has a great deal to do with spirituality in one form or another.

From the most beautiful works of art and the artistic perception of culture to all the diverse cultures in the world and the organizational forms and structures of different species, there is no doubt that culture possesses a remarkable capacity to act as a gateway to spirituality because everything is there in the final analysis when it is added up and considered in totality. This is because culture makes it possible to move horizontally as well as vertically—in breadth as well as in depth—across virtually every domain and activity that exists in the world, from the human to the non-human, the simple to the complex, the individual to the collective, the local to the global, and the mundane to the profound. As Barbara Ward asked many years ago when she observed that the chief environmental insight is that all things are linked, "Where is the thread that will lead us through the maze?" It is now clear that culture is this thread.

And this is not all. While an important part of spirituality involves

---

[9] Jin Li, *Cultural Foundations of Learning: East and West* (New York: Cambridge University Press, 2012), p. 8.

going "outside the self" in order to expand awareness of the external world, a much greater part involves going "inside the self" in order to become much more conscious of the internal world. In the final analysis, this is what is required to become a whole person, live in the whole, in the good, and in the beautiful, follow one's bliss, and achieve balance and harmony among all the diverse factors and faculties that constitute life. To do so is not only to experience more and more and higher and higher moments of spirituality, but also to move closer and closer to a permanent state of spirituality.

Why is this so essential? It is essential because this will not only bring people a great deal more fulfillment and happiness in life, it will also reduce the huge demands we are making on the natural environment and make it possible for us to tread more lightly on the land. This is because a much better balance will be realized between people's material and non-material requirements. This is imperative if humanity is to come to grips with the difficult and demanding problems that have loomed up on the global horizon in recent years.

No challenge is greater in this respect than the need to come to grips with the relentless march of human numbers compared to the finite carrying capacity of the earth. In recent years, it has become crystal clear that the world's population of seven billion is exerting tremendous pressure on the natural environment and the globe's scarce resources. Given this fact, and the fact that world population is expected to increase significantly in the years and decades ahead in absolute if not relative terms, there is no doubt that major environmental catastrophes are inevitable if humanity does not bring its material appetites under control and reduce the colossal ecological footprint it is making on the earth. Already, climate change and the increased frequency of floods, hurricanes, droughts, forest fires, and the devastation of coastal areas are revealing that severe consequences lie in store for humanity if it persists in this practice.

Clearly much more emphasis will have to be placed on humanity's internal and non-material—rather than external and material—requirements if this problem is to be dealt with effectively in the future. Hence the need for a quantum leap in the spiritual and qualitative side of life compared to the material and quantitative side. In global terms, a leap of this magnitude would bring about a great deal more environmental conservation while simultaneously making it possible for people to live on a much higher plane of existence and experience a great deal more spirituality in life. It would also bring about much more caring, sharing, cooperation, and compassion in the world, thereby reducing the major income inequalities and social inequities that exist throughout the world.

And this brings me back to my own situation and the personal experiences I have had with spirituality over the years. Each of the experiences I have had with the principal perceptions of culture—from the arts to the organizational forms and structures of different species—has enriched my life in countless ways and made it possible for me to move progressively from specific moments of spirituality to something much closer to a permanent state of spirituality.

I am not there yet, but feel I am moving in the right direction in this regard. I have the sense that the cultural way of life I am living at present is slowly but surely being transformed into a spiritual way of life. I hope this is the case, since culture is without doubt one of the best vehicles of all for opening the doors to spirituality and unlocking the secrets of the sublime and perhaps even the divine.

Relevant Books and Articles
by D. Paul Schafer

Books

Revolution or Renaissance: Making the Transition from an Economic Age to a Cultural Age. Ottawa: University of Ottawa Press, 2008.

Culture: Beacon of the Future. Westport, Conn.: Praeger, 1998.

The Challenge of Cultural Development. Markham, Ont.: World Culture Project, 1994.

The Cultural Personality. Markham, Ont.: World Culture Project, 1991.

Arguments for the Arts: Towards a Dynamic and Innovative Arts Policy. Scarborough, Ont.: Arts Scarborough, 1982.

Articles

"Towards a New World Order: The Age of Culture." *UNESCO Cultures* 2: 3 (1975).

"The Age of Culture: Prospects and Implications." *UNESCO Cultures* 2: 4 (1975).

"The Culturescape: Self-Awareness of Communities." *UNESCO Cultures* 5: 1 (1978).

"Culture and Cosmos: The Role of Culture in the World of the Future." *UNESCO Cultures* 7: 2 (1980).

"Culture and the New World Order." *Proceedings of the Conference on the New International Economic Order: Philosophical Basis and Socio-cultural Implications.* Vienna: International Progress Organization, 1980.

"The Cultural Interpretation of History: Beacon of the Future." Reprinted in part in *The Future of the Past: Historical Identity and Permanence and*

Change. Buffalo, N.Y.: Center for Integrative Studies; Durango, Col.: Center of Southwest Studies; Mexico City: Center for Economic and Social Studies of the Third World; and Paris: UNESCO, 1980. Reprinted in full in Robin Blazer and Robert Dunham, eds., *Arts and Reality: A Casebook of Concern*. Introduction by Northrop Frye. Vancouver: Talon Books, 1986.

"The New World Order: A Contribution to the World Decade for Cultural Development." *Major Programme I: Reflection on World Problems and Future Oriented Studies*. Paris: UNESCO, 1989.

"Culture: Beacon of the Future." *Razvoj Development International* 6: 2–3 (1991). Published by the Institute for Development and International Relations, Zagreb, Croatia.

"The Evolution and Character of the Concept of Culture." *World Futures: The Journal of General Evolution* 38: 4 (1993).

"Culture as It Might Be." *Futures: The Journal of Forecasting, Planning and Policy* 26: 1 (1994).

"Cultures and Economies: Irresistible Forces Encounter Immovable Objects." *Futures: The Journal of Forecasting, Planning and Policy* 26: 8 (1994).

"Towards a New World System: A Cultural Perspective." *Futures: The Journal of Forecasting, Planning and Policy* 28: 3 (1996).

"The Millennium Challenge: Making the Transition from an 'Economic Age' to a 'Cultural Age.'" *World Futures: The Journal of General Evolution* 51 (1998).

"A New Model of Development for the New Millennium." *World Futures: The Journal of General Evolution* 55 (2000).

"Culture and Cultures: Key Learning Requirements for the Future." Published online as a chapter in a book on creating learning communities. http://www.creatinglearningcommunities.org (2001).

"The Arts in Turbulent Times." *The Artspaper* 11: 1 (2001).

"The Arts and Cities." *The Artspaper* 12: 3 (2002).

"Diversity and Sustainable Development: Contemporary Concerns or Permanent Realities?" *Culturelink* Special Issue (2002/2003) on "Cultural Diversity and Sustainable Development." Published by Culturelink and the Institute for International Relations, Zagreb, Croatia, 2003.

"A New System of Politics: Government, Governance, and Political Decision-making in the Twenty-first Century." *World Futures: The Journal of General Evolution* 61: 7 (2005).

"Feasting on Cultures to Solve Our Problems and Enrich Our Lives." Posted in 2006 in the "Hot Topics" section of the World Culture Project website. http://www3.sympatico.ca/dpaulschafer.

"The New Politics: Government and Governance in the Twenty-first Century." *Humanitad World Leadership Magazine*, no. 1 (2006). Published in London.

"The Cultural Imperative: The Role of Culture in the World of the Future." Posted in 2010 in the "Hot Topics" section of the World Culture Project website.

"A Cultural Model of Development." Posted in 2010 in the "Hot Topics" section of the World Culture Project website.

"The Future of Culture." Posted in 2010 in the "Hot Topics" section of the World Culture Project website.

"Foundations for Life: How an Education in the Arts Can Transform Your Entire Life." Included in a collection of articles on arts education published by the Institute of Spiritual Development of Man and UNESCO Chair on Spiritual Cultural Values of Upbringing and Education at the Volodymyr Dahl East-Ukrainian National University in Luhansk, Ukraine (2011), and accessible in the "Hot Topics" section of the World Culture Project website.

"Culture and Spirituality: Key to Life and Living in the Twenty-First Century." Included in a collection of articles on spirituality published by the Institute of Spiritual Development of Man and UNESCO Chair on Spiritual Cultural Values of Upbringing and Education at the Volodymyr Dahl East-Ukrainian National University in Luhansk, Ukraine (2013), and accessible in the "Hot Topics" section of the World Culture Project website.

Acknowledgements

This book would not be possible without a great deal of help, support, and encouragement from many people over the years. I would especially like to thank the following people in this regard: Walter Pitman, Biserka Cvjetičanin, Gao Xian, Jack Fobes, Guy Métraux, André Fortier, Sheila Jans, Eleonora Barbieri Masini, Prem Kirpal, Erika Erdmann, Henri Janne, Paul Braisted, Jeremy Geelan, Maurice Strong, Ervin Laszlo, Herman Greene, James Peacock, Joyce Zemans, John Hobday, Galyna Shevchenko, Isabella Stasi Castriota Scanderbeg, Mochtar Lubis, Robert Vachon, Magda Cordell McHale, Augustin Girard, Andreas Wiesand, Dirk Heinze, Tom Symons, Kurt Blaukopf, Peter Brokensha, Michael Marien, Bill McWhinney, Vincent Tovell, Mavor Moore, James Gillies, Milton Carman, Ian Morrison, Tony Saadat, Sal Amenta, Joy MacFadyen, Elfriede and Attila Bimbo, Arthur Witkin, Barry Witkin, Réal Bédard, Brian Simpson, Steven Thorne, Frank Pasquill, John Gordon, Peter Sever, Polly Tong, Thierry Dufay, Leslie Oliver, and Greg Baeker.

I would also like to thank my parents—Harold and Belle—as well as my family—Nancy, Charlene, Susan, and Alan—for their indispensable contributions to my work on culture over many years. Finally, I would like to express my deep gratitude to Federico Mayor for writing the Foreword to the book, and David Stover for proposing the book in the first place and making my thoughts on a cultural age known to a broader public through publication of the book and writing the Introduction to it. While recognizing these contributions, I nevertheless assume responsibility for everything contained in the text.

D. Paul Schafer
2014

www.ingramcontent.com/pod-product-compliance
Lightning Source LLC
Chambersburg PA
CBHW062211270326
41930CB00009B/1709